MEDIAEVALITAS: READING THE MIDDLE AGES

The essays collected in this volume, from the 1995 J.A.W. Bennett Memorial Symposium, are centred on the idea of 'mediaevalitas' as constructed in the centuries, following three main lines of enquiry. Thus we have medieval authors reading other medieval authors, modern authors who rewrite medieval works, and modern critics discussing medieval texts in relation to new critical projects such as 'New Historicism' and gender analysis. The volume opens with a study of medieval representations of Nature in the light of modern environmental ethics, followed by an essay which shows the *Clerk's Tale* as a narrative of debated readings joined in a hermeneutic project. Two readings of Chaucer's works are then proposed: one by Charles of Orleans who is influenced by Chaucer's dream visions, the other by the friar-poet Bokenham who uses the *Legend of Good Women* as a structural model for his female legendary. The case of Alice Chaucer is seen as emblematic both of the issue of women's access to books and of the question of how to read *now* the cultural role of women in the late Middle Ages. There follows a section which illustrates the idea of medievalism in Spenser, Blake, and Browning by showing their different responses to tradition and authority. The volume ends with two articles devoted to modern reworkings of medieval texts: Soseki's Arthurian novella is examined in relation to its sources, while the use of the mythical potential of the story of Arthur and his Court in contemporary German drama is viewed as an illustration of the end of utopian ideals.

Piero Boitani / Anna Torti (eds.)

MEDIAEVALITAS: READING THE MIDDLE AGES

The J.A.W. Bennett Memorial Lectures
Ninth Series
Perugia, 1995

D. S. Brewer

© Contributors 1996

All Rights Reserved. Except as permitted under current legislation no part of this work may be photocopied, stored in a retrieval system, published, performed in public, adapted, broadcast, transmitted, recorded or reproduced in any form or by any means, without the prior permission of the copyright owner

First published 1996
D. S. Brewer, Cambridge

ISBN 0 85991 488 7

ISSN 1361–7621

D. S. Brewer is an imprint of Boydell & Brewer Ltd
PO Box 9, Woodbridge, Suffolk IP12 3DF, UK
and of Boydell & Brewer Inc.
PO Box 41026, Rochester, NY 14604–4126, USA

British Library Cataloguing in Publication Data
Mediaevalitas: reading the Middle Ages. – (The J.A.W. Bennett memorial lectures. Ninth series)
1. Literature, Medieval – History and criticism 2. Criticism, Medieval
I. Boitani, Piero II. Torti, Anna
809'.02
ISBN 0859914887

Library of Congress Cataloging-in-Publication Data
Mediaevalitas : reading the Middle Ages / Piero Boitani, Anna Torti, eds.
    p.   cm.
Papers presented at the ninth symposium in honor of J.A.W. Bennett, Perugia, 3–5 Apr. 1995.
"The J.A.W. Bennett memorial lectures."
Includes bibliographical references and index.
ISBN 0–85991–488–7
1. Literature, Medieval – History and criticism. 2. Middle Ages in literature. 3. Criticism, Textual. 4. Medievalism. I. Boitani, Piero. II. Torti, Anna.
PN671.M37 1996
809'.02 – dc20   96–17095

This publication is printed on acid-free paper

Printed in Great Britain by
Boydell & Brewer Ltd, Woodbridge, Suffolk

Contents

List of Plates

Contributors

Preface

Lisa J. Kiser
Alain de Lille, Jean de Meun, and Chaucer:
Ecofeminism and Some Medieval Lady Natures 1

Robert R. Edwards
'The sclaundre of Walter':
The *Clerk's Tale* and the Problem of Hermeneutics 15

Julia Boffey
Charles of Orleans Reading Chaucer's Dream Visions 43

Sheila Delany
The Friar as Critic: Bokenham Reads Chaucer 63

Carol M. Meale
Reading Women's Culture in Fifteenth-Century England:
The Case of Alice Chaucer 81

Thomas P. Roche
Spenser's Virtue of Justice and the Four Daughters of God 103

Stefania D'Agata D'Ottavi
Blake's Chaucer: Scholasticism *post litteram* 115

Angelo Righetti
Browning's Medievalism 129

Toshiyuki Takamiya
Love and Transgression in Soseki's Story of the Maid of Ascolat . . 139

Joerg O. Fichte
The End of Utopia – The Treatment of Arthur and His Court in
Contemporary German Drama 153

Index 171

Plates

Plates appear between pages 102 and 103

Reading Women's Culture in Fifteenth-Century England: The Case of Alice Chaucer

1 Half-figure of Alice Chaucer, St Mary's Church, Ewelme
2 London, British Library MS Arundel 119, fol. 4 recto
3 BL MS Arundel 119, fol. 1 recto
4 BL MS Royal 15.E.VI, fol. 439 verso
5 BL MS Royal 16.G.II, fol. 8 recto
6 BL MS Royal 16.G.II, fol. 33 recto
7 Oxford, Jesus College MS 124: Margaret of Anjou's prayer-roll
8 Tomb of Alice Chaucer, St Mary's Church, Ewelme

Plates 1 and 8 are reproduced by courtesy of J. Marshall; Plates 2–6 are reproduced by kind permission of the British Library Board; Plate 7 is reproduced by kind permission of the Principal and Fellows of Jesus College, Oxford.

Blake's Chaucer: Scholasticism *post litteram*

9 William Blake, *The Canterbury Pilgrims*

Plate 9 is reproduced by courtesy of Glasgow Museums and Art Galleries, Stirling Maxwell Collection, Pollock House.

Spenser's Virtue of Justice and the Four Daughters of God

10 Canterbury Psalter, fol. 150B (M.R. James)
11 Utrecht Psalter, fol. 49v (E.T. DeWald)

Photos for Plates 10 and 11 are by C.A. Bozelko.

Contributors

Lisa J. Kiser	Ohio State University
Robert R. Edwards	Pennsylvania State University
Julia Boffey	University of London
Sheila Delany	Simon Fraser University
Carol M. Meale	University of Bristol
Thomas P. Roche	Princeton University
Stefania D'Agata D'Ottavi	Rome
Angelo Righetti	University of Verona
Toshiyuki Takamiya	Keio University
Joerg O. Fichte	University of Tübingen

Preface

The ninth Symposium dedicated to the memory of J.A.W.Bennett was held in Perugia, 3–5 April 1995, in the Palazzo Donini. The theme of 'Mediaevalitas' which was chosen for the Symposium attracted a number of scholars from various countries. The papers delivered in Perugia are contained, in a revised form, in the present volume.

The idea of discussing the topic according to at least three guidelines – the way medieval poets read other medieval poets, the modern reworking of medieval matter, modern criticism as applied to medieval literature – turned out to be successful. While some contributors focus on the problematic relationship of medieval and 'modern' poets to their sources, others are concerned with the relevance to medieval texts of modern critical analyses.

The first essay by Lisa Kiser discusses the gendered conceptions of Nature in Alain de Lille, Jean de Meun, and Chaucer by using modern ecofeminist theories in order to understand the continuity between the human and the natural. Robert Edwards sees in the *Clerk's Tale* the *via media* Chaucer finds between Boccaccio's hermeneutic multiplicity and Petrarch's closure in dealing with the Griselda story.

Among the papers devoted to medieval authors reading other medieval authors, Julia Boffey's highlights the centrality of Anglo-French political and cultural relations as exemplified both in the way Charles of Orleans reads Chaucer's dream poetry and in English interest for Charles's French poems in the late fifteenth century. Osbern Bokenham's legendary is taken by Sheila Delany as evidence of opposing as well as imitating veneration towards Chaucer's *Legend of Good Women*. Carol Meale's essay bears in its own title the ambiguity of the term 'reading' which is to be understood – the author makes clear – both in the sense of how Alice Chaucer had access to books and of the way we *now* interpret the role of women in late medieval England.

The section on modern writers reading medieval ones opens with a piece by Thomas Roche, who sees Spenser, at the end of Book V of the *Faerie Queene*, playing with the narrative of recent history against the paradigm of the Four Daughters of God. By looking at the 1808 picture and at the *Descriptive Catalogue*, Stefania D'Agata D'Ottavi draws attention to Blake's 'misreading' of Chaucer's Pilgrims in terms of an allegorization of the General Prologue. Angelo Righetti offers a fresh investigation of the relevance of Browning's medievalism within his poetical activity.

The volume closes with two articles, written by the representatives of Eastern and Western scholarship, Toshiyuki Takamiya and Joerg Fichte, who discuss Japanese and German reworkings of Arthurian material. While Soseki's *Kairo-ko* makes use of Malory's and Tennyson's Arthurian versions in order to express the author's sense of transgression, the appropriation of the Arthurian myth by contemporary German drama aims at emphasizing the 'pastness' of the Round Table experience and the decline of all utopian ideals in the present time.

We would like to thank all the institutions who made the Symposium possible: the New Chaucer Society, the Universities of Perugia and Macerata, the British Council, the City of Perugia and the Regional Council of Umbria, in the person of its President Claudio Carnieri. We also wish to express our gratitude to the session chairmen, Domenico Pezzini, Sergio Rufini, and Enrico Giaccherini for their help in making the discussion lively.

We thoroughly enjoyed the papers, the debate, and the company of our contributors. We hope our readers will find the volume as stimulating.

14 July 1995   Anna Torti
                                                                                                                       Piero Boitani

ALAIN DE LILLE, JEAN DE MEUN, AND CHAUCER: ECOFEMINISM AND SOME MEDIEVAL LADY NATURES

LISA J. KISER

> Now who put *us*, we should like to know, in *Her* manage?
> – W.H. Auden, 'Dame Kind'

It hardly needs to be demonstrated that women have been closely identified with Nature in the western cultural tradition, an identification widely embraced by western writers since antiquity and one of interest to modern proponents of ecofeminism, ecocriticism, environmental ethics, and the philosophy of nature.[1] In the medieval philosophical and literary traditions, for example, especially those of the twelfth through fifteenth centuries, Nature is overwhelmingly configured as a woman, occasionally cast in the role of mother, but more often seen metaphorically as a goddess, the viceregent of God and the conveyor of his natural laws to the physical world. There are major exceptions to this generalization, however. J.A.W. Bennett, whose memory we are honouring at this symposium, reminds us emphatically in his survey of medieval conceptions of Nature that Langland, in *Piers Plowman*, envisions Nature (Kynde) as a male: he is 'the fader and fourmour of al that ever was maked'.[2] But Nature, in the late medieval period, is usually configured as feminine, with the impetus for this configuration coming, we can assume, partly from the grammatical gender of the Latin noun *natura* and partly from the linking of Nature's regenerative powers with the biological capacities of the female sex.

---

[1] For a convenient survey of this connection in pre-nineteenth-century Europe, see Carolyn Merchant, *The Death of Nature: Women, Ecology and the Scientific Revolution* (New York, 1983), pp. 1–41. Women's identification with nature in general is treated in, among other works, Susan Griffin, *Women and Nature: The Roaring Inside Her* (San Francisco, 1978); Rosemary Radford Ruether, *New Woman/New Earth: Sexist Ideologies and Human Liberation* (New York, 1975); Katherine Davies, 'Historical Associations: Women and the Natural World', *Women & Environments* 9 (1987) 4–6; Judith Plant, ed., *Healing Our Wounds: The Power of Ecological Feminism* (Boston, 1989); Karen J. Warren, 'The Power and the Promise of Ecological Feminism', *Environmental Ethics* 12 (1990) 125–46; Val Plumwood, *Feminism and the Mastery of Nature* (New York, 1993); and Karen J. Warren, ed., *Ecological Feminism* (New York, 1994).

[2] B IX 27. This line, from Skeat's edition, is cited and discussed in J.A.W. Bennett, *The Parlement of Foules: An Interpretation* (Oxford, 1957), p. 209.

Studying some of the medieval period's central representations of Nature with modern environmental ethics in mind can be enlightening (as I will momentarily argue), but it can also – if we are not careful – serve to distract us from the specifically medieval emphases of some of these primary texts. In one of Alain de Lille's sermons, for example, he preaches eloquently against what might be construed as the rape of the environment, personifying Nature as an aggrieved and embattled mother. She laments,

> 'Why do you do injury to your mother? Why do you do violence to me who brought you forth from my womb? Why do you disturb me with the plough, so that I may return your investment in seed an hundredfold? Why do you dig into me, your mother, to make me give up my gold? Are those things not sufficient which I give you abundantly and of my own free will, that you should tear things from me by force?'[3]

We might be tempted here to foreground Alain's environmentalism, to note his objection to the over-cultivation of the land for profit and applaud his rhetorical move of configuring the land as our mother, one to whom we owe our life and therefore our respect. Indeed, Alain may be displaying some form of what we would call environmentalism here, but he is, in fact, intending to make quite a different case; this passage is less about nature than it is about sin, coming as it does in a sample sermon on avarice, one which needs to be historically contextualized and analyzed as an argument serving Alain's larger moral ends and directed to his particular medieval audience.[4]

This point, namely, that medieval configurations of nature are always about something else as well, needs to be emphasized – yet feminist ecological theory is nonetheless still useful in helping us to analyze the cultural results of a specifically gendered identity for nature and the natural world. When nature is gendered as female in a culture such as that which prevailed in the medieval European scholastic environments of the late twelfth and thirteenth centuries, she is very often made a partner in various sets of binaries, being placed in opposition to concepts such as 'maleness' and 'reason,' binaries that have their origins in pre-medieval cultures but which persisted with special tenacity in the European middle ages. Ecofeminist theorists such as Karen J. Warren and Val Plumwood, whose cultural analyses are especially persuasive, argue that the engendering of nature as female has unfortunately brought with it a chain of other related conceptions, all of which depend implicitly on the acceptance of binaristic

---

[3] Alan of Lille, *The Art of Preaching*, trans. Gillian R. Evans, Cistercian Studies Series 23 (Kalamazoo, 1981), pp. 40–41.

[4] Pliny, Ovid, and Seneca also connected mining to avarice and associated the earth with the maternal body. For an ecofeminist analysis of these tropes, see Merchant, *The Death of Nature*, pp. 30–41.

paradigms and most of which are still with us today: if Nature is not male, then she is not rational; if she is not rational, she is not human; if she is not human, she is not culture/technology, etc. As Plumwood writes, 'In [this] dualism, the more highly valued side (males, humans) is construed as alien to and of a different . . . order of being from the "lower" inferiorized side (women, nature)'; and Karen Warren adds that 'the feminization of nature and the naturalization of women have been crucial to the historically successful subordinations of both'.[5] The result of such essentialism and binary thinking is not only to locate women in an inferior position, one which requires them to be mastered, but also to place nature in that category as well, hindering – both for the medieval and the modern world – genuinely revisionist ecological arguments against the need to master the natural world. Not every medieval text that speaks about nature speaks exactly to these positions as I have outlined them, but one thing is very clear: these texts are as much about power relations as they are about nature, and this is owing, in large part, to nature's gendered identity in the masculinized theological environments that constructed her.

There is a surprising amount of variation, however, in the ways in which each major literary embodiment of Nature envisions and empowers her. She displays varying degrees of authority, from a substantial amount (despite her strict subordination to God's governing ordinances) to very little. She is configured as belonging to, originating from, or serving several different social classes and as occupying a number of social roles, with both rural and – surprisingly – urban connections, roles both traditionally possible for actual medieval women and those which would have been only rarely adopted by females. She sometimes displays gender instability, reflecting some traits and behaviours that were almost certainly construed as masculine. She is also closely enough allied to sexual behaviour to have posed a problem for the clerical communities who theorized her, a problem which was partially addressed by the development of a male companion for her – Genius. The texts I will be discussing in light of these issues are the major ones: Alain de Lille's *De Planctu Naturae*, Jean de Meun's section of the *Romance of the Rose*, and Chaucer's *Parliament of Fowls*. But I want to begin with a few remarks about Brunetto Latini's *Il Tesoretto*, because this text expresses so clearly some of the major social tensions and gender-dependent conceptual schemes surrounding the medieval allegorical analysis of Nature.

First of all, unlike the other writers I will cover, Latini has a genuine interest in identifying Nature's sphere of influence and differentiating it from extra-natural realms; his poem is a kind of descriptive compendium, in allegorical form, of the major components of the universe. He at times takes hints from Alain and Jean de Meun, both clearly literary models for him, but his text does not reflect their obvious scholastic agendas. Indeed, Latini's

---

5   Plumwood, *Feminism*, p. 32 and Warren, 'The Power and the Promise', p. 133.

Nature is something of an inscrutable figure. She resides in a *selva* (190)[6] which is off the narrator's well-travelled pilgrim route (*gran cammino*, 189), a location suggesting a realm of secrecy, privacy and mystery. Like Alain de Lille, Latini briefly finds it convenient to adapt the model of Boethius's Lady Philosophy to describe his figure's ability to change her size and her expression (218–30), but he does not stay with this empowering model long. Nature very quickly begins to be constructed as a model of ideal feminine beauty by means of the standard rhetorical *effictio*, with her gender being fixed and conventionalized through Latini's deployment of the secular descriptors that begin with her hair (golden tresses) and move down through her forehead, brows, eyes, nose, lips, teeth, and throat (249–61). When Nature speaks, her theme is 'alwey oon', as Chaucer might say – she discusses at length the limitations of her power, being quite obsessed with delineating – in great detail – what it is that she *cannot* do vis-à-vis God's superior creative and intellectual abilities. In addition, Latini aligns her with medieval conceptions of femininity by stressing her ideological affinities with the vernacular language (*volgare*, 425, 911, 1119) and with prose rather than rhyme (despite the fact that her speeches, like the whole *Tesoretto*, are in verse). When Lady Nature does get around to mentioning her actual accomplishments, they are nervously contextualized as just the insignificant final stages in God's plan of creation, and she focuses especially on animal rather than human realms, avoiding discourse about the stars or anything other than sublunary creation. Discussion of sexual matters is also rigorously avoided; although we are told that people ask her to 'fulfil their need' (513), this euphemism is never explained or analysed further. She in fact tells us that she dislikes the God of Love, and she gives the narrator a mysterious badge to ward off the deity's arrows. She closes her discourse with a list of things under her purview, a list which is largely composed of natural oddities: weird or unusual animals, far-away oceanic tidal behaviour, the rivers of Paradise, and magical stones and herbs. Lady Nature's realm is truly mystified here – but also trivialized, extending largely to an array of things most people never see, things falling outside most people's experience of the natural world.

Latini's *Tesoretto* is worth examining because it encodes the linkage between nature and gender identity fairly clearly, and it also expresses the cultural effect of such a linkage: Nature has no real power or importance largely because it is homologous to the feminine. Nature's fixed gender identity as a woman in fact seems to interfere with Latini's primary design – to account for the important place of the natural world in the medieval Christianized universe – since his assignment of gender to Nature results in the occlusion of its powers; readers are never sure about the extent of Nature's dominion, except to see that it has little relevance to the larger Christian

---

[6] All quotations from *Il Tesoretto* are from the edition of Julia Bolton Holloway, Garland Library of Medieval Literature, vol. 2, Series A (New York, 1981).

scheme. We cannot account for the tensions in Latini's text by simply attributing them to his most important source, Alain de Lille's *De Planctu Naturae*, because Alain's text has a vastly different construction of Lady Nature; his Nature, in fact, has a much less stable gender identity than Latini's, and her authority is greater. But Alain's text, too, betrays the interesting results of binary linkages between nature and gender.

Alain's poem, a product of the late twelfth-century schools, was written in the rarefied atmosphere of the Chartrian academic tradition, which promoted views about the physical world that are crucial to an analysis of the Western history of representations of nature. Alain de Lille and his literary mentors (especially Guillaume of Conches and Bernardus Silvestris) were united in their goal of attempting to eliminate dualistic thought about creation, namely, the idea that the physical world is separate from (and subordinate to) spiritual forces.[7] Alain was also actively involved in combating heresies such as Catharism, which affirmed that the natural world was evil.[8] Alain thus had a stake in representing Nature as empowered and as closely connected to divine spiritual mysteries. And indeed, her power and importance are stressed repeatedly in Alain's opening characterizations of her. She lives not in Latini's *selva* but in a *palacio* in Heaven (2.2); she shines with a light of her own, not a reflected one (she is *propria scintillans*, 2.3);[9] and she delivers a resoundingly confident speech about her powers and achievements, sprinkled with phrases attesting to her agency (*pro meo arbitrio*, 6.42; *mee potentie*, 6.43). She appropriates an imperious argument used by theologians and philosophers that spiritual mysteries and powers (such as hers) should be hidden from the vulgar throng (6.121 ff.),[10] and she notes that she has arrived from the 'innermost depths of the secret heavens' to visit the 'common brothels of earth' (8.4–5).[11]

To elevate her status, Alain has configured her in the opening of his work

---

[7] For the cosmological, philosophical, and theological significance of Alain's treatment of Natura, see especially George D. Economou, *The Goddess Natura in Medieval Literature* (Cambridge, Mass., 1972); M.-D. Chenu, 'Nature and Man: The Renaissance of the Twelfth Century', in *Nature, Man, and Society in the Twelfth Century*, ed. and trans. Jerome Taylor and Lester K. Little (Chicago, 1968), pp. 18–32; and Winthrop Wetherbee, *Platonism and Poetry in the Twelfth Century: The Literary Influence of the School of Chartres* (Princeton, 1972), pp. 187–219.

[8] Alain's Natura speaks out against heresy in 7.143–44, mentioning Manichaeism and Arianism in particular. For Alain's participation in the church's fight against heresy, see G.R. Evans, *Alan of Lille: The Frontiers of Theology in the Later Twelfth Century* (Cambridge, 1983), pp. 11, 116–24 and John M. Trout, *The Voyage of Prudence: The World View of Alan of Lille* (Washington, D.C., 1979), pp. 10–17.

[9] All quotations from *De Planctu Naturae* are from the edition of Nikolaus M. Häring, *Studi Medievali* 19 (1978) 797–879.

[10] Macrobius, *Commentary on the Dream of Scipio*, 2.17, trans. William Harris Stahl (New York, 1952), p. 86.

[11] These translations are James J. Sheridan's, from *Plaint of Nature*, Medieval Sources in Translation, 26 (Toronto, 1980), p. 130.

as a powerful member of the upper feudal aristocracy, one of the few possible empowering social identities for a woman in Alain's time. She wears a royal diadem (2.40) and fine linen (*sindo . . . non plebea vilescens materia*, 2.196–97), and she is treated by the narrator as well as by the natural world around her with deferential feudal posturing – the narrator employs the language of secular social service in her presence by paying 'homage' to this 'queen' from whom he desires 'favour' (6.194–95), and the natural world seeks her 'grace' with *obsequium* (4.64). As a powerful aristocrat, Alain's Nature is unproblematically gendered here as female, and he works to stabilize her gender identity in the *effictio*-like lines that Latini borrowed later – her hair, skin, eyebrows, eyes, nose, and teeth are mentioned, and we are even given a glimpse of her through the sexually-motivated male gaze when the narrator notes that her lips invite kisses (2.20–21), her arms suggest embraces (2.28–29), and his 'faith' imagines the veiled parts of her body to be even more inviting than what is disclosed to him (2.32).

Yet in spite of Nature's opening construction as a female, her gender identity undergoes some curious modifications when Alain introduces the subject of sexual behaviour, one of the most important topics of his work. As soon as Nature begins her complaint against the human practices of sexual excess and perversity, she begins to display social traits and roles conventionally assigned, in the late twelfth century, to men. Her frequent use of grammatical metaphors, for example, to describe sexual perversity, is clearly imitating discourse associated with scholastic communities, and she quickly casts herself in the role of the schoolmaster, lecturing to pupils whose understanding of Latin grammar needs to be improved: humanity's perversion of the rules of sexual 'rightness' is for her closely analogous to poor writing ('*sophista . . . falsigraphus*', 7.56–59).[12] Her role as a teacher of Latin is further developed as she describes her gift of a reed pen, along with strict orthographic and grammatical rules to prevent erroneous writing, to Venus, who, as her pupil, is also taught the principles of logic and argumentation. Nature's literacy here, her ability to compose in Latin and to write down her compositions, distinctly sets her apart from most twelfth-century women, and her role as a university master of grammar, logic, and dialectic places her entirely outside the sphere of twelfth-century women's gender roles, for

---

[12] Nature's grammatical metaphors have been the subject of much discussion. See especially Maureen Quilligan, 'Words and Sex: the Language of Allegory in the *De planctu naturae*, the *Roman de la Rose*, and Book III of *The Faerie Queene*', *Allegorica* 2 (1977) 195–215; Economou, *The Goddess Natura*, p. 87; R. Howard Bloch, *Etymologies and Genealogies: A Literary Anthropology of the French Middle Ages* (Chicago, 1983), pp. 133–36; R. H. Green, 'Alain of Lille's *De planctu naturae*', *Speculum* 31 (1956) 649–74; Wetherbee, *Platonism and Poetry*, pp. 189 and 194. It is worth noting that in Alain's probable sources, Claudian's *Consulship of Stilicho* and Bernard Silvestris's *De mundi universitate*, she is not represented as being a writer or as having literacy skills.

women were prohibited from becoming involved in the university, either as teachers or as students.[13] In fact, one might not imprudently say that Nature here has come to resemble Alain de Lille himself.

Alain continues to destabilize Nature's gender identity when he introduces Nature's companion Genius.[14] Genius is a character deserving some attention, because he is actually said to be Nature's 'other self' (*sibi alteri*, 16.188). When she looks at him, she thinks she has looked into a mirror (16. 189–91); the two bear a close resemblance to one another, being doubles of each other in dress, physical traits, and ideological attitudes. It is here, I would assert, that Nature most clearly begins to be masculinized. In fact, we might be tempted to say that Alain's mingling of genders in this remarkable union of Nature and Genius is a further (and very daring) breakdown of dualistic thinking on the part of this poet, who clearly wanted to elevate the status of the physical world. But a more accurate analysis reveals that Alain is expressing something much more conventional here. Unwilling to allow a female to be in charge of humanity (especially human sexual behaviour), he creates a male identity for her. Genius, her male side, is the aspect of her that polices sexual matters, and in addition to his male gender identity, he is given the social role of priest. To be sure, Genius is in some sense subordinate to Lady Nature, but it is he (not her) who is actually in control of the generation and stewardship of humanity.[15]

Here, then, Alain de Lille's conception of Nature becomes somewhat conflicted. Although his moral and theological commitments require that he avoid any binary separation between spiritual and natural realms and that he present a powerfully unified configuration of Nature's dominion over moral and spiritual truth, he is reluctant to allow an entity that is gendered as female to oversee human existence, especially that part of it – human sexual behaviour – traditionally policed by the Church and assumed to be in moral jeopardy as a result of uncontrollable female sexual excess. Thus, Nature's control over humanity is 'masculinized' (and clericalized) through Genius, and Alain's poem begins to ally itself with the very binaries its author had hoped to avoid, here setting up a division (which is in fact an opposition)

---

[13] See Joan M. Ferrante, 'The Education of Women in the Middle Ages in Theory, Fact, and Fantasy', in Patricia H. Labalme, ed., *Beyond Their Sex: Learned Women of the European Past* (New York, 1980), pp. 9–42.

[14] On the history and theological function of the character Genius, see Jane Chance Nitzsche, *The Genius Figure in Antiquity and the Middle Ages* (New York, 1975); Economou, *The Goddess Natura*, pp. 90–97; Wetherbee, *Platonism and Poetry*, pp. 202–10; George D. Economou, 'The Character Genius in Alan de Lille, Jean de Meun, and John Gower', *Chaucer Review* 4 (1970) 203–10; and Denise N. Baker, 'The Priesthood of Genius: A Study of the Medieval Tradition', *Speculum* 51 (1976) 277–91.

[15] On Genius's connection both to maleness and to human nature, see Wetherbee, *Platonism and Poetry*, pp. 206–7; Nitzsche, pp. 7–15 and 90–97; and Economou, *The Goddess Natura*, pp. 90–92.

between the 'human' and the 'natural', gendering them as 'male' and 'female' respectively. Indeed, Nature has been empowered in some daring ways in this work, but Alain's ideological affinities with the moral philosophy of the twelfth-century schools have finally taken control of his intellectual colonization of the natural world.

When we move to Jean de Meun's Nature, created nearly one hundred years after Alain's, we find a strikingly different configuration, even though Jean de Meun's connection with the University of Paris suggests that, like Alain, he was writing out of an academic tradition.[16] Interpreting Jean's Nature, who is an ecofeminist's nightmare, as any sort of serious meditation on the natural world, is inadvisable since Jean is almost certainly perpetrating a series of clerical jokes; his loquacious Lady Nature and her false priest-confessor, Genius, are portrayed as rather shameless recruits in Amant's campaign to deflower his lady. Nor is this the place to revisit the subject of Jean de Meun's most overt forms of misogyny in his characterization of Lady Nature; the fact that Reason has been removed from Nature's bailiwick and made into a separate character reinforces the ecofeminist claim about rationality being denied to what is identified as the 'natural' – but this move, as well as the openly misogynistic comments made by Genius, have been noted before.[17] Yet in spite of the jocular tone and the crude antifeminist comedy in Jean de Meun's poem, in Nature's long speech, she raises a variety of philosophical points about the extent of her authority, an issue that medieval readers of the *Roman* responded to seriously in their marginal comments and in their scribal rewritings of Jean's work.[18] In other words, Jean de Meun's conception of Nature entered the mainstream as an authoritative rendering.

[16] Jean de Meun's affiliation with the University of Paris is demonstrated by his most recent editor, Félix Lecoy, in *Le Roman de la Rose*, vol. 1, Les Classiques Français du Moyen Âge (Paris, 1965), p. 18.

[17] Jean de Meun's misogyny, especially that which emerges in Lady Nature's section of the *Roman*, has been the frequent subject of scholarly commentary. See, for example, Lionel J. Friedman, ' "Jean de Meung", Antifeminism, and "Bourgeois Realism", ' *Modern Philology* 57 (1959) 13–23; Rosamund Tuve, *Allegorical Imagery: Some Medieval Books and Their Posterity* (Princeton, 1966), p. 269; and Economou, *The Goddess Natura*, pp. 120–21. On the relationship between Natura and Raison and on Natura's 'de-allegorization' in the *Roman*, see especially Winthrop Wetherbee, 'The Literal and the Allegorical: Jean de Meun and the *de Planctu Naturae*', *Medieval Studies* 33 (1971) 264–91. Also see Lucie Polak, 'Plato, Nature and Jean de Meun', *Reading Medieval Studies* 3 (1977) 80–99.

[18] Sylvia Huot, in *The Romance of the Rose and its Medieval Readers: Interpretation, Reception, Manuscript Transmission* (Cambridge, 1993), notes the marginal glossing of Nature's speech (p. 36) and the rewriting of it to assign a few of her powers to God instead (p. 138–39), an attempt to make Jean's text cohere better with received cosmological and theological belief. She also discusses Gui de Mori's 1290 reworking of the *Roman de la Rose*, which edits Nature's speech so that it conforms more closely to Alain de Lille's conception (pp. 110–14). Clearly, these readers were responding to Jean's work as if it were a genuine contribution to the philosophical tradition of describing the natural world, even if, like Jean Gerson (see Huot, p. 22), they quibbled

In developing his personification, Jean de Meun is careful to foreground Lady Nature's female identity. He does not detail her bodily traits, as do Brunetto and Alain, but he does – in an extended *occupatio* – assert that she is one of God's loveliest female creations (16199–219).[19] Her gender identity is also firmly fixed by her priest Genius,[20] who essentializes women (like Nature) by noting, among other character flaws, how easily they become upset and how changeable they are. We might note here that Genius too is essentialized as conforming to stereotypes of the male anti-feminist cleric; like the Wife of Bath's husband Jankyn, he is replete with *exempla* about women being unable to keep secrets. But on this score, Lady Nature agrees, saying, 'I am a woman and cannot keep silent; from now on I want to reveal everything, for a woman can hide nothing' (19188–90). Indeed, Lady Nature briefly displays stereotypical academic and clerical tendencies herself as she demonstrates an interest in oral debate and argument (17697 ff.) and as she voices some of the commonest antifeminist anecdotes drawn from the misogamous literature of male Christian communities (18100 ff.). At odd moments such as these, when Nature seems to be a traitor to her sex in the gender wars, we might be tempted to analyse her as gender-destabilized – but I think that the effect is just the opposite: these misogynistic remarks serve to remind us repeatedly that we are in the presence of a woman (as constructed by thirteenth-century clerical males) and that her doctrines about the natural world should be received with that fact in mind. Jean de Meun also robs Lady Nature of her literacy. Her priest-confessor Genius does all of the writing, fulfilling a common socio-cultural pattern of illiterate women using their confessors as scribes (16253–54; 19376–77); moreover, all of the complex analogies between sexuality and writing that Alain de Lille had created are given to Genius rather than to Nature (19513–38; 19599–606).[21] Lady Nature also praises clerks for their ability to read (18605 ff.), and she directs the inquisitive to seek out clerks in order to learn more about the intricacies of Fortune's role in earthly affairs (17705–6).

Jean de Meun's debasement and containment of Nature is most visible, however, in his assignment of a habitation, occupation, and social class to his

---

with some of its details. See also Sylvia Huot, 'Authors, Scribes, Remanieurs: A Note on the Textual History of the *Roman de la Rose*', in *Rethinking the 'Romance of the Rose': Text, Image, Reception*, ed. Kevin Brownlee and Sylvia Huot (Philadelphia, 1992), esp. pp. 206–7.

19 All quotations from the *Roman de la Rose* are taken from the edition of Félix Lecoy. Translations are from Charles Dahlberg, trans. *The Romance of the Rose* (Princeton, 1971).

20 On Genius's role in the *Roman*, see especially Baker, 'The Priesthood of Genius', 284–86; Economou, 'The Character Genius', 205–8, and *The Goddess Natura*, pp. 111–18; Nitzsche, *The Genius Figure*, pp. 116–25; and Wetherbee, 'The Literal and the Allegorical', 282–86.

21 See Huot, *The Romance of the Rose*, pp. 267–69, for a discussion of Genius's writerly functions and their reception by later French poets.

poem privileges, are there to accept Nature's 'dom and yeve hire audience' (308), to follow her 'statut' and accept her 'governaunce' (387).[25] Moreover, Nature imposes other forms of social control on the wildfowl around her. She orders each bird to 'take his owene place' (320) in her parliament in a fashion strictly consonant with their social standing: noble birds of prey are highest (and get to choose their mates first), then come the worm-fowl, water-fowl, and seed-fowl in a descending order of social status, an arrangement that – in keeping with aristocratic will – discourages the idea of social mobility or intermarriage between social classes. This method of classifying wild creatures by means of human social categories might, in another poem, seem jarring or ridiculous. Yet Chaucer has worked hard to make that system seem, well, perfectly natural. Supporting each of his birds' social identities with lore drawn from scientific sources and/or stores of proverbial wisdom, Chaucer asks his readers to accept the rightness of such a classification of the natural world, even though, on close analysis, it is a classification heavily biased in favour of aristocratic interests.[26]

For all her wisdom and laudable skills in mediation and governance, Chaucer's Nature is nonetheless serving dominant social ideologies. His Nature is wholly constructed to bolster and confirm a set of aristocratic beliefs about the innate superiority of the upper class, beliefs presumably held by his noble audience. Nature's function is to preserve social hierarchies and reinforce dismissive stereotypes of those classes beneath the aristocratic ones; only the aristocrats are given full space to display their courtly mating rituals, whereas the classes below them are given short shrift (and are even implied to be unable to comprehend noble behaviour).[27] Tellingly, Nature is not shy about informing us who her favourite birds are – they are the royal formel eagle ('. . . of shap the gentilleste / That evere she among hire werkes fond / The moste benygne and the goodlieste', 373–75) and the royal tercelet ('. . . the gentilleste and most worthi / Which I have wrought', 635–36).

Finally, Nature's law, as expressed in this poem, contains many gender-specific doctrines which not only bear directly on her own gendered identity but also on the social codes of Chaucer's day. Nature calls for males to choose

---

[25] On the legal atmosphere of this scene, and on how its vocabulary recalls fourteenth-century parliamentary discourse, see Bennett, *The Parlement of Foules*, p. 140; and D.S. Brewer, ed. *The Parlement of Foulys* (London, 1960), pp. 37–38.

[26] Chaucer has carefully selected his bird lore from Vincent of Beauvais's *Speculum naturale*, Bartholomaeus Anglicus's *De proprietatibus rerum*, Isidore's *Etymologies*, Pliny's *Natural History*, and a variety of popular sources, some of them distilled in bestiaries of the period. For identifications of some of the sources behind specific lines, see the notes to the *Parliament* in *The Riverside Chaucer*.

[27] On courtship practices as markers of social class in this poem, see Macdonald Emslie, 'Codes of Love and Class Distinctions', *Essays in Criticism* 5 (1955) 1–17; also relevant is Lee Patterson's discussion of the self-legitimization of the aristocratic classes through social display in his chapter on the 'Knight's Tale' in *Chaucer and the Subject of History* (Madison, 1991), esp. pp. 168–74, 181–94.

their mates first, but females must be given a chance to agree to the match (407–11), a restriction that appears to be binding for birds of all classes. Thus, Chaucer's Nature is working against the practice of forced marriages (a point that Bennett made long ago) and for a woman's right to have a say in the choice of her marriage partner, a right not always happily recognized among the fourteenth-century noble classes.[28] And for the noble bird in question here, Nature is actually willing to alter her decrees to empower this female even more, for she gives the usually male prerogative of initial choice to her ('Thanne wol I don hire this favour', 626–30), also allowing for a delay to suit the woman's desire to remain temporarily unmarried. Here, then, the aristocratic female is seemingly allowed special powers above and beyond those normally accorded her in late medieval society, a move that Chaucer makes in order to assert how firmly his Lady Nature is enlisted in the service of aristocratic – especially female – interests.[29]

Yet Nature's advocacy of female interests is only a mirage. The fact that the marriage delay is only temporary and that the formel's 'choice' is largely illusory (feudal interests will ultimately force her to pick one of her three suitors, whether she wants him or not),[30] raises questions about just how empowered Chaucer's formel – and his Lady Nature – really are. As with the female formel eagle, Chaucer's Nature *seems* to exhibit substantial control and power over her own sphere of existence, but upon closer analysis, that sphere reveals itself to be organized around class- and gender-based ideologies much larger than can be affected by her individual will. Both Nature and the formel can only delay the inevitable, not prevent it; and the parliamentary rules, though bendable, are not breakable, persisting, as they do, 'alwey, fro yer to yeere' (411). Like Alain's and Jean de Meun's, then, Chaucer's Lady Nature encodes his culture's dominant conceptions about the distribution of power in the social order, – and that power is obviously not vested in women or in the natural world, which is represented as feminized and thus subordinate to the cultural dominance of males.

In analysing medieval representations of nature, we must agree with the ecological feminists that 'the problematic of nature has been . . . closely interwoven with that of gender'.[31] We also need to recognize that to medieval

---

[28] Bennett, *The Parlement of Foules*, pp. 143–44. For a recent discussion of the degree of female consent in marriage practices among the English nobility of the late medieval period, see Jennifer C. Ward, *English Noblewomen in the Later Middle Ages* (London, 1992), pp. 12–33.

[29] We should remember also that this poem may well be alluding to the actual marriage negotiations between Richard II and Anne of Bohemia. See *The Riverside Chaucer*, p. 994.

[30] For a gender-based reading of the *Parliament* that addresses in greater detail the submerged conflict between feudal interests and courtly codes, see Elaine Tuttle Hansen, *Chaucer and the Fictions of Gender* (Berkeley, 1992), pp. 117–28.

[31] Plumwood, *Feminism and the Mastery of Nature*, p. 1.

Christians, nature existed only in a fallen state, a state that was brought about in part by the effects of Eve's transgressive feminine will. The connection between nature and the feminine thus runs deep in medieval culture, and it clearly serves to reaffirm the logic of a dualism that places fallen nature and the female in opposition to everything that is not fallen, i.e., God. But I would like to point out that these medieval configurations of nature (to the extent that they are bona fide attempts to theorize the natural world) achieve something that some modern ecological feminists and philosophers of nature might see as laudatory, namely, that nature has a human face. The natural world is, in other words, continuous with – not separated from – humanity and culture; humans are thus theorized not as 'outside' nature but as 'inside' it, a point that significantly undermines some of the other damaging ontological dualisms that have kept nature in a position of subordination in western culture, especially those that place nature in opposition to culture, to mind, to the self, and to the human; indeed, as ecofeminists argue, '[T]he separation of humanity and nature is the linchpin of patriarchial ideology'.[32] Although we can't pretend to be able to empty these poems of the oppressive social programs they promote, the medieval Lady Natures who live in them actually may help us to theorize about how we can find a '*non-reductionist* basis for recognizing continuity'[33] between the human and the natural, and to come up with 'a form of knowledge which grants to the world around us its independent integrity but does so in a way which remains cognisant of, indeed relies on, our connectivity with that world'.[34] Perhaps modern ecofeminist philosophers can find in medieval visions of Nature the seeds of a theory that will free nature from its domination as an 'other'. Yet we also have much to learn about the negative social consequences of the domestication of nature in the gendered conceptions used by Alain, Jean de Meun, Chaucer – and Auden, with whom this paper began. For Auden surely owes much to his medieval forebears when he writes of Dame Kind, 'She mayn't be all She might be but She *is* our Mum'.[35]

---

[32] Ariel Salleh, 'Class, Race, and Gender Discourse in the Ecofeminism/Deep Ecology Debate', *Environmental Ethics* 15 (1993), p. 225. See also Salleh's 'The Ecofeminism/Deep Ecology Debate: A Reply to Patriarchal Reason', *Environmental Ethics* 14 (1992), p. 209, in which she cites and approves of Ynestra King's statement that 'ecofeminsts would like to see men give up their attempts to control women and nature and join women in their identity with nature'.

[33] Plumwood, *Feminism and the Mastery of Nature*, p. 123. This 'non-reductionist' basis would not simply consist of wholesale anthropocentrism, but would, of course, recognize difference at the same time that it sought integration.

[34] Evelyn Fox Keller, *Reflections on Gender and Science* (New Haven, 1985), p. 117; quoted in Plumwood, *Feminism and the Mastery of Nature*, p. 123. See also Elizabeth M. Harlow, 'The Human Face of Nature: Environmental Values and the Limits of Nonanthropocentrism', *Environmental Ethics* 14 (1992) 27–42.

[35] Quotations from Auden's 'Dame Kind' are taken from the edition of Edward Mendelson, *W.H. Auden: Selected Poems* (New York, 1989).

'THE SCLAUNDRE OF WALTER': THE *CLERK'S TALE* AND THE PROBLEM OF HERMENEUTICS

ROBERT R. EDWARDS

Over the last decade or so, scholars have turned to the record of Chaucer's historical reception as a way of reading the *Clerk's Tale* in a context that defines the poem as both a literary text and a cultural product. To judge from Lydgate's reference in the *Temple of Glass* (75–76) to 'Grisildis innocence, / And al hir mekenes, & hir pacience' and from his distinct echoes of the tale's Envoy in the Christmas mumming at Hertford castle, Chaucer's poem was regarded in the century after his death as an *exemplum* of patience applicable to courtly figures and brawling rustics alike.[1] Textual evidence indicates that, apart from its inclusion in complete manuscripts of the *Canterbury Tales*, the story was popular in fifteenth-century excerpts and anthologies.[2] Showing

---

[1] *Lydgate's Temple of Glas*, ed. J. Schick, EETS ES 60 (1891), p. 3; cf. Venus's remark to her petitioner, 'Griseld[e] was assaied at[te] ful, / That turned aftir to hir encrese of Ioye' (405–6). In the text printed by Eleanor P. Hammond, 'Lydgate's Mumming at Hertford', *Anglia* 22 (1899) 364–74, the wives answer their husbands' complaint of mistreatment by citing the Wife of Bath (168) and affirming their intent 'to clappen as a mylle' (cf. *Clerk's Tale* IV. 1200). Chaucer's claim, 'Griselde is deed, and eek hire pacience, / And bothe atones buryed in Ytaille' (1177–78) undergoes a shift in which the patience is not Griselde's specifically but the wives' generally: 'ther pacyence was buryed long agoo / Gresyldes story recordethe pleinly soo' (175–76). I have regularized *thorn* to *th*. See Caroline F.E. Spurgeon, *Five Hundred Years of Chaucer Criticism and Allusion: 1357–1900*, 3 vols. (Cambridge, 1925), 1: 17, 18, 36. All quotations of Chaucer's text will use *The Riverside Chaucer*, ed. Larry D. Benson (Boston, 1987).

[2] The independent versions are as follows:

Ha1   (British Library, Harley 1239): *Knight's Tale*, *Man of Law's Tale*, *Wife of Bath's Tale*, *Clerk's Tale*, and *Franklin's Tale*.
Ll1   (Longleat 257): *Knight's Tale* and *Clerk's Tale*.
Np   (Naples, Royal Library 13.B.29): *Clerk's Tale* only.
Ph4   (Phillipps 8299; now Huntington Library, HM140): *Clerk's Tale*, 'Truth', and *Anelida and Arcite*.
Ra4   (Bodleian Library, Rawlinson C.86): *Clerk's Tale* and parts of the *Prioress's Tale*.
Si   (London, Sion College, Arch L.40.2/E.23; now Tokyo, T. Takamiya, MS 22): *Clerk's Tale* followed by Fragment III of *Canterbury Tales*.

A fragment of the *Clerk's Tale* (IV. 808–91) is preserved in Hl4 (British Library, Harley 5908) but begins and ends in the middle of stanzas. J.J. Griffith, 'A Re-examination of Oxford, Bodleian Library, MS Rawlinson C.86', *Archiv für das Studium der neueren Sprachen und Literaturen* 219 (1982) 381–88, argues that Ra4

few traces of correction and supervision, the anthologies compiled roughly in the third quarter of the century give us a picture of how the tale was represented to late-medieval readers. Frequently, it came to them as an independent narrative named after its heroine.[3] Sometimes, it was classified generically as a romance and associated with the *Knight's Tale* and *Anelida and Arcite*.[4] Undoubtedly, it was seen as a philosophical and moral tale, just the sort of preaching the Host makes a point of instructing the Clerk to avoid in the Prologue.[5]

Building on the literary testimony and textual evidence, the most persuasive of modern historicist readings have situated the *Clerk's Tale* in a period of social anxiety, in which the poem appeals to an audience more decentralized, more socially mobile and diverse than Chaucer's original circle of court functionaries, yet still conservative, backward-looking, and now belated.[6] David Lawton observes that the portion of the Chaucer canon most cited by fifteenth-century poets is a group of 'uniformly serious works' and that 'Griselda's patience, the supreme public virtue of the fifteenth century, is

    dates to the early sixteenth century and originates in or near London. The starting point for discussion of these manuscripts by recent scholars is Charles D. Owen, 'The *Canterbury Tales*: Early Manuscripts and Relative Popularity', *JEGP* 54 (1955) 104–10; and Daniel S. Silvia, 'Some Fifteenth-Century Manuscripts of the *Canterbury Tales*', in *Chaucer and Middle English Studies in Honour of Rossell Hope Robbins*, ed. Beryl Rowland (London, 1974), pp. 153–63. For recent discussion of the anthologies in the period, see Julia Boffey and John J. Thompson, 'Anthologies and Miscellanies: Production and Choice of Texts', in *Book Production and Publishing in Britain 1375–1475*, ed. Jeremy Griffiths and Derek Pearsall (Cambridge, 1989), pp. 279–315.

[3] Np (beginning at IV. 92) entitles the tale 'Griselda'; Ll1 (beginning at IV. 57) 'Grisild'; Ra4 (beginning at IV. 57) 'Grysill'. The identification of the tale as 'Griselda' is not, however, unique to manuscripts recording the *Clerk's Tale* apart from the Canterbury sequence. Ra3 (Rawlinson Poetry 223) calls the *Clerk's Tale* 'Griselde'; see John M. Manly and Edith Rickert, eds., *The Text of the Canterbury Tales*, 8 vols. (Chicago, 1940), 1: 466. Tc2 (Trinity College Cambridge R.3.15) has the indication 'hic gresild' for placing the Clerk's headlink and tale next in a mutilated copy of the *Canterbury Tales* (Manly and Rickert, 1: 529). Np is defective, and it probably lost a leaf; yet the title 'Griselda' would presumably have applied to both the Prologue and the tale. Ll1 and Ra4 clearly begin at the start of the narrative.

[4] Manly and Rickert say of Np, 'Griselda is included here merely as a romance' (1: 377). Derek Pearsall, *The Canterbury Tales* (London, 1985), p. 323, describes Ll1: 'Knight's Tale and Clerk's Tale in a "romance" collection'. The extract from David Laing's *Reliquae Antiquae*, 2 vols. (1841–43), 2: 58–70 (which lists the contents of Np) in Spurgeon, 2: 247–48 also suggests that the MS is a collection of romances.

[5] The arrangement of Ph4 may reflect a moralizing context for the tale; the text begins without heading or prologue and runs without any indication of a break into Chaucer's 'Balade de Bon Conseyl' ('Truth'), which is transcribed without the Envoy to Vache.

[6] Thomas J. Heffernan, 'Aspects of the Chaucerian apocrypha: animadversions on William Thynne's edition of the *Plowman's Tale*', in *Chaucer Traditions: Studies in Honour of Derek Brewer*, ed. Ruth Morse and Barry Windeatt (Cambridge, 1990), p. 166 n13, remarks that the shift in Chaucer's audience from a court circle to wealthy country households in the fifteenth century involved both appropriation and the creation of a new image of the poet.

exalted as a model of behaviour rather than censured for submission to the monstrous Walter'.[7] Paul Strohm argues that where fourteenth-century audiences valued tales (like the *Franklin's Tale*) which destabilized genre and challenged the social values associated with it, fifteenth-century readers favoured works (like the *Clerk's Tale*) which were stable in genre and traditional in their outlook on social values and relations.[8] Incorporating Strohm's points about genre and outlook, Seth Lerer reads the version of the *Clerk's Tale* preserved in one of the fifteenth-century anthologies (Ph4) as a text that has been removed from an autonomous literary sphere and made to function as 'a fable for apprentice readers' addressed as children who need to learn the lessons of patience, governance, and stability in the face of authority.[9]

The historicist approach has the considerable advantage of locating reception in a world of readers sufficiently different from us, but it brings along with it several anomalies. In some measure, it is the old historicism inverted or at least refurbished to accommodate modern themes of power and dominance and critical styles that seek to render visible the sunken understructure of ideology. The period of Chaucer's reception remains withal the age of glory departed as it was described nearly fifty years ago by H.S. Bennett, who was then revising an earlier view that the age was altogether barren of poetry.[10] Though it assigns different meanings to historical forces, our contemporary narrative of the fifteenth century does not much disturb the shape of Bennett's account of war abroad, and war and social upheaval at home. A further anomaly is that the historicist approach concedes from the outset that the *Clerk's Tale* is indeed the right story for an age and readership that made dullness not just an authorial pose of humility, as in Hoccleve and Lydgate, but a psychological strategy and even a social and public virtue. On this view, Chaucer's beleaguered readers in the fifteenth century did not merely impose a constructed meaning on the text; rather, they turned to a text that they understood properly, without mediation. Though they feel the loss of Chaucer at one level, at another they occupy a position before the need for hermeneutics. As Gadamer and others assert, historical understanding of an artwork means integrating rather than restoring what has been lost.[11] Our

---

7   David Lawton, 'Dullness and the Fifteenth Century', *ELH* 54 (1978), p. 780.
8   Paul Strohm, 'Chaucer's Fifteenth-Century Audience and the Narrowing of the "Chaucer Tradition" ', *Studies in the Age of Chaucer* 4 (1982), p. 26.
9   Seth Lerer, *Chaucer and His Readers: Imagining the Author in Late-Medieval England* (Princeton, 1993), p. 113.
10 H.S. Bennett, *Chaucer and the Fifteenth Century*, vol. 2, pt 1 of The Oxford History of English Literature (Oxford, 1947; rpt 1961), pp. 98–123.
11 Hans-Georg Gadamer, *Truth and Method*, trans. Garrett Barden and John Cumming (New York, 1975). I cite Gadamer in this context as a figure who defines the philosophical ground for the subsequent extension of hermeneutics into literary studies by Wolfgang Iser and Hans Robert Jauss and for the political dimension of hermeneutics emphasized by Jürgen Habermas and absorbed into much contemporary historicist practice.

contemporary view of Chaucer's belated audience for the *Clerk's Tale* suggests, however, that nothing is lost for them. These readers are not estranged from Chaucer's poem; they are able to respond to it without any sense of its difference from them – which is to say, without a sense of its historicity or theirs.

Historical reception is just one part of what I have called in the title of my essay the problem of hermeneutics, but it serves to signal a larger constellation of interpretive issues. For one thing, the work of interpretation in the *Clerk's Tale*, is not deferred in time and external to the narrative but already present in the text as a condition of its poetic meaning. Interpretation operates before, around, and within the tale, most notably in the literary tradition Chaucer inherits and exploits. Furthermore, the hermeneutic problems in the tale, not just the overt seriousness and moralizing, carry a deep resonance for Chaucer's fifteenth-century readers. Rather than a stable genre and correspondingly stable values, the *Clerk's Tale* offers a structure of debated readings, and these readings characterize the tale as a narrative of social challenge and resolution. In this essay, I want to show how text and reception, formal meaning and historical application are intimately joined in a hermeneutic project. I shall look first at the literary tradition of the Griselda story, emphasizing Petrarch's formulation of the interpretive issues. I shall then turn to Boccaccio's *Decameron* not as a direct influence for Chaucer but as a hermeneutic model that the subsequent tradition seeks to efface. Finally, I shall examine Chaucer's response to the readings that emerge in Boccaccio and Petrarch. My aim is to suggest that aesthetically Chaucer finds a middle ground between Boccaccio's hermeneutic multiplicity and Petrarch's closure and that historically his mediation of these readings produces a context of understanding in which Griselde's example of patience finds a rationale and application.

I

The literary heritage of the *Clerk's Tale*, defined in its main outlines by J. Burke Severs, has three constant and interrelated features.[12] The Griselda story is primarily a narrative, the narrative is coterminous with hermeneutics, and the hermeneutics are contested. However much Griselda becomes a figure standing topically for patience, wifely submission, or political obedience, her exemplarity depends essentially on narrative, on what Robin Kirkpatrick calls the 'strong image of temporal sequence' recounting the increments of her testing and the constancy of her patience.[13] The importance attached to

---

[12] J. Burke Severs, *The Literary Relationship of Chaucer's 'Clerkes Tale'*, Yale Studies in English 96 (New Haven, 1942).

[13] Robin Kirkpatrick, 'The Griselda Story in Boccaccio, Petrarch, and Chaucer', in *Chaucer and the Italian Trecento*, ed. Piero Boitani (Cambridge, 1983), p. 232. Recent accounts of imitations of the *Clerk's Tale* and of Griselde's exemplarity are given by

narrative as a sequence of action can be seen in a fifteenth-century manuscript at Montpellier recording the 'pia historia Griseidis' (Bibliothèque de l'École de Médicine, MS 432). In this manuscript, the story has escaped the generic confusion of history and fable introduced by Petrarch (*Epistolae seniles* 17.4) and announces itself as history.[14] The rubrics include the divisions familiar from the *Clerk's Tale* but offer a much closer articulation of the main parts of the story, charting a sequence of action. They begin by labelling the description of the marquis, the interview with his followers, his response to them, the introduction of Griselda, and her marriage to Valterius; in the middle of the story, they mark the first two trials ('experienciae') of Griselda, the contrived second marriage, and the expulsion of Griselda ('Tertia experiencia'); at the end, they indicate the arrival of the supposed new wife and finally Griselda's restoration and the disclosure of the children's identity.[15] Boccaccio's authorship and Petrarch's translation are present in the

---

Helen Cooper, *The Canterbury Tales*, Oxford Guides to Chaucer (Oxford, 1989), pp. 422–24; Anna P. Baldwin, 'From the *Clerk's Tale* to *The Winter's Tale*', in *Chaucer Traditions*, pp. 199–212; and the essays collected in *La storia di Griselda in Europa*, ed. Raffaele Morabito (L'Aquila, 1990).

14 Here the claim to historical status underwrites Griselda's exemplarity and reflects an outlook quite different from the one Middleton attributes to Petrarch, though not to the reader mentioned in Petrarch's letter who rejects the story as fable: 'Petrarch clearly finds this distinction [between history and fable] arbitrary and literarily trivial, and thereby suggests that with respect to their emotional, spiritual, and ethical value to the hearer, there is no functional difference between *historia and fabula*; the good of a story, whether it is historical or fictive, lies in its use as *fabula*' (p. 135). Boccaccio, who received neither of Petrarch's letters about Griselda, describes the story as a *fabula* in writing to Petrarch's son-in-law to request copies of the letters (quoted in Severs, p. 11). Philippe de Mézières, describing Petrarch as a 'docteur-poete' who composes books 'remplis de tres grant devocion et de vraye doctrine catholique', places such faith in his account and local tradition that he believes the story must be founded on historical fact; see Elie Golenistcheff-Koutouzoff, *L'histoire de Griseldis en France au XIVe et au XVe Siècle* (Paris, 1933; rpt 1975), pp. 155–56.

15 The rubrics for Montpellier MS 432 read as follows (correspondences indicated for Severs's division of Petrarch's text based on the anonymous French translation):

'Descripcio Marchionis Saluciar[um]' (fol. 130r; Severs's Pars I.1 'Est ad Italie')

'Oracio subditi ad Marchion*um* pro sum*e*nda uxorem' (fol. 130v; before I.25 'Id aliquamdiu')

'Responsio Marchionis et dispo*s*icio eius ad uxorem' (fol. 131v; before I.51 'Moverunt pie')

'Oracio griseidis et eius assumpcio in uxorem' (fol. 132r; at II.1 'Fuit haud procul', beginning of Severs's Pars II)

'Desponsatio [MS: Dispencio] grise[idis]. et celebratio nupciarum' (fol. 134r; before II.62 'Satis est')

'Prima experien*c*ia. de filia jussa mori' (fol. 135v; at III.1 'Cepit, ut fit', corresponding to Severs's Pars III)

'Secunda experien*c*ia grise[idis]. de filio jusso mori' (fol. 137r; at III.51 'Valterius interea sepe [sepe *om.*] vultum coniugis', sentence before Severs's Pars IV)

make-up of the manuscript, but the narrative holds the central place, much like the detached versions of the *Clerk's Tale* in the fifteenth-century English manuscripts.

The poetic lesson contained in the rubrics applies directly to Chaucer's art. Though the *Canterbury Tales* establish a fully realized dramatic framework for the story, Chaucer's tale is basically a narrative. In his reading of the *Clerk's Tale*, Lerer suggests that the literary qualities and aesthetic complication depend strongly on the Prologue and Envoy; when they are absent, as in the anthology versions like Ph4, the tale, Lerer argues, gives itself up to uninflected moral exemplification and becomes fit material for the literature of instruction.[16] It is a debatable point, however, whether complex literary representation depends solely on a dramatic framework anywhere in the *Canterbury Tales*.[17] Rather, poetic meaning in the *Tales* derives chiefly from Chaucer's narrative art and from the power of the story. For the *Clerk's Tale*, John M. Manly and Edith Rickert suggest it may even be possible to detect a stage of composition that precedes the *Canterbury Tales* (1, 286–87), a version thus standing solely and unambiguously as narrative.

If the story of Griselda is fundamentally a narrative text, it is one that nonetheless comes already marked by interpretation. As Anne Middleton and Charlotte C. Morse note, the beginnings of the Griselda story are simultaneously the beginnings of its interpretive and literary history.[18] Despite its origin and analogues in folklore, the history of the tale properly speaking starts with Boccaccio who sets the narrative within the multiple

'Simulacio secunde sponse assumpte' (fol. 138v; at IV.53 'Ceperat sensim de Valterio decolor [decolor *om.*] fama')

'Tercia experiencia griseidis. de expulsa sua' (fol. 139v; at V.1 'Hec [Hec *om.*] inter Valterius solito', beginning of Severs's Pars V)

'Adventus secunde sponse' (fol. 141r; at VI.1 'Iam Panici comes propinquabat', beginning of Severs's Pars VI)

'Reassumpcio gri*seidis* in uxorem et recogni*cio* filiorum' (fol. 142r; at VI.32 'Valterius eo ipso in tempore')

With only slight differences, the same text of the rubrics appears in Munich, Bayerische Staatsbibliothek, MS. 78, which also contains *Seniles* 17.3 (see Severs, pp. 50–51). Vittore Branca, *Boccaccio medievale* (Florence, 1956), p. 227 n, gives a preliminary list of manuscripts containing Petrarch's translation without the accompanying letter.

[16] Lerer says of the Prologue and Envoy, 'what happens is that the narrative fiction they enclose is progressively subordinated to the social fact of its telling. We might say that the Prologue and Envoy swell out of proportion; they become read as the most salient features of the *Tale*, offering stories of authorial and patronly subjection and the strategies for praising the source and placating the public' (p. 39; cf. pp. 88, 100).

[17] See C. David Benson, *Chaucer's Drama of Style: Poetic Variety and Contrast in the Canterbury Tales* (Chapel Hill, 1986) for a critique of the 'dramatic principle' of the *Canterbury Tales*.

[18] Anne Middleton, 'The Clerk and His Tale: Some Literary Contexts', *Studies in the Age of Chaucer* 2 (1980), p. 124; Charlotte C. Morse, 'The Exemplary Griselda', *Studies in the Age of Chaucer* 7 (1985), p. 73.

interpretive frames of the *Decameron*. In his Latin translation of the story, Petrarch dramatizes interpretation and reception as a warrant for translation. Though he admits to only a cursory reading of the *Decameron*, attending chiefly to the opening and ending of the collection, he nonetheless recognizes its mixture of amusing and serious material: 'Inter multa sane iocosa et levia, quaedam pia et gravia deprehendi'.[19] He responds specifically to Griselda's story because of its strangeness and dissimilarity with the stories preceding it: 'multis precedencium longe dissimilem' (Severs, p. 291). It is this dissimilar – in a precise sense, monstrous – story that he memorizes to recount for his friends in conversation and later to translate for the benefit of others. In his *Livre de la Vertu du Sacrement du Mariage*, Philippe de Mézières fashions Petrarch's translation as a 'miroir des dames marieés' in which Griselda's constancy and obedience to her twin husbands – Gautier and Christ, 'son espous immortel' – earn her a place among the nine worthy women recorded by ancient historians as heroic counterparts to the nine chivalric worthy. In comparison with their martial exploits, Griselda's valour, he says, consists in conquering herself and overcoming (*efforsant*) nature:

> Mais qui vaudra bien peser à la balance, qui rent à chascun le pois de sa valour, la grant vertu du corage invincible de la noble marquise de Saluce, fille d'un povre laboureur, en vaincant et surmontant soy meisme et en efforsant nature, qui est une chose de plus grant merite que n'est de vaincre autrui . . .[20]

> But whoever wishes to weigh the balance which tells each one the weight of his virtue [should think of] the great virtue of the invincible heart of the noble marquise of Saluzzo, daughter of a poor laborer, in conquering and mastering herself and overcoming nature, which is a thing of greater merit than conquering someone else . . .

As Kevin Brownlee points out, Philippe recovers the literal sense that Petrarch had suppressed in favour of a figural meaning, and his work consequently addresses two audiences – married women and every good Christian.[21]

The compiler of the *Menagier de Paris*, who inserted Philippe's translation into his work of domestic instruction, eliminates the pseudo-historical furnishings but still locates the story within a framework of direct reception by a specific reader: 'une leçcon generale vous sera par moy escripte et a vous baillee' ('a general lesson will be written by me for you and handed over to

---

[19] Text in Severs, p. 290. For convenience, I shall cite the translations reprinted by Robert M. Miller, *Chaucer: Sources and Backgrounds* (New York, 1977), pp. 136–52. Glending Olson, 'Petrarch's View of the *Decameron*', *MLN* 91 (1976) 69–79, argues that Petrarch's assessment is generally the one held by Boccaccio's contemporaries.

[20] Elie Golenistcheff-Koutouzoff, p. 154. In Golenistcheff-Koutouzoff's listing of manuscripts for Philippe's translation (pp. 34–37), the Griselda story appears with *Le Livre du Chevalier du Tour Landry pour l'enseignement des ses filles*.

[21] Kevin Brownlee, 'Commentary and the Rhetoric of Exemplarity: Griseldis in Petrarch, Philippe de Mézières, and the *Estoire*', *South Atlantic Quarterly* 91 (1992) 867–70.

you').[22] The Griselda story teaches his young wife what is necessary to acquire God's love, the salvation of one's soul, a husband's love, and peace in marriage in this world. As the husband enumerates these items in the plan of his book, they are arranged as a distributive proportion with corresponding terms: God's love is to a husband's love as salvation is to domestic peace. The spiritual goal of the Christian soul is analogous in the domestic sphere to a husband's peace: 'salvacon de l'ame et la paix du mary'. In this interpretive scheme, the wifely humility and obedience exemplified by Griselda are the efficient cause, not the final cause. The anonymous French version (*Le Livre Griseldis*) on which Chaucer relied for help in translating Petrarch directs the tale not only to wives but to other women as a model of conduct. The story is written, the translator tells us, 'a l'exemplaire des femmes mariees et toutes autres' (Severs, p. 257). There is, in short, no point at which the Griselda story is a narrative without hermeneutics.

The contested hermeneutics of the Griselda story begin with the interpretive categories Boccaccio sets out. As I want to show below, Boccaccio invents a sophisticated provocation to literary understanding. Petrarch responds to Boccaccio's story and its interpretive complexity in ways that promise, then forestall debate over meaning. He establishes what becomes the departure point for subsequent interpretation by rejecting direct imitation of Griselda as a wife and treating her instead as an example of female constancy ('ad imitandam saltem femine constanciam' [Severs, p. 288]). The aim of this allegorical shift is overtly hermeneutic. Petrarch does not intend merely to represent a virtue; rather, he wants to affect the reader's understanding: 'ut nobis nostra fragilitas notis ac domesticis indicijs innotescat' ('that our weakness should be made plain to ourselves by obvious and familiar proofs' [Severs, p. 288]). Self-conscious reading by a general reader thus displaces a prior, literal interpretation prescribing conduct for women ('matronas nostri temporis').

In his second letter about the Griselda story (*Seniles* 17.4), Petrarch orchestrates but again cancels interpretive debate. The initial dispute is about the genre and truth value of the story – whether it is *historia* or *fabula*. In her analysis, Middleton argues that for Petrarch there is no functional difference between history and fable (p. 135). But Petrarch has, I think, chosen a less radical course than annulling a venerable distinction from the rhetorical tradition he invokes elsewhere. He operates within a Ciceronian taxonomy of discourse that is signalled by debating whether the story is *historia* or *fabula*.[23] In suggesting that Griselda's patience is comparable to a class of

---

[22] *Le Menagier de Paris*, ed. Georgine E. Brereton and Janet M. Ferrier (Oxford, 1981), p. 3. The actual plan of composition as set out at the beginning of the *Menagier* is not realized exactly.

[23] For discussion of the Ciceronian distinction among *historia*, *argumentum*, and *fabula* in the High Middle Ages, see Robert R. Edwards, *Ratio and Invention: A Study of Medieval Lyric and Narrative* (Nashville, 1989), pp. 75–89.

extraordinary feats performed by well-known classical figures, he treats Griselda's story as a form of *argumentum*. Her tale belongs to a narrative discourse standing between documented history (*res gesta*) and sheer invention (*fabula*); it occupies the domain of the logically probable, where meaning is open to deliberation and contested understanding.

The possibility of such debate is the topic of the two narratives of reading that serve as the other focus of the letter. Petrarch recounts that a Paduan reader of the story is so overcome by its pathos that he bursts into tears and cannot continue. Later, a Veronese reader, hearing of the first reader's response, asks for the story and reads it through without displaying emotion. He readily admits to its pathetic appeal, but he rejects the tale as mere fable because no equal to Griselda can be found. Petrarch declines to answer his sceptical reader at this point, fearing to provoke dissension amidst friendly discussion. His letter is, however, a tacit refutation, listing men and women of antiquity who have performed comparably extraordinary feats. It is also a demonstration of the privileged position of his authorial intent, for the alternate responses he allows his circle of readers amount to silence and inadequacy.

As these narratives of reading suggest, the hermeneutics dramatized in Petrarch's letters are at base a strategy of displacement, moving our attention from a troubling story toward a spiritual application. The French versions following Petrarch's translation return the story to domestic instruction, the 'miroir des dames mariées' that Petrarch rejects but Philippe recommends. The literal application is no less debated, however, than the figural. Philippe ends his prologue with the exegetical figure of separating the wheat from the chaff, but like the Nun's Priest he provides no guidance for which is wheat and which chaff.[24] The husband in the *Menagier* gives up on topical allegorical correspondences. Recognizing the social constraints imposed on him by his wife's superior lineage, he comments that the story cannot apply exactly: 'je ne suis mie marquis ne ne vous ay prise bergiere' (p. 73). He apologizes for its excess: 'Et me excuse se l'istoire parle de trop grant cruaulté, a mon adviz plus que de raison'. Yet he insists both on Petrarch's superior authority and his own pedagogical aims: 'je . . . seulement pour vous endoctriner l'ay mise cy' (p. 72). In staging and withdrawing their readings, these responses reflect an effort to domesticate Boccaccio's story, in both senses of the term. They direct the story to the sphere of private relations between husband and wife. At the same time, they carry out the project,

---

[24] 'Et pour ce que cestui livre traitte de la vertu du sacrement de mariage, et la dicte marquise souverainement la garda, pour un miroir des dames mariées le dit Solitaire en la fin de son livre leur presente ceste piteuse, vertueuse et merveilleuse histoire, en priant à Dieu qu'elle leur vaille si en prendront le grain et en laisseront la paille' (Golenistcheff-Koutouzoff, p. 156). It is worth noting as well that Philippe locates the story in the same rhetorically emphatic final position that Petrarch notices in the *Decameron*.

famously re-enacted at the end of the *Clerk's Tale*, of dissipating the disruptive force of poetic representation into narratives of reception. So successful has the aesthetic strategy been that the original ground of hermeneutic dispute, drawn carefully in Boccaccio, has dropped out of our field of vision and Petrarch's displacement has modelled our reading of the story. Nonetheless, the hermeneutic problems Boccaccio first put in place reveal much about the story, and they reflect the poetic multiplicity that Chaucer reinscribes in his translation of Petrarch.

II

Boccaccio frames Griselda's story with an intricate, multi-levelled structure of interpretation. Panfilo, elected king for the final day of storytelling, establishes a unifying theme for the tales. Dioneo, who narrates Griselda's story, offers interpretive commentary at the beginning and end of his recitation. When he finishes, the women in the *brigata* take up debate, 'chi d'una parte e chi d'altra tirando, chi biasimando una cosa e chi un'altra intorno ad essa lodandone' ('some taking one side and some another, some finding fault with one of its details and some commending another').[25] Their comments provide a structural balance for Panfilo's instructions, while recasting his theme in a multiplicity of moral and aesthetic judgements. They offer as well a point of origin in the vernacular of feminine discourse for the learned conversations of the historical-imaginary 'Petrarchan Academy' that David Wallace has defined as 'a small, consciously exclusive, masculine group of initiates dedicated to the pursuit of Latin culture'.[26] These frames create a chiasmic structure of interpretation around the story, and within this structure interpretation operates as an element of the narrative itself, working through formal speeches and the reports of what people are saying and thinking. We have, then, a narrative encompassed by interpretation repeatedly dramatizing the theme and problems of its meaning.[27] As it does so, the ground of debate shifts, but Boccaccio's artistic and conceptual focus remains strikingly consistent.

Panfilo decides that the final day of storytelling will be devoted to tales that

---

[25] Giovanni Boccaccio, *Il Decameron*, ed. Carlo Salinari (Bari, 1963), p. 768. All citations will be taken from this edition. For convenience, I add an English translation from *The Decameron*, trans. G.H. McWilliam (Harmondsworth, 1972).

[26] David Wallace, ' "Whan She Translated Was": A Chaucerian Critique of the Petrarchan Academy', in *Literary Practice and Social Change in Britain, 1380–1530*, ed. Lee Patterson (Berkeley, 1990), p. 160.

[27] For recent discussion of Boccaccio's attitude toward literary interpretation, see Susan Noakes, *Timely Reading: Between Exegesis and Interpretation* (Ithaca, 1988), pp. 68–97; and Francesco Bruni, 'Interpretation within the *Decameron*', in *Interpretation: Medieval and Modern*, ed. Piero Boitani and Anna Torti (Cambridge, 1993), pp. 123–36.

demonstrate generosity or magnificence – or, more significantly, tales about people who show these qualities: 'di chi liberalmente o vero magnificamente alcuna cosa operasse intorno a' fatti d'amore o d'altra cosa' (the acts of 'those who have performed liberal or munificent deeds, whether in the cause of love or otherwise', p. 733). By setting a narrative theme, he restores 'la legge usata' that Emilia had temporarily suspended on the previous day, and he announces that the stories have the moral purpose of instilling the desire to act virtuously. As Neifile remarks at the start of the tenth day, the theme involves a pre-eminent virtue: 'come il sole è di tutto il cielo bellezza ed ornamento, è chiarezza e lume di ciascuna altra vertù' ('even as the sun embellishes and graces the whole of the heavens, [magnificence] is the light and splendour of every other virtue', p. 680). The two categories Panfilo specifies – generosity and magnificence – derive from Aristotle's discussion of moral virtues in Book 2 of the *Nicomachean Ethics* (1107b8–21), and they provide an initial, if subsequently contested, framework for interpreting the tale.

Aristotle discusses generosity and magnificence under the rubric of getting and spending money; their sphere of action is 'external goods'.[28] In his analytical scheme, generosity and magnificence differ primarily in scale and secondarily in scope: the former has to do with smaller, the latter with larger, sums of money. A magnificent man is thus always generous, but a generous man does not rise to the level of the magnificent. In a later discussion (Book 4.i, 1119b22), Aristotle extends the meaning of generosity to include property generally. He points out that generosity and magnificence have a public dimension, but magnificence, unlike ordinary transactions of giving and spending, is concerned only with expenditures; furthermore, it entails connoisseurship, a large outlay done in good taste (1122a17). Under the terms Panfilo establishes, Griselda's story will concern matters of property and actions that regulate external goods and not patience *per se*, which is the mean in the sphere of anger. Equally important, by invoking Aristotle, Panfilo's categories establish a criterion of judgement for the tale. Aristotle points out that generosity and magnificence operate in accord with the disposition of the giver, not the objects of his generosity. At issue is character, and disposition, the natural inclination of character, is what measures the ethical qualities of action – whether it is generous, prodigal, or miserly; magnificent, vulgar, or petty.

In the prefatory and closing remarks that bracket his story, Dioneo introduces a competing hermeneutics that complicates and challenges Panfilo's frame.

---

28 St Thomas Aquinas, *In decem libros Ethicorum Aristotelis ad Nicomachum Expositio*, ed. Raimundo M. Spiazzi (Turin, 1949), p. 96; trans. C.I. Litzinger, *Commentary on Aristotle's 'Nicomachean Ethics'* (Chicago, 1964), p. 113. Since Aquinas's commentary uses the Antiqua Translatio of the *Ethics* by William of Moerbeke known to Boccaccio and Dante, I cite both Aristotle and Aquinas in Spiazzi's edition and Litzinger's translation. John Larner, 'Chaucer's Italy', in *Chaucer and the Italian Trecento*, p. 24, notes that Boccaccio transcribed Aquinas's commentary on the *Ethics*.

Dioneo shifts the heuristic categories from moral virtues to the matter of disposition. He begins by saying, 'vo' ragionar d'un marchese non cosa magnifica ma una matta bestialità' ('I want to tell you of a marquis, whose actions . . . were remarkable not so much for their munificence as for their senseless brutality', p. 758). This shift brings character emphatically to the fore. By calling Gualtieri's action brutishness, Dioneo directly signals a textual and philosophical background. His phrase 'matta bestialità' echoes the passage in *Inferno* 11 where Vergil explains the plan of Hell and refers Dante specifically to the *Ethics* which treats 'le tre disposizion che 'l ciel non vole, / incontenenza, malizia e la matta / bestialitade' (11.81–83).[29]

Dioneo's claim that Gualtieri acts out of brutishness is, however, significantly misapplied. Aristotle says that brutishness rarely occurs; when it does, it occurs mostly among barbarians, and among Greeks the causes for it are sickness and loss or the prevalence of vice (1145a33). Paraphrasing Aristotle, Aquinas explains that just 'sicut virtus divina raro in bonis invenitur, ita bestialitas raro in malis' ('as divine virtue is rarely found among the good, so brutishness is rarely found among the vicious' [Spiazzi, p. 353; Litzinger, p. 410]). Brutishness exists in the realm of the subhuman, beyond judgements of virtue and vice. It is illustrated by the compounding of atrocity and carnality, such as ripping open the bellies of pregnant women to devour the fetuses or the practice of cannibalism among barbarians (Antiqua Translatio, section 967; Spiazzi, p. 368). The exemplary brutish figure is Phalaris, the notoriously cruel tyrant of Sicily whom Aristotle credits with such extreme acts as devouring children or using them for sexual pleasure (1149a14). Despite the model of tyrannical rule afforded by Phalaris, Dioneo's application of brutishness to Gualtieri fails the test of subhuman extremity. Such usage, as Aquinas notes in his discussion of the passage in Aristotle (Antiqua Translatio, sections 976–77), must be meant *metaphorice* rather than *simpliciter* (Spiazzi, p. 370).[30] Dioneo's claim is, instead, a hermeneutic response; rejecting the ethical framework of Panfilo's categories, Dioneo seeks to register, by his partial and defective analogy, the alarm that Gualtieri's actions provoke. Like Boccaccio in the rubrics, Dioneo responds as a reader – in this case, a reader even before the telling of his own story.[31]

---

[29] Dante Alighieri, *The Divine Comedy*, trans. Charles S. Singleton, 6 vols. (Princeton, 1970–75), 1: 114. For discussion of Boccaccio's use of the phrase, see Charles Haines, 'Patient Griselda and *matta bestialitade*', *Quaderni d'Italianistica* 6 (1985) 233–40.

[30] In the *Ethics* 7.i (1145a33), Aristotle accepts a semantic definition of brutishness: 'We also use the word brutish to express reprobation of extremely vicious persons' (*Ethics*, trans. J.A.K. Thomson [Harmondsworth, 1953; rpt 1981], p. 226). The Antiqua Translatio portrays a rhetorical excess that matches an excess of vice: 'et propter malitiam autem hominum superexcedentes, sic superinfamamus' (Spiazzi, p. 351).

[31] For Boccaccio as a reader in the rubrics, see Jonathan Usher, 'Le rubriche del *Decameron*', *Medioevo romanzo* 10 (1985), p. 417n.

Dioneo is a licensed figure of dissonance.[32] At the end of the previous day (9.10), he had described his function as radically contrastive; he plays the black crow to the ladies' white doves, the apparent fool to wise men. Here he introduces a story that refuses hermeneutic containment at several levels. His challenge to Panfilo's framework of moral virtues is only the most obvious example. As a narrator, Dioneo intensifies the hermeneutic problems of the story, frustrating expectations by granting Gualtieri precisely the happiness he seeks: 'gran peccato fu che a costui ben n'avvenisse' ('it was a great pity that the fellow should have drawn any profit from his conduct', p. 758). As his tale rejects Panfilo's strictures, he in turn rejects his tale. At the end of his recitation, Dioneo draws attention to the disparity between precepts and outcome by invoking again the shadowy contraries of god-like virtue and brutishness: 'anche nelle povere case piovono dal cielo de' divini spiriti, come nelle reali di quegli che sarien più degni di guardar porci che d'avere sopra uomini signoria' ('celestial spirits may sometimes descend even into the houses of the poor, whilst there are those in royal palaces who would be better employed as swineherds than as rulers of men', p. 768). He then imagines a different ending to the story he has told, in which Griselda, turned out only in the shift Gualtieri allows her, trades her sexual favours for a better dress. Up to this point, the story has moved through the epicycles of fortune that generate a sequence of provisional endings – comic in Griselda's marriage, tragic in her suffering, then comic again in her restitution. Dioneo's fabliau alternative cancels the tale's hardwon comic resolution; indeed, it is a parodic reworking of moral categories, in which generosity and magnificence are replaced by crude commerce and rough justice. Furthermore, Dioneo cancels out a potential, allegorizing reading of his story which is made possible by labelling Gualtieri brutish. Brutishness is conventionally defined by contrast to divine virtue.[33] Gualtieri's brutishness thus implies Griselda's superhuman virtue and potentially carries the story from matters of practical virtue and human character into the realm of the sublime. Dioneo's hypothetical ending, fashioning Griselda as a vengeful and shrewd sexual entrepreneur, forestalls this possibility, rejecting the sublime for the carnivalesque. Seen in this context, Petrarch's exemplary reading of the story is not only a displacement of meaning but a rescue of sorts.

The framing devices I have been describing in Boccaccio not only dramatize the story as a hermeneutic problem; they also furnish a means for analysing the tale that drives it toward a problematic understanding. One

---

32 Itala Tania Rutter, 'The Function of Dioneo's Perspective in the Griselda Story', *Comitatus* 5 (1974), p. 34.

33 Giuseppe Mazzotta, *The World at Play in Boccaccio's 'Decameron'* (Princeton, 1986), p. 125, notes that in his commentary on *Inferno* 11 (*Esposizioni sopra la Comedia*) Boccaccio refers to brutishness and divine wisdom (not divine virtue) as contraries: 'E adunque questa bestialità similmente vizio dell'anima opposto, secondo che piace ad Aristotile nel VII dell'Etica, alla divina sapienza'.

critical tradition sees the tale as a story of humility triumphant, lending a final rising moral action to the *Decameron* as a whole.[34] Giuseppe Mazzotta has argued that Dioneo's story is built on the allegory of marriage and that Boccaccio's artistic motive is to reveal the distance between idealized allegorical meaning and human experience (p. 126). The explanation I want to propose locates the interpretation within the human sphere and practical judgements. Panfilo calls for stories about persons who act generously or magnificently. His focus is on the agent. The rubric introducing the story, which Jonathan Usher characterizes as Boccaccio's readerly reponse, portrays Gualtieri as an agent who will choose a wife 'a suo modo' – on his own and in a way appropriate to him. For all their disruptive potential, Dioneo's remarks about character are directed toward agents capable of the virtue of magnificence, even as they fail to achieve it. If the conceptual focus is on agents and Gualtieri is the chief agent, it follows necessarily, albeit paradoxically, that the moral index of the tale must be defined by his disposition.

This focus on paradoxical moral agency is a key feature of the narrative itself and represents Boccaccio's commitment to a literary world. Gualtieri's aim, expressed from the outset, is to achieve an appropriate match of temperaments that will guarantee his peace of mind. When his men approach him with their request that he marry, he resists on the grounds of incompatibility:

> Amici miei, voi mi strignete a quello che io del tutto aveva disposto di non far mai, considerando quanto grave cosa sia a poter trovare chi co' suoi costumi ben si convenga, e quanto del contrario sia grande la copia, e come dura vita sia quella di colui che a donna non bene a sé conveniente s'abbatte. (p. 759)

> My friends, you are pressing me to do something that I had always set my mind firmly against, seeing how difficult it is to find a person who will easily adapt to one's own way of living, how many thousands there are who will do precisely the opposite, and what a miserable life is in store for the man who stumbles upon a woman ill-suited to his own temperament.

As the vocabulary makes clear, the emphasis falls on Gualtieri's disposition. He says what he is inclined (*disposto*) not to do, asserts the need to find someone with habits (*suoi costumi*) appropriate to this inclination (*ben si convenga*), and warns of the perils of marrying someone ill-suited to one's habits of character (*non bene a sé conveniente*). Griselda is first described as a character satisfying his disposition: 'Erano a Gualtieri buona pezza piaciuti i costumi d'una povera giovanetta che d'una villa vicina a casa sua era, a parendogli bella assai, estimò che con costei dovesse potere aver vita assai consolata' ('Now, for some little time, Gualtieri had been casting an

---

[34] See Victoria Kirkham, 'The Last Tale in the *Decameron*', *Mediaevalia* 12 (1989 for 1986), 203–23.

appreciative eye on the manners of a poor girl from a neighbouring village, and thinking her very beautiful, he considered that a life with her would have much to commend it', p. 759). Even Griselda's acceptance of his repudiation echoes Gualtieri's concern with the apt correspondence to his disposition: 'Signor mio, io conobbi sempre la mia bassa condizione alla vostra nobilità in alcun modo non convenirsi' ('My lord, I have always known that my lowly condition was totally at odds with your nobility', p. 764). In the moral scheme debated by Panfilo and Dioneo, Gualtieri remains a moral agent acting virtuously.

A similar claim of moral action informs Gualtieri's exposition of his goals in the final speech that balances his earlier discussion with his men. Gualtieri addresses Griselda to explain the purpose of her suffering and speaks to the others to refute their contentions that he has been cruel, unjust, and brutish. Breaking the frame of the narrative, he also addresses the charge ('matta bestialità') that Dioneo has lodged even before telling the story. Gualtieri says he has acted with clear ends in mind ('ciò che io faceva ad antiveduto fine operava', p. 767): 'volendoti insegnar d'esser moglie ed a loro di saperla e tôrre e tenere, ed a me partorire perpetua quiete mentre teco a vivere avessi' ('I wished to show you how to be a wife, to teach these people how to choose and keep a wife, and to guarantee my own peace and quiet for as long as we were living beneath the same roof', p. 767). As in his earlier speech, Gualtieri is motivated by rational ends, clearly articulated in a patriarchal hierarchy in which teaching Griselda and the people is a secondary good and securing his peace is the higher good. Griselda's patience and humility are subordinate and complementary, as Petrarch's French translators surmised. In the hermeneutic logic of the story, her virtues are the means to his ends. Ironically, it is Gualtieri who grasps Aristotle's moral teaching that our activities aim at some good and that the good every person desires is happiness, expressed in this instance as peace and contentment. It is Gualtieri, too, who understands that such a good must be judged not absolutely in itself but in respect to the agent and his disposition.

The hermeneutic framework established for the final tale of the *Decameron* produces, then, a monstrous story – not in the way James Sledd described Chaucer's Griselde as monstrous in her abjection but in the perversion of the ethical structure that contains moral virtues like generosity and magnificence.[35] True to his disposition and fully conscious of his ends, Gualtieri is a grotesque of Aristotelian moral virtue; he is a prudent agent who understands the workings but not the spirit of the Mean and thereby deforms it. If Dioneo's narratorial comments reject this monstrous hermeneutic and seek to move our understanding of the story onto different grounds, such

---

[35] James Sledd, 'The *Clerk's Tale*: The Monsters and the Critics', *Modern Philology* 51 (1953–54), 73–82; repr. in *Chaucer Criticism, Volume I: 'The Canterbury Tales'*, ed. Richard Shoeck and Jerome Taylor (Notre Dame, 1960), pp. 160–74.

commentary is only a gesture of containment, not rebuttal. In its full dimensions, Griselda's story remains radically problematic because it destabilizes virtue from within, using the logic of moral virtue and character as the instrument of a troubled understanding. As Mazzotta remarks, Dioneo's tale 'suggests that nothing is definitive and final in this narrative universe' (p. 130). One might add that the corollary of narrative indeterminacy is a universe of debated interpretation.

III

In framing Griselda's story by interpretation, Boccaccio and Petrarch move in different directions and to opposite ends. Boccaccio's hermeneutics work to establish a domain of independent literary representation in which competing interpretations reflect the story's profound moral and aesthetic complexity. By contrast, Petrarch's hermeneutics force closure by alienating our understanding from our experience of the story. Where we anticipate the lesson of domestic obedience that subsequent French writers reflexively drew, Petrarch closes off meaning by defining a prior, authorial intent that overmasters us by turning the story on his readers: he has rewritten Boccaccio's story so that we recognize our weakness. Chaucer's version of the story stands between these two hermeneutic strategies. Grounded like its predecessors in dramatized interpretation, the *Clerk's Tale* absorbs and reorders the claims of Boccaccian multiplicity and Petrarchan closure.

Petrarch's hermeneutics are present from the start of the tale, in the Clerk's answer to the Host's instructions to '[t]elle us som myrie tale' (IV. 9). His response is an ambitious claim concealed under Griselde-like obedience. Telling 'a tale which that I / Lerned at Padowe of a worthy clerk' (IV. 26–27), the Clerk enrolls in the Petrarchan Academy, presenting himself as one of those cultivated friends for whose benefit Petrarch memorized and recited Boccaccio's story. Similarly, the ending of his tale dutifully preserves the substance of Petrarch's *moralitas*: Griselde is not a wifely model to imitate but an example of patience and constancy in the face of adversity. Between these points, the textual layout of the tale, as the Ellesmere, Hengwrt, and other manuscripts indicate, augments the Clerk's narrative with Petrarch's own glosses.[36] Petrarch's regulation of the text extends from his immediate circle of friends to his *legentes* and to their readers as well.

---

[36] Manly and Rickert, 3: 505–8. Germaine Dempster, 'Chaucer's Manuscript of Petrarch's Version of the Griselda Story', *Modern Philology* 41 (1943–44), p. 6, argues that Hengwrt preserves the glosses from the parent copy Chaucer used and that Corpus Christi College, Cambridge MS 275 is the witness closest to Chaucer's text of Petrarch. Thomas J. Farrell, 'The Style of the *Clerk's Tale* and the Function of Its Glosses', *Studies in Philology* 86 (1989), p. 290, says, 'the glosses highlight important thematic material at the moment of its introduction, and they focus attention on the style of the *Clerk's Tale*, particularly in contrast to that of its source'.

But if Chaucer begins and seems to end with the closure imposed by Petrarch's authorial intent, he moves as well toward the complexity signalled by Boccaccio's contested hermeneutics. The Host correctly, if unwillingly, intuits that the story is a 'sophyme' (IV. 5), a tale that by its very nature embodies problematic meaning and the resources of human understanding, chief among them logic.[37] Although Petrarch's *moralitas* is present, it is defective and only temporary. The Clerk grasps the pattern of analogy between domestic and spiritual obedience in Petrarch. Each person, he says, should suffer 'in his degree' (1145) and the example of a patient mortal woman should teach us all to receive what God sends us. But as Kirkpatrick observes, 'the responsibility for the analogy seems to be transferred firmly to Petrarch' (p. 235). The element of self-knowledge that Petrarch announces as his final end ('nostre fragile humanité' in the anonymous French translation) also drops out, and we are left with the pious application: 'Lat us thanne lyve in vertuous suffraunce' (1162). This moment of interpretive certainty gives way, in turn, as the Clerk pushes beyond the limit of Petrarch's text (1162) to recontextualize Griselde in the female hermeneutics of the Wife of Bath and the archwives. Petrarchan closure is the ironic foil to Boccaccian multiplicity. This tension hovers over Chaucer's retelling of the story and gives his version its distinctive qualities.

Like Boccaccio and Petrarch, Chaucer locates interpretive problems early in his story. Boccaccio gives rhetorical prominence to Gualtieri's first speech to his retainers and thereby portrays him as a character prudently aware of the difficulties of finding someone appropriate to his disposition. Petrarch grants the retainers their own speech of supplication in a fine display of how one speaks to rulers. Martin McLaughlin argues that Petrarch describes Valterius as an ideal ruler, but Petrarch carefully omits Boccaccio's suggestion that the marquis acts as a prudent, rational agent.[38] Every trace of Gualtieri's speech on the need for a wife with a complementary disposition disappears, along with his clearly stated aim of acting to achieve a domestic peace that mirrors tranquil relations with his men. Instead, Petrarch's Valterius quickly resigns his *omnimoda libertas* and stakes his belief on the prudence and good faith of his subjects: 'Ceterum subiectorum michi voluntatibus me sponte subicio, et prudencie vestre fisus et fideo' ('I willingly submit to the wishes of my

---

37 James A. Weisheipl, O.P., 'Curriculum of the Faculty of Arts at Oxford in the early Fourteenth Century', *Mediaeval Studies* 26 (1964), p. 178, notes that in fourteenth-century academic usage, *sophisma* 'signified a proposition which could be defended by logical arguments' and consequently that the term is not limited to a negative sense of *aenigmata* and *obscuritates*. John M. Ganim, 'Carnival Voices and the Envoy to the *Clerk's Tale*', *Chaucer Review* 22 (1987–88), p. 117, argues that Chaucer's use of 'sophyme' is semantically related to 'study', a term he takes to mean both intellectual inquiry and melancholy.

38 Martin McLaughlin, 'Petrarch's rewriting of the *Decameron*, X.10', in *Renaissance and Other Studies: Essays Presented to Peter M. Brown*, ed. Eileen A. Millar (Glasgow, 1988), pp. 47–50.

subjects, trusting in your prudence and devotion', Severs, p. 258). Trust in God rather than his own power of judgement will be the means to his ends: 'ipse [Deus] michi inveniet quod quieti mee sit expediens ac saluti' ('He will find for me that which shall be expedient for my peace and safety', Severs, p. 258).

Chaucer's treatment of this opening scene shifts the narrative elements to disclose a new array of motives and a different vision of political relations. In Petrarch, Valterius's aversion to marriage is the most prominent of his subjects' complaints: 'quodque in primis egre populi ferebant' (Severs, p. 256). Chaucer narrows the range of complaint to Walter's absorption in 'his lust present' (80): 'Oonly that point his peple bar so soore' (85). Petrarch identifies Valterius as the progenitor and exemplar of a line of noble rulers ('unus primusque omnium et maximus'); the crisis provoked by his reluctance to marry is a crisis of origins, and the outcome is consequently a civic foundation myth. Like Boccaccio, Chaucer places Walter within an established lineage, with 'his worthy eldres hym bifore' (65). The crisis is consequently the threat of dynastic interruption:

> For if it so bifelle, as God forbede,
> That thurgh youre deeth youre lyne sholde slake,
> And that a straunge successour sholde take
> Youre heritage, O wo were us alyve! (136–39)

In Petrarch, the noble wife whom Valterius's subjects propose to choose for him offers the best hope ('spes optima') in a future yet to unfold. In Chaucer, her nobility signifies a known value because she will confer '[h]onour to God and yow' (133).

The changes in the *Clerk's Tale* imply a political vision in Chaucer that is more heterogeneous and nuanced than Petrarch's absolutism. Valterius deals with his subjects, while Walter negotiates the complex relations that bind him to his lords and his 'commune' (70). As Chaucer uses the term, 'comune' means a third estate distinct from nobility and clergy.[39] Though recent critics have described Walter's rule as feudal or autocratic, Judith Ferster rightly observes: 'What is remarkable about the body politic of Walter's realm is not that there is hierarchy or tension and suspicion among the various groups, but that influence travels up as well as down the hierarchy'.[40] Rather than sheer absolutism, Chaucer's constellation of ruler, greater and lesser nobles, and *commune* portrays a moment of political transition and complication between traditional and emerging forces.[41] The spokesman who addresses Valterius

---

[39] *MED*, s.v. 'commune', sense 2.
[40] Judith Ferster, *Chaucer on Interpretation* (Cambridge, 1985), p. 110.
[41] Lynn Staley Johnson, 'The Prince and His People: A Study of the Two Covenants in the *Clerk's Tale*', *Chaucer Review* 10 (1975–76) 17–29, sees the relations as feudal; Lars Engle, 'Chaucer, Bakhtin, and Griselda', *Exemplaria* 1 (1989) 429–59, sees only an autocratic state; Michaela Paasche Grudin, 'Chaucer's *Clerk's Tale* as Political

gives voice to the silent wishes ('tacitas voluntates') of an obedient people ('qui nullum tuum imperium recusarent', Severs, p. 256). In the corresponding lines, Chaucer suggests a dual, if unequal, authority. The spokesman seeks audience 'to shewen oure requeste', while Walter retains the prerogative 'to doon right as [he] leste' (104–5). The passage suggests the kind of distributive justice Aristotle locates in monarchy and finds analogous to the relations between a husband and wife (Antiqua Translatio, sections 1199, 1209), with the provision that differential rights now extend over several classes of subordinates.

The relations suggested by this differentiation in authority find expression, too, in the lexicon of political anxiety. Valterius leaves his subjects with 'molesta solicitudine' because he is unmarried: he is a 'firste stok,' as Chaucer phrases it in 'Gentilesse' (1), but without the prospect of further branches. The equivalent term for the people's anxiety in the *Clerk's Tale* – 'bisy drede' (134) – resonates against other uses. The dual bond uniting Walter to his nobility and citizens is affection and fear. Walter is 'Biloved and drad' (69), and though he promises to marry so as to relieve popular fears, the people remain anxious: 'For yet alwey the peple somwhat dredde, / Lest that the markys no wyf wolde wedde' (181–82). Even as the promised day approaches, the people nurture dread 'whan they were in privetee' (249), wondering, in lines that Chaucer adds, 'Why wole he thus hymself and us bigile?' (252). The *commune*'s concern for Walter and itself – panegyric 'wo' turned to statecraft – reflects a system of stratified political power. Whereas Petrarch, like Boccaccio, sees a coincidence of interests in which the marquis does not want to be left without a successor and the people without a governor, Chaucer portrays a system of subtle reciprocity in which the end of Walter's line and the introduction of a 'straunge successour' would cancel one of the proportional elements in a larger political equation.[42] Continuity of lineage underwrites the stability of complex political and social relations with a network of differentiated authority rather than absolutism.

In the middle sections of the *Clerk's Tale*, which focus on Griselde, the problem of hermeneutics coincides with politics. Griselde represents the site of interpretive and political contest. Like Emily in the *Knight's Tale*, she is the object at once of desire and knowledge. In effect, desire becomes identical with hermeneutics. This conflation is most apparent in Walter's appreciation of Griselde, an innovation that Petrarch introduces and Chaucer recontextualizes. In Boccaccio, Griselda attracts Gualtieri's attention with the

---

Paradox', *Studies in the Age of Chaucer* 11 (1989) 63–92, argues for an exploration of absolute monarchy.

42 Petrarch: 'ne si quid humanitus tibi forsan accideret, tu sine tuo successore abeas, ipsi sine votivo rectore remaneant' (Severs, p. 300). Boccaccio: 'La qual cosa a' suoi uomini non piacendo, più volte il pregaron che moglie prendesse, acciò che egli senza erede né essi senza signor rimanessero' (pp. 758–59).

appearance of her good habits and beauty (p. 759), but Petrarch makes her the occasion of Valterius's penetrating insight:

> In hanc virgunculam Valterius, sepe illac transiens, quandoque oculos non iuvenili lascivia sed senili gravitate defixerat, et virtutem eximiam supra sexum supraque etatem, quam vulgi oculis conditionis obscuritas abscondebat, acri penetrarat intuitu. (Severs, p. 260)

> Walter, passing often by that way, had sometimes cast his eyes upon this little maid, not with the lust of youth, but with the sober thoughts of an older man; and his swift intuition had perceived in her a virtue, beyond her sex and age, which the obscurity of her condition concealed from the eyes of the common throng.

Valterius's wandering, the symbolic extension of his search for prey in hunting and hawking, finds a point of attention and arrest in Griselda. There his gaze transforms from sensual passion to judgement, from youth to maturity. As Carolyn Dinshaw points out, Griselda is associated with a text to be read and interpreted by men.[43] Petrarch describes Valterius's gaze as insight, an intellectual virtue (*Ethics* 1139b18) that allows Valterius to penetrate the opaque surface of Griselda's appearance and grasp her hidden and inherent virtue. Insight also distinguishes his perception from the common understanding that her social condition obscures. Valterius's insight thus demonstrates prudence: 'quodque eximiam virtutem tanta sub inopia latitantem tam perspicaciter deprehendisset, vulgo prudentissimus habebatur' ('because he had so shrewdly discovered the remarkable virtue hidden under so much poverty, he was commonly held to be a very prudent man', Severs, p. 266). In Valterius and Griselda, we find as well a congruence of excess. Valterius goes beyond the wisdom of his age, while Griselda's unusual qualities ('virtutem eximiam') place her beyond the norms of her sex and age. By stressing excess, Petrarch establishes a basis for exemplarity and gestures toward recuperating the sublimity that Boccaccio tries to forestall in Dioneo's narration.

Chaucer's version of this passage (232–45) follows the details of Petrarch's narrative outline but sets the scene in a different framework of understanding. Walter's gaze is not an intellectual virtue *per se*. Rather, Chaucer defines it by a series of literary contrasts. It is the lover's gaze in the *Romance of the Rose*, now chastened and redirected from 'wantown lookyng of folye' (236) to moral reflection: 'in sad wyse / Upon hir chiere he wolde hym ofte avyse, / Commendynge in his herte hir wommanhede' (237–39). Walter's encounters with Griselde are a reversal of the collapsed *chanson d'aventure* that ends in rape in the *Wife of Bath's Tale*. His insight seeks to penetrate Griselde's 'rype and sad corage' (220), to know her as a creature utterly different from his desires; and as Ferster remarks, to know her as other is also to know her as she

---

[43] Carolyn Dinshaw, *Chaucer's Sexual Poetics* (Madison, 1989), p. 133.

is known by others.⁴⁴ Chaucer thus stages Walter's decision to marry Griselde as a reform of courtly conventions and particularly of the circular, solipsistic desire that serves as its primary model. As desire becomes the equivalent to hermeneutics, the tale banishes passion for knowledge.⁴⁵

Walter's gaze is the constant element in a shifting array of interpretive positions, which express the strangeness of what he finds stable and seek to locate it within its proper social forms. Though Petrarch claims a dual descent for Valterius's lineage ('nec minus moribus quam sanguine nobilis', Severs, p. 252), it is Griselde's natural virtue that makes fully concrete and present the mystifying ideology of *gentilesse* in the story. She calls the question on the proposition, widely celebrated by the Dolce Stil Nuovo, examined by Dante in the *Convivio*, and illustrated by the Wife of Bath in her tale, that nobility of character is more important than noble descent.⁴⁶ But if 'unto vertu longeth dignitee / And noght the revers' ('Gentilesse' 5–6), virtue devoid of lineage is still a powerfully confusing sight when it actually arrives. Chaucer follows Petrarch by reinscribing Griselde in the hereditary lineage she singularly disproves. Her integration is a consummate hermeneutic manoeuvre. She seems 'by liklynesse' (396) to have been 'norissed in an emperoures halle' (399), and those who have known her cannot now, on present evidence, believe she is really Janicula's daughter. In Ellesmere, Hengwrt, and other manuscripts, the marginal gloss emphasizes the point: 'Atque apud omnes supra fidem cara et venerabilis facta est vix quod hijs ipsis qui illius originem nouerant persuaderi posset Ianicule natam esse tantus vite tantus morum decor ea verborum grauitas atque dulcedo quibus omnium animos nexu sibi magni amoris astrinxerat' (Manly and Rickert, 3, 506). Griselde is, says Chaucer in a deft addition, 'another creature' in their estimate (406), embodied virtue estranged from its origin and now at odds with the very ideology thought to promote character over lineage as the sign of true nobility. It is the strangeness of her virtue that produces Griselde's reputation and keeps her the object of continuing observation as 'men and wommen, as wel yonge as olde, / Goon to Saluce upon hire to biholde' (419–20). Once she has

---

44 Ferster, pp. 94–109. This reciprocity, as Ferster notes, sets up not only Walter's oppression but also Griselda's collaboration in his oppression.

45 For discussion of the tale's epistemological concerns, see Kathryn L. Lynch, 'Despoiling Griselda: Chaucer's Walter and the Problem of Knowledge in *The Clerk's Tale*', *Studies in the Age of Chaucer* 10 (1988) 41–70.

46 The opening of Guido Guinizelli's doctrinal canzone ('Al cor gentil rempaira sempre amore') reappears in *Troilus and Criseyde*, deriving from Dante's discussion in the *Convivio*, which is also the source for the hag's disquisition in the *Wife of Bath's Tale*; see J.S.P. Tatlock, 'Dante and Guinicelli in Chaucer's Troilus', *Modern Language Notes* 35 (1920), p. 443. D'Arco Silvio Avalle, 'Due tesi di Andrea Capellano', in *Ai luoghi di delizia pieni: Saggio sulla lirica italiana del XIII secolo* (Milan, 1977), argues that the thesis about virtue and lineage has two distinct formulations in Capellanus's *De amore*, one egalitarian and the other aristocratic.

been properly displayed, common people see openly what was reserved to Walter's exceptional insight. Griselde's strangeness in turn underwrites Walter's reputation as a 'prudent man' (427), a point reinforced by the marginal gloss: 'Quodque eximiam virtutem tanta sub inopia latitantem tam perspicaciter deprendisset vulgo prudentissimus habebatur' (Manly and Rickert, 3, 506).

As Walter begins to test Griselde, these readings of his character produce another hermeneutic problem. He remains perversely steadfast in his purposes and searches vainly for 'variance' (710) in Griselde's response to her losses. His scrutiny depends, of course, on disguising his own difference in feeling and appearance. Meanwhile, the 'sclaundre of Walter' replaces his reputation for prudence: 'where as his peple therbifore / Hadde loved hym wel, the sclaundre of his diffame / Made hem that they hym hatede therfore' (729–31).[47] When Griselde is turned out, '[t]he folk hire folwe, wepynge in hir weye' (897). But the forged papal edicts, purporting to restore peace between the marquis and his subjects, deceive the 'rude peple' (750) who are subsequently beguiled by the sight of Walter's new bride. Chaucer accepts Petrarch's point that Walter is wrongly rehabilitated as a prudent man (986) by the false documents, but he goes on to expose the popular wish that Griselde's virtue has suppressed and deferred. Not only is the new bride fairer and younger, but 'fairer fruyt bitwene hem sholde falle, / And moore plesant, for hire heigh lynage' (991–92). If the new bride introduces 'noveltee' (1004) into the city, she is a familiar aristocratic figure whose social standing the people recognize, even as they perceive no fault in Griselde's conduct (1018). (With nobility apparently restored, virtue can evidently be separated again from lineage.) Chaucer's innovation is to emphasize the paradox of encountering natural virtue. Amidst wavering popular allegiance, Walter's perverse steadfastness is one of the few stable positions. Besides him, only the 'sadde folk in that citee' (1002) reject the 'stormy peple! Unsad and evere untrewe' (995). Chaucer adds the stanza of their repudiation, and Ellesmere and other manuscripts designate it by the notation 'Auctor' (Manly and Rickert, 3, 508).

Chaucer further accentuates the hermeneutic problems of the tale by reintroducing a tension present in Boccaccio but largely contained by Petrarch. Giulio Savelli notes that both Boccaccio and Dioneo assume authorial and interpretive functions at various points in the story.[48] Chaucer's equivalent is to add a series of comments by the Clerk that punctuates the course of Walter's testing and represents what Derek Pearsall sees as

---

[47] The marginal gloss reads at this point: 'Ceperit sensim de Waltero decolor fama crebescere' (Manly and Rickert, 3: 507). The manuscript owned by Jean d'Angoulême (Paris, Bibliothèque Nationale, Fonds Anglais 39) adds the lines at this point: 'And thus he lost here loue euery deel / For though a man by hygh on fortunes wheel' (Manly and Rickert, 6: 330).

[48] Giulio Savelli, 'Struttura e valori nella novella di Griselda', *Studi sul Boccaccio* 14 (1983–84) 278–301.

Chaucer's most systematic and audacious departure from Petrarch.[49] Petrarch describes Valterius's obsession with proving his wife as 'mirabilis quedam quam laudabilis . . . cupiditas' (Severs, p. 268). Chaucer's text cites the passage from Petrarch in a marginal gloss (Manly and Rickert 3, 506–7), but the Clerk amplifies the point rhetorically. He does not see the testing as 'subtil wit': 'But as for me, I seye that yvele it sit / To assaye a wyf whan that it is no nede, / And putten hire in angwyssh and in drede' (459–62). When Griselde's son is taken from her, the Clerk stops short of saying Walter is brutish, but he charges him with moral vice in going beyond the mean: 'O nedelees was she tempted in assay! / But wedded men ne knowe no mesure, / Whan that they fynde a pacient creature' (621–23). After Griselde returns to her father's house, the Clerk comes close to sounding like the Wife of Bath comparing Griselde to Job and lamenting clerks' habitual neglect of women's virtue (932–38).

Chaucer brings a narrative resolution to his story that again renegotiates the hermeneutic positions of his sources. Petrarch largely cancels the final speech Gualtieri makes in the *Decameron*; he consequently disrupts the structural symmetry of the first and last speeches and nullifies Gualtieri's claims to instruct both wife and vassals and to establish peace in his household. In Boccaccio the decisive point occurs when Griselda banishes Gualtieri's doubts:

> Gualtieri, al qual pareva pienamente aver veduto quantunque disiderava della pazienza della sua donna, veggendo che di niente la novità delle cose la cambiava, ed essendo certo, ciò per mentecattaggine non avvenire, per ciò che savia molto la conoscea, gli parve tempo di doverla trarre dell'amaritudine la quale estimava che ella sotto il forte viso nascosa tenesse. . . . (p. 767)

> Gualtieri felt that he had now seen all he wishes to see of the patience of his lady, for he perceived that no event, however singular, produced the slightest change in her demeanour, and he was certain that this was not because of her obtuseness, as he knew her to be very intelligent. He therefore considered that the time had come to him to free her from the rancour that he judged her to be hiding beneath her tranquil outward expression.

For Gualtieri, Griselda proves her patience and her intelligence; and she disproves, by her generous reception of the new bride, the lingering suspicion that she has been dissembling. Petrarch changes the issue, however, from Griselda's proof to Walter's knowing. The moment of decision occurs when Valterius declares, 'Satis . . . mea Griseldis, cognita et spectata michi fides est tua' ('It is enough, my Grisildis! Your fidelity to me is made known and proved', Severs, p. 286). In other words, Petrarch stages a moment of

---

[49] Derek Pearsall, *The Canterbury Tales*, p. 273.

self-recognition in which Valterius knows that he knows enough. Nor is Valterius suspicious of Griselda's intelligence or honesty. She has proved herself as a wife to his satisfaction, as his phrasing makes apparent: 'nec sub celo aliquem esse *puto* qui tanta coniugalis amoris experimenta perceperit' ('nor do *I think* that under heaven there is another woman who has undergone such trials of her conjugal love', my emphasis). When he reveals the intention of his testing, he simultaneously confesses his own flaw: 'Sciant qui contrarium crediderunt me curiosum atque experientem esse, non impium; probasse coniugium, non dampnasse; occultasse filios, non mactasse' ('Let all know, who thought the contrary, that I am curious and given to experiments, but am not impious; I have tested my wife, not condemned her; I have hidden my children, not destroyed them'). Valterius's self-recognition corresponds in kind to the self-recognition Petrarch seeks for his readers; like the circle of cultivated readers, he learns his fragility.

The *Clerk's Tale* reformulates Petrarch's emphases in ways that lend further nuance to their meaning. Chaucer renders the decisive line in Petrarch with complete accuracy: 'This is ynogh, Grisilde myn' (1051). As Jill Mann has shown, *ynogh* has a broad semantic range in Middle English, and Chaucer has extended Petrarch's use of the term to punctuate the structural divisions of his narrative.[50] The word is introduced here in a close echo of Griselde's wish that God send Walter and his new bride prosperity and '[p]lesance ynogh unto youre lyves ende' (1036). Walter's intention is an accurate rendering, too, of Petrarch's *fides*: 'Now knowe I, dere wyf, thy stedfastnesse' (1056). The term signifies more than loyalty, however. As Chaucer indicates in his balade to King Richard, steadfastness implies union, reciprocity, and virtue acting through proper social hierarchy; the compelling image is domestic: 'wed thy folk agein to stedfastnesse' (28).[51] Likewise, the passage that corresponds to Valterius's second address to his people deals with different issues:

> And folk that ootherweys han seyd of me,
> I warne hem wel that I have doon this deede
> For no malice, ne for no crueltee,
> But for t'assaye in thee thy wommanheede,
> And nat to sleen my children – God forbeede! –
> But for to kepe hem pryvely and stille,
> Til I thy purpos knewe and al thy wille. (1072–78)

Walter's curiosity is only implicit, and the charge he refutes is not impiety, as in Petrarch, but malice and cruelty – that is to say, moral instead of spiritual failings. Rather than test his wife by proofs of conjugal love ('coniugalis

---

[50] Jill Mann, 'Satisfaction and Payment in Middle English Literature', *Studies in the Age of Chaucer* 5 (1983) 17–48. Mann's discussion emphasizes that the definition of satisfaction generally involves a notion of the mean.

[51] See *Riverside Chaucer*, pp. 1085–86, for the problems of dating 'Lak of Stedfastnesse'.

amoris experimenta'), as Valterius phrases it, Walter seeks something much closer to Gualtieri's purpose – to know her purpose and will, just as he has earlier seen the people's 'trewe entente' (127, 148). Walter, like Gualtieri, wants to dispel the worry that there may be a disparity between his wife's visible actions and her private motives. That he himself has cultivated a similar disparity throughout the tests, as Kathryn Lynch points out (pp. 53–55), complicates his project and compromises his own standing, but it does not shift the focus of the story.

The ending of the *Clerk's Tale* takes shape, then, from the hermeneutic problems that bear on the narrative in its literary tradition and intertextual relations. Interpretations of intent and character converge in a cultural and political transformation debated successively through Boccaccio, Petrarch, and Chaucer. The integration of Griselde into the social order, for all her investitures and reversals of fortune, is secured finally when Janicula is brought to court.[52] Boccaccio says after the final test that Gualtieri takes the old man from his 'lavorìo' and installs him honourably as his father-in-law. Petrarch makes the delay part of Valterius's strategy: he has deferred taking Janicula in so as not to have him obstruct his plans for testing Griselda. Chaucer has him brought to live 'in pees and reste' (1132). Meanwhile, Griselde's daughter is suitably married to a lord of high social standing, proving thereby that she has the cultural value that originally led Walter's subjects to propose a noble wife who would confer honour on him. Boccaccio says nothing of the son, but Petrarch and Chaucer make succession an issue.[53] Valterius leaves his son as his successor and lives happily with his wife and heirs. Chaucer writes an additional passage in which the son, enjoying the same 'reste and pees' (1136) as Janicula, is 'fortunat' in marriage, without having to prove his wife. The males of three generations, now connected by a shared and unified heritage, live under the conditions of 'concord' and 'reste' that define Walter's marriage (1129). In other words, Chaucer's Walter enjoys the complementarity of temperament and the domestic peace that Boccaccio's Gualtieri originally sees respectively as means and ends.

In this transformation, Chaucer's ending consolidates and absorbs the

---

52 Norman Blake, 'Chaucer's Text and the Web of Words', in *New Perspectives in Chaucer Criticism*, ed. Donald M. Rose (Norman, 1981), pp. 227–28, offers a different interpretation of these lines based on Hengwrt. The accepted text reads: 'His wyves fader in his court he [Walter] kepeth' (1133). Hengwrt reads: 'His wyues fader and his court he kepeth'. Blake says of Hengwrt, 'This reading implies that Walter looked after his wife's father (though not necessarily by transferring him from the cottage to live at his own palace) and that he maintained his court (that is, his household, which symbolizes his estate and management) in dignified peace until he, Walter, died'.

53 Usher, pp. 410–17, usefully analyses the discrepancy between the tale's chiasmic structure, which places the birth of Gualtieri's son at the centre of the narrative, and the opening rubric, which obscures the narrative structure and emphasizes the importance of marriage bonds.

competing explanations of natural virtue and lineage. Griselde's qualities, operating alike in the domestic and political spheres, do not stand apart and independent from hierarchy and lineage. The strangeness she presents to those who would understand her is consciously and conspicuously brought into courtly life. Chaucer brilliantly expresses the point in a phrase that evidently confused fifteenth-century scribes but has fascinated modern critics: 'Whan she translated was in swich richesse' (385).[54] Her 'translation', like the removal and installation of relics, a bishop, or a literary text, is the movement of a given value to a new locale. In this movement, what renders Griselde knowable and displays her qualities is dress; and the rituals of investiture and devestiture accordingly punctuate her movement into, out of, and then back into courtly culture. The most interesting detail occurs in the first investiture, in which Griselde is clothed not just in a garment with the appropriate social badges but in clothes that have been measured for her beforehand (256–59). In the symbolism of this act, natural virtue finds its proper form in an antecedent hierarchy that signifies descent and lineage. Griselde's children, heirs to her virtues and to Walter's, have themselves been raised in such a hierarchy, and the qualities apparent on their return to Saluzzo legitimate both natural virtue and lineage. In a sense, the final test of Griselde, which prompts Walter to realize that he knows enough, is for her to recognize the legacy of her natural virtue in the two young aristocrats who stand before her as her successors. Her instinctive response to them is the pendant to Walter's 'greet insight' (240) about her. Like the *Man of Law's Tale*, the *Clerk's Tale* gives us a narrative that explains how new elements are brought into established political structures, how the margin (Janicula's 'throop' no less than the geographical limits of a Christianized Roman empire for Custance) is absorbed into the centre. In this respect, we can discover a rationale as well for Chaucer's rejection of Petrarch's idea that Valterius stands at the start of a noble lineage. Chaucer locates Walter further up the family tree with 'his worthy eldres hym bifore' (65) because he wants to demonstrate the power of grafting rather than the point of origins.

It is this idea of integration within hereditary hierarchy that may allow us to explain fully why the *Clerk's Tale* proved so popular in the century after Chaucer's death. However compelling it may be as a figure for personal, spiritual, domestic, and political obedience, Griselde's patience is not self-sufficient in Chaucer's poem, though Petrarch makes it so in his version of the story. Her patience requires belief of some sort that Walter endeavours to act prudently and wisely, that his testing is not merely pathological but motivated by responsible concerns for personal and public interests, that the

---

[54] Manly and Rickert, 6: 286–87, record the following variants for *translated*: transmuwed, transmuted, transnewid, transformed, transposed. In Petrarch, the relevant phrase is 'insignatam gemmis et corona velut subito transformatam'; in the *Livre Griseldis*, 'ainsi ordonnee et paree de couronne et de pierrerie tres grandement, comme soudainement transmuee et changié' (Severs, pp. 306, 307).

excess of curiosity is governed finally by calculation and judgement. It requires readers to believe, with Griselde in virtually her last words, that Walter is a 'benyngne fader' (1097) who has preserved his line and so the social and cultural forms dependent on it. This belief is where, moreover, the problem of hermeneutics rejoins the problem of historicism. Modern critics suggest that for fourteenth-century readers the *Clerk's Tale* bears a historical meaning because it serves as an analogue to monarchic excess and authoritarianism under Richard II's rule.[55] I propose that for fifteenth-century readers the tale bears a different historical meaning, which grows out of its hermeneutic problems. The *Clerk's Tale* is a narrative in which political authority lives up to the ideological commonplace of natural virtue. Griselde's noble qualities find their proper place and form in noble lineage. The tale is resolutely conservative in maintaining hierarchic rule, but it portrays an established hierarchy acting on the reasonable claims that the *commune* makes of its ruler, and it is optimistic in its belief that natural nobility can be not only recognized but accommodated into structures of power. The *Clerk's Tale* is not just a conduct book, extolling the value of obedience for a troubled age; it incorporates the political fantasy of Chaucer's new audience of country and mercantile gentry. It expresses what lies behind abjection, the deep wish for a place within benevolent, purposive, rational authority. For these readers, Griselde's patience is a means that must imagine and endorse Walter's ends and accept the scandal of his moral agency.

---

[55] Wallace, pp. 208–13; Carol Falvo Heffernan, 'Tyranny and *Commune Profit* in the *Clerk's Tale*', *Chaucer Review* 17 (1982–83), pp. 334–35.

CHARLES OF ORLEANS READING CHAUCER'S DREAM VISIONS

JULIA BOFFEY

One of the most famous images of Charles of Orleans, French poet and English prisoner for twenty-five of his seventy-six years, comes from a manuscript produced in the last years of the fifteenth century, some decades after his death in 1465.[1] It accompanies a selection of Charles's French poems, specifically a *ballade* in which Charles, restored to France, thanks the Duke of Burgundy for his help in negotiating a release, and it depicts the prisoner in the Tower of London, during the final stages of his English captivity.[2] Charles is represented three times in the miniature: in the centre, alone at a window of the White Tower; on the right, signing documents concerning his release; and to the left, tightly clutching the roll of documents, ready for departure. In what follows I should like to explore some of the issues of fifteenth-century Anglo-French cultural exchange which this image, with its fusion of bustling English metropolis and important departing French detainee, so elegantly focuses. The issues have to do with courtly poets writing in English in a tradition which was saturated with French precedents, but was also, by the early to mid-fifteenth century, alive to Chaucer's example and to the possibilities of a vernacular literary tradition. The issues can be

---

[1] In London, British Library, MS Royal 16. F. ii, fol. 73r, and invoked by J.A.W. Bennett in a discussion of *The Kingis Quair* of James I of Scotland: 'A King's Quire', in *The Humane Medievalist and Other Essays in English Literature and Learning, from Chaucer to Eliot*, ed. Piero Boitani (Rome, 1982), pp. 67–88. The manuscript is described in Sir George Warner and Julius Gilson, *Catalogue of Western Manuscripts in the Old Royal and King's Collections in the British Museum*, 4 vols. (London, 1921) II: 203–04, and has been more recently discussed by Janet Backhouse, 'Founders of the Royal Library: Edward IV and Henry VII as Collectors of Illuminated Manuscripts', in *England in the Fifteenth Century: Proceedings of the 1986 Harlaxton Symposium*, ed. Daniel Williams (Woodbridge, 1987), pp. 23–41.

[2] The miniature is reproduced in John Fox, *The Lyric Poetry of Charles d'Orléans* (London, 1969), frontispiece, and the illumination of the manuscript briefly discussed in Thomas Kren, ed., *Renaissance Painting in Manuscripts: Treasures from the British Library* (London and New York, 1983), pp. 56–58. For the *ballade*, 'Des nouvelles d'Albion', see Pierre Champion, ed., *Charles d'Orléans: Poésies*, 2 vols. (Paris, 1923–27, rpt. 1971), I: 143–44. Further references to the French poems of Charles d'Orléans will be to this edition. For biographies of Charles, see Pierre Champion, *Charles d'Orléans, joueur d'échecs* (Paris, 1908), and Enid McLeod, *Charles of Orleans: Prince and Poet* (London, 1969).

pointedly illustrated with reference to the approximately parallel bodies of poems, in English and French, for which Charles of Orleans was evidently responsible.[3] Since they have been often overlooked in favour of commentary on the shorter lyrics, I should like to look in particular at the two dream episodes which give a structure to Charles's body of English poems to see what they might reflect of his own reading of Chaucer's dream visions.

Charles's English poems survive in London, British Library MS Harley 682 as a 'book' or sequence made up of short lyrics in the traditional fixed forms of ballade and roundel, and of some longer sections, generally in seven-line rhyme royal or eight-line stanzas. The French poems, as collected in Charles's personal and partly autograph manuscript, Paris, Bibliothèque Nationale f.fr. 25458, and in anthologies related to it, also preserve a narrative framework, but there are several points, especially concerning poems towards the end of MS Harley 682, where there is no correspondence between English and French (occasionally these result from losses in the MS).[4] Scholars remain divided on the issue of authorship. Some (including the Early English Text Society editors) believe the same individual to have been responsible for both versions, and admit the possibility that at least some of the French redactions may postdate the English ones. Others hold to the idea that an 'English translator' of uncertain identity rendered Charles's French poems into English and organized them (perhaps with some additions of his own) into the coherent sequence of MS Harley 682. Whichever view one takes (and I tend to the first, so calling the author of both French and English versions 'Charles'), it is hard to overlook the pronounced Chaucerian cast of some of the writing in the English 'book'. There are echoes of lines and phrases from a number of Chaucer's poems, from the lyrics to *Troilus and Criseyde* and certain of *The Canterbury Tales*, sufficient to suggest that whoever worked on the English poems had an intense and discriminating understanding of Chaucerian idiom. The complex infiltration of this idiom into Charles's English sequence deserves some attention.

The 'story' distilled by the poems is a love allegory, and it begins with an introductory series of verse pseudo-documents which recount the narrator's swearing of fealty to Cupid and his undertaking to follow the rules of love in his courtship of a sometimes distant lady. Some lyrics further into the

---

[3] See Champion, ed., and Robert Steele and Mabel Day, eds., *The English Poems of Charles of Orleans*, EETS OS 215, 220 (rpt. in one volume, 1970). Questions concerning the authorship of the English poems, and their status as translations or sources of the French, have prompted much debate: see Mary-Jo Arn, 'Charles of Orleans and the Poems of BL MS, Harley 682', *English Studies* 74 (1993) 222–35. I was not able to consult Professor Arn's edition of the poems, *Fortunes Stabilnes* (Binghamton, NY, 1994) until this article was completed.

[4] Mary-Jo Arn, 'Poetic Form as a Mirror of Meaning in the English Poems of Charles of Orleans', *Philological Quarterly* 69 (1990) 13–29, and Thomas E. Vesce, 'The Pose of Love: The Early English Ballad Cycle of Charles d'Orleans', *Fifteenth-Century Studies* 17 (1990) 439–56. For descriptions of the manuscripts, see Steele and Day,

sequence we learn that the lady dies, and the first dream-episode, termed by its Early English Text Society editors the 'Vision in Complaint', and surviving in both English and French versions, follows lyrics which refer in various ways to a period of desolation and mourning.[5] After the 'karfulle payne' of his daylight hours the narrator goes to bed as the light fails and the sun sets. The dream which follows is of Age, who before had given instructions to Nature to consign the narrator first to Childhood, then to Youth, and has come to warn him now of the approach of 'Elde', a state inimical to love, since (in an echo of a line from Chaucer's 'Miller's Tale', I 3230) 'loue and elde are falle at gret debate' (2576).[6] Age delivers warning words on Fortune and her deceptive blandishments, and these are so frightful a prospect that the dreamer wakes with a start. He decides to petition for retirement from Love's court, is granted a 'quytance', and accompanied by 'Comfort' from Love's court to 'the Castelle of no care', where he remains with 'passid tyme' for company.

There follows a *jubilee* or feast of roundels and other short lyric forms offered by the narrator (who defines himself throughout as a poet), from his retreat of 'No Care', to other lovers. He represents himself at this point as short of creative inspiration – 'Baladis songis and complayntis / God wot they are forgote in my party' (3071–72) – but he experiments with the shorter roundel form as if to provide material for others' use. Asked by one of his acquaintance to write a poem which will 'biwayle fortunes stabilnes' (4660), he takes his writing materials outside and produces a 'complaint' against Fortune – a labour which induces sleep and the second dream episode, entitled 'Love's Renewal' by its editors, which persuades him that it will not be impossible to love again. When, after waking, he meets a new lady, he initiates a correspondence which constitutes a new series of poems. There is an apt symmetry in these two dream episodes which mark off, firstly, abdication from Love's service and its inspiration of poems of true feeling, and subsequently, the commitment to a new lady and a new source of inspiration. Both dreams in effect serve to objectify or externalize processes of thought or reflection which draw together the action of the sequence with what seems to be one of its larger themes: the business of poetic composition. They help to clarify the narrator's reasons for writing or not writing the love poems which serve as the primary index of his claim to creative worth.

Outside these actual dream episodes, several of the ballades recall dream poems in one way or another. Some for example invoke the familiar circumstances in which dreams habitually occur, only to tell how the anticipated movement into sleep was somehow frustrated. The narrator

---

eds., pp. xi–xxx, and Pierre Champion, *Le Manuscrit autographe de Charles d'Orléans* (Paris, 1907).
5   The French version, 'Le Songe en complainte', is discussed by J.A. Burrow, *The Ages of Man: A Study in Medieval Writing and Thought* (Oxford, 1988), pp. 182–86.
6   All references to Chaucer's works are to Larry D. Benson, ed., *The Riverside Chaucer* (Boston, 1987).

suffers the lover's habitual sleeplessness – 'Bi nyght to slepe as I haue no power' (561); he courts insomnia because his heart persists in re-reading the 'romance of plesaunt pancer' (412);[7] on another occasion the noise of mating birds wakes him up and stops him sleeping (2455). One ballade even consists of a small, self-contained dream episode, in which a flower rebukes the lover for his service to the leaf (2264 ff.).

Points such as these in the sequence inevitably recall Chaucer's dream poems, and it is not hard to find further common matter and themes. The death of the narrator's first lady, and his subsequent melancholy and search for consolation, for instance, seem to duplicate the concerns shared by the narrator and the Man in Black in *The Book of the Duchess*. The allegorical cast of the sequence, with a central lover/poet/dreamer who encounters figures such as Cupid, Venus, and Fortune, allows for opportunities along the lines of the dreams of *The Parliament of Fowls* or *The Prologue to the Legend of Good Women*, where different aspects of love are personified. Clearly, too, Charles's concern with the network of relationships between desire, imagination, and poetry is close to Chaucer's preoccupation, in the dream visions generally, and especially in *The House of Fame*, with the status and inspiration of the professional poet of love.[8] Equally, though, it might be objected that such concerns, and the strategies by which they are addressed, were for Chaucer focused by his reading of fourteenth-century French *dits amoureux* (as perhaps by the wider European tradition of the erotic pseudo-biography), and that the poems of MS Harley 682 simply articulate in English some of the devices and conventions which were Charles of Orleans's native heritage. We might look for example at the patterns of complaint and consolation effected through sleep and dreams in Machaut's *La Fonteinne Amoureuse*, or Froissart's *La Prison Amoureuse*; or at these French poets' pervasive interest in reflection on their own oeuvres, duplicated in Chaucer's *House of Fame* and *Prologue to the Legend of Good Women*, and again parallelled by Charles's anxieties over the relationship between his writing and his role as a lover.[9]

Such difficulties in unravelling the nature of Charles's possible Chaucerian

---

[7] Eleanor P. Hammond, *English Verse between Chaucer and Surrey* (Durham, NC, 1927), p. 215, reads this as 'the romaunce of plesaunt chaucer', but Steele and Day's reading of 'pancer' is clearly the correct one.

[8] On these preoccupations, see most recently Robert Edwards, *The Dream of Chaucer: Representation and Reflection in the Early Narratives* (Durham, NC, 1989).

[9] R. Barton Palmer, ed. and trans., *Guillaume de Machaut: The Fountain of Love (La Fonteinne Amoureuse) and Two Other Love Vision Poems* (New York, 1993); Anthime Fourrier, ed., *Froissart: La Prison Amoureuse* (Paris, 1974). For the specifics of Chaucer's debts, see B.A. Windeatt, ed. and trans., *Chaucer's Dream Poems: Sources and Analogues* (Cambridge, 1982); James I. Wimsatt, *Chaucer and his French Contemporaries: Natural Music in the Fourteenth Century* (Toronto, 1991), and William Calin, 'Machaut's Legacy: the Chaucerian Inheritance Reconsidered', *Studies in the Literary Imagination* 20 (1987) 9–22.

debt extend beyond the general conception of his sequence to local points of style and diction. Verbal echoes and borrowed phrases which occasionally suggest his recall of Chaucer's dream visions may turn out to have a more complex and layered history. In two separate ballades on the theme of a lover's distress, for instance, it is immediately tempting to locate memories of *The Book of the Duchess*. Charles's narrator declares:

> Who so that lust aqueynt him silfe with sorowe
> As come to me and seche no ferthir way ...
> Thus ay diyng y lyue and neuyr deed ... (2529–30; 2536),

and he later elaborates on the same invitation with some extra detail:

> For alle my ioy is turnyd to hevynes
> Myn ese in harme my wele in woo
> Mi hope in drede in dowt my sikirnes
> And my delite in sorow lo ...
> For who so with sorwe list acqueyntid be
> As come to me and spille no ferthir wey
> For sorwe is y and y am he (5848–51; 5856–58).

The figures and phrasing here instantly bring to mind Chaucer's Man in Black:

> For whoso seeth me first on morwe
> May seyn he hath met with sorwe,
> For y am sorwe, and sorwe ys y.
> Allas! and I wol tel the why:
> My song ys turned to pleynynge,
> And al my laughtre to wepynge,
> My glade thoghtes to hevynesse ... (595–601),

and some of the overlap must clearly reflect an attempt to cultivate a Chaucerian idiom. But, as the notes to any scholarly edition of Chaucer will point out, certain elements of this passage were themselves probably influenced by earlier texts which were doubtless known to Chaucer and Charles alike: the opening couplet of Alain de Lille's *De planctu naturae*; *Le Roman de la Rose* (4293–334); Machaut's *Remede de fortune* (1198) and *Le Jugement dou roi de Behaigne* (177–87).[10] Charles's several allusions to games of draughts, 'tablis' and chess, in ballades 22, 46, and 61 respectively, may seem insistently to recall the game of chess with Fortune played by *The*

---

[10] James J. Sheridan, trans., *Alan of Lille: The Plaint of Nature* (Toronto, 1980), p. 67; Felix Lecoy, ed., *Guillaume de Lorris and Jean de Meun: Le Roman de la Rose*, 3 vols. (Paris, 1963–70), I: 133–34; James I. Wimsatt and William W. Kibler, eds., *Le Jugement du roy de Behaigne and Remede de Fortune of Guillaume de Machaut* (Athens, GA, 1988), p. 235.

Book of the Duchess's Man in Black (652–86), but again it is possible to locate similar motifs in the *Remede de fortune* (1190–91), and, with still greater weight of authority, in *Le Roman de la Rose* (6620–726); 'the trope was a common one', as we are roundly told by the Riverside notes.[11] Exercises such as this, which expose the pre-history of certain apparently 'Chaucerian' debts in Charles's poems, are instructive warnings about the complex combination of sources on which he doubtless drew.

Some of the 'Chaucerian tinges' which it is tempting to locate in the sequence may of course, in the words of Eleanor Hammond, 'have filtered to our author through a second dilution':[12] that is to say, they are Chaucerian echoes and allusions which reached Charles through the poems of intermediaries such as Lydgate. An example of this is the ostensible echo of *The Parliament of Fowls* in Charles's ballade about Maytime observance, where his visit to the woods to hear 'the birdis synge and pley / Right as the wood therwith shulde forshyuere' (1694–95) seems to recall Chaucer's 'The noyse of foules for to ben delyvered / So loude rong, "Have don, and lat us wende!" / That wel wende I the wode hadde al to-shyvered' (491–93). But his phrasing may equally have been influenced by lines in Lydgate's *The Complaint of the Black Knight*, which relate that in this dream landscape the birds 'So loude songe that al the wode ronge, / Lyke as hyt sholde sheuer in pesis smale' (45–46).[13] Once we situate Charles in a context such as this, where many of the fifteenth-century English poets whose works he was likely to encounter were probably essaying a Chaucerian strain, it often seems pointless to expect to identify precise influences or precedents.

The survival of both French and English versions of some of the poems does at least offer the occasional foothold in these muddy waters, since it is sometimes the case that a 'Chaucerian tinge' in the English (however derived) is not reflected in the French. Whichever way the translator or redactor was working – from French into English, with some purpose of enhancing the Chaucerian flavour, or from English to French, with the intention of expunging it – it seems quite clear that a Chaucerian mode was considered appropriate in the English poems, and sometimes actively sought. One stanza of Charles's ballade on the perils of 'hasty biholdyng' and sudden love,

>   Which causith oft fulle paynfulle abidyng
>   Or he may passe the gate of Iupardy
>   The tyme so long vnsure the releuyng
>   As of comfort to fynden remedy   (279–82),

---

[11] Wimsatt and Kibler, eds., p. 235, and Lecoy, ed., I: 203–6.
[12] Hammond, *English Verse*, p. 215.
[13] Henry Noble MacCracken, ed., *The Minor Poems of John Lydgate*, 2 vols., EETS ES 107 and OS 192 (1911 and 1934), II: 384, and also John Norton-Smith, ed., *John Lydgate: Poems* (Oxford, 1966), p. 48.

contains a reminiscence of the cadence of the opening of *The Parliament of Fowls* ('The lyf so short, the craft so long to lerne') in lines which are contrived rather differently in the French:

> Car mains maulx lui fault endurer,
> Et de Soussy passer le port,
> Avant qu'il puisse recouvrer
> lacointance de Reconfort (Champion, ed., p. 20).

The cadence recurs in lines such as 'This long dilay this hope without comfort' (5576) and 'The long dilay the hope without comfort' (5940) in two further English poems to which no parallel French versions have survived.[14]

Another very specific infiltration of Chaucerian flavour into the English poems can be noted in ballade 64, where commemoration of the first lady turns into a more generalized statement about the inescapableness of death. The second stanza lists famous beauties of the past whom death has taken:

> Ou vieil temps grant renom couroit
> De Creseide, Yseud, Elaine,
> Et maintes autres qu'on nommoit
> Parfaittes en beaute haultaine (Champion, ed., p. 85)

In the English the list of women is changed to 'dido cresseid Alcest and Eleyne', an emendation necessary on metrical grounds (since a longer line is required), but also perhaps recalling *The Prologue to the Legend of Good Women*, where the balade in praise of Alceste lists all these names (F24969, G203–23).[15] It is not impossible, I think, that the first line of Charles's ballade, 'When y revolue in my remembraunce', might have somehow sparked associations with the 'remembrance' discussed at the start of *The Prologue to the Legend of Good Women*. There is in fact a nexus of reference to the *Prologue* in both this and the following two ballades (both of which are interestingly matched by quite close French versions: Champion ed., pp. 85–87). After the meditation on death and remembrance comes a poem in which the narrator recalls a Maytime sortie during which he was asked to state his allegiance to either flower or leaf; naturally he chose the latter, 'syn thorugh deth y lost haue welawey / She which was sorse and flowre of alle bewte . . . Of othir flowre god wott y take no quere' (2239–40, 2244). The following ballade takes the form of a short recollected dream in which the spurned flower visits the dreamer to ask an explanation for his choice of the leaf. In the context of the sequence of French poems, the French credentials of this small sequence are impeccable, with connections to poems by Deschamps

---

[14] Derek Pearsall, *John Lydgate* (London, 1970), pp. 52–53, points out Lydgate's fondness for lines modelled on this chiasmus.

[15] Cf. also *PF* 288–92, where all but Alceste appear.

and others;[16] the very slight differences in the English poems re-draw the pedigree in a subtle but significant way.

Keeping in mind these special qualifications which attach to any attempt at source-spotting in the English poems attributed to Charles, I'd like now to look more closely at the Chaucerian infiltration of the second and longer of the dream episodes in the sequence, 'Love's Renewal'. Unlike the earlier dream of Age (the so-called 'Vision in Complaint'), and indeed unlike the mini-dream about the protesting flower, this has no surviving parallel in the body of French poems, although it serves a clear structural purpose in the English 'book' in rounding off the 'jubilee' and indicating changes in the poet-narrator's circumstances which ostensibly redirect his creative energies in a more positive way. It is introduced by a group of stanzas in which the narrator speaks of the 'wakyng dremys sad' (4640) which have oppressed him since his lady's death, and the 'ydille thought' (4641) which now does duty for the imaginative exercise he previously expended in the composition of love-poems. There are analogies here, we might think, with both the dulled narrator and the mourning Man in Black of *The Book of the Duchess*, and with the uninspired poet of love who becomes the prey of the eagle in Book II of *The House of Fame*. An acquaintance brings a commission: he wants a complaint which will 'biwayle fortunes stabilnes' (4660), and presumably with the sense that this fits his own preoccupations very well the narrator agrees to take it on. Settled on a grassy bench overlooking the sea, oppressed by the tedium of the exercise, he writes, 'syn it must nede be doon' (4675); the resulting complaint, which has more than a little in common with the words of 'Le Pleintif' in Chaucer's *Fortune*, is incorporated as part of the narrative. Appropriately enough, given his lack of enthusiasm and the constraining repetitiveness of the undertaking, the effort of writing induces sleep; perhaps this is a witty variation on the framing device which involves Chaucerian narrators in reading[17] or in otherwise speculating about their lack of creative inspiration.

The recollection of the dream is prefaced by a very brief gesture towards the debate about the significance of dreams which is invoked at the start of *Le Roman de la Rose* and *The House of Fame* (1–58).[18] Next the narrator recounts how he dreamed that 'A lady nakid alle thing saue hir here / And on hir hed lijk as a crowne she were' (47601) came somehow 'fletyng' towards him over the waves (the dream, like the waking introduction, is located by the sea). Although the lady appears to expect some familiar acknowledgment

---

16 Wimsatt, *Chaucer and his French Contemporaries*, p. 261; D. A. Pearsall, ed., *The Floure and the Leaf and the Assembly of Ladies* (Manchester, 1962), pp. 22–29.
17 M.W. Stearns, 'Chaucer Mentions a Book', *Modern Language Notes* 57 (1942) 28–31.
18 Lecoy, ed., I: 1–20, and cf. the translation attributed to Chaucer, *The Romaunt of the Rose*, Benson, ed., pp. 686–87.

from the dreamer, and indeed addresses him as 'Charlis' (4788), he does not at first recognize her, and only some way into their conversation realizes 'þat venus then hit was' (4795). Part of the joke about the narrator's confusion resides in the improbable combination of attributes with which the goddess is here credited, and their assortment warrants a moment's pause. She is virtually naked, crowned, and comes from the sea surrounded by pairs of doves: not difficult to identify as marine Venus, and in fact much like the goddess illustrated alongside Chaucer's conjoined *Complaints of Mars and Venus* on fol. 14v of Oxford, Bodleian MS Fairfax 16, a manuscript which includes lyrics connected with the English poems of Charles of Orleans.[19] Details of the iconography recall the depiction of Venus in Part III of 'The Knight's Tale',

> ... naked, fletynge in the large see,
> And fro the navele doun al covered was
> With wawes grene, and brighte as any glas ...
> Above hir heed hir dowves flikerynge   (I. 1956–68, 1962),

and in the dream-temple of *The House of Fame* (132–39), whose significance has been exhaustively discussed by J.A.W. Bennett and Meg Twycross.[20] Here, though, to justify the dreamer's confusion, he also perceives

> About hir wast a kercher of plesaunce
> And on hir hond an Owle y sigh sittyng   (4764–65).

There is, I think, a reasonable argument for reading these details as a reminiscence of the Venus presented in *The Parliament of Fowls* (260–73). While a 'kercher of plesaunce' which has figured earlier in the sequence in a ballade about the lover's retention of his lady's heart, where it is used as a kind of wrapper (1168), seems simply parallel to the item described as 'ung cueuvrechief de Plaisance' in the matching French *ballade* (Champion ed., p. 51), in the context of the dream episode its echo of the 'subtyl coverchef of Valence' (273) with which the *Parliament*'s Venus is artfully veiled seems inescapable.[21] It is to play a very material role later in the dream, and is appropriately to be foregrounded in anticipation.

---

[19] See the facsimile: John Norton-Smith, intro., *Bodleian Library MS Fairfax 16* (London, 1979). On the poems in the manuscript which have been associated with Charles (and by association, with one of his English guardians, the Duke of Suffolk), see J. P. M. Jansen, 'Charles d'Orléans and the Fairfax Poems', *English Studies* 70 (1989) 206–24, and ed., *The Suffolk Poems: An Edition of the Love Lyrics in Fairfax 16 Attributed to William de la Pole* (Groningen, 1989).

[20] J.A.W. Bennett, *Chaucer's Book of Fame: An Exposition of The House of Fame* (Oxford, 1968), pp. 16–24; Meg Twycross, *The Medieval Anadyomene: A Study in Chaucer's Mythography* (Medium Aevum Monographs NS 1, Oxford, 1972); Earl G. Schreiber, 'Venus in the Medieval Mythographic Tradition', *Journal of English and Germanic Philology* 74 (1975) 519–35.

[21] As described in Boccaccio's *Teseida* VII 50–66, Chaucer's source for this section of

The owl on Venus's hand has more complex associations. Marine Venus is of course often represented with a conch shell, as in the Fairfax 16 miniature; through various more or less comprehensible chains of association, she sometimes carries other items of her toilette, like the comb of *The House of Fame*, or a stringed instrument of some kind – the 'citole' of 'The Knight's Tale', for example.[22] I have not been able to trace any other relevant examples of her association with an owl. While it is quite possible that the scribe of MS Harley 682 has miscopied 'Owle' in place of some more predictable item,[23] or indeed, as Steele and Day point out, that the owl has been inadvertently misplaced as details from a source were taken over and reworked,[24] it seems

> the *Parliament*, Venus is naked to the waist, 'and the other part was covered by a garment so fine that scarcely nothing was concealed':
>> le braccia e 'l petto e' pomi rilevati
>> si vedean tutti, e l'altra parte d'una
>> veste tanto sottil si ricopria,
>> che quasi nulla appena nascondia;
>
> A. Limentani, ed., *Tutte le Opere di Giovanni Boccaccio*, II, ed. V. Branca (Milan, 1964), p. 476 (65), trans. Windeatt, *Chaucer's Dream Poetry*, p. 83.

[22] Twycross, *The Medieval Anadyomene*.

[23] The peculiarities of the text in MS Harley 682, some of which have been revised in different stages of correction, are preserved in Steele and Day, eds., who comment (p. xxvii): 'The copy given to the scribe was then in a rough state, the spelling phonetic and not regularised, while a number of the words were hardly English at all, so that the scribe had to make the best of them he could'. Among the peculiarities, we might note at 5096 the words 'Owlle septe' which in context must presumably mean 'Owtte-septe' (= except).

[24] Steele and Day, eds., p. 292, refer to Lydgate's version of the Judgement of Paris, *Troy Book*, II 2556, where Pallas and her owl are described immediately after Venus and her doves, and suggest that an inattentive reader could have confused the attributes; see Henry Bergen, ed., *Lydgate's Troy Book*, 4 vols, EETS ES 97, 103, 106, 126 (1906–35), I: 218. It is indeed possible that Charles's owl may have been suggested in some way by an illustration to the Judgment of Paris in a version of the story of Troy. On the tradition of illustration in Benoît and Guido, see Hugo Buchthal, *Historia Troiana: Studies in the History of Medieval Secular Illustration* (London, 1971), pp. 37–38, and for illustrated copies of Lydgate's *Troy Book*, Lesley Lawton, 'The Illustration of Late Medieval Secular Texts, with Special Reference to Lydgate's *Troy Book*', in *Manuscripts and Readers in Fifteenth-Century England*, ed. Derek Pearsall (Cambridge, 1981), pp. 41–69. The only copy of Lydgate's poem which appears to illustrate this episode is Manchester, John Rylands Library MS English 1; the representation of Venus is linked by Lawton (p. 66 n. 68) with that in Bodleian MS Fairfax 16. For a reproduction, see Margaret H. Ehrhart, *The Judgment of the Trojan Prince Paris in Medieval Literature* (Philadelphia, 1987), facing p. 221, and for analysis, p. 228: 'Reading the picture from the lower right, we see Paris hunting . . . We then see his riderless horse tethered to the branch of a tree. Above the horse, Paris reclines with closed eyes against a rock as Mercury taps him with his caduceus . . . Mercury is accompanied by his cock, which is perched above Paris's head . . . Behind Mercury is Pallas . . . her owl sits in a tree above Paris. Next is Juno . . . followed by a peacock. Above, in a river that descends from the top of the scene, is Venus, nude and surrounded by doves'.

to me not at all unlikely that it should have been allotted to this Venus as a very significant emblem. As the bird conventionally associated with Minerva, it suggests the wisdom and often chastity which she represents (it is also of course associated with sleep, and sometimes with death, states of some significance to this dreamer).[25] Ample precedent for the association of Minerva and Venus existed in literary and visual representations of the Judgement of Paris, and some witty interchanging of attributes would not have been incomprehensible.[26] Perched here on Venus's hand, the owl gives this goddess additionally something of the aspect of Nature as she appears in *The Parliament of Fowls* with the formel eagle (372–75): an odd, but in context not at all inapposite reminder. Unlike the Venus of the *Parliament*, Charles's Venus, despite initial appearances, is not in the least lascivious: the 'kercher of plesaunce' significantly conceals her nakedness, and when the possibility arises that she will be spied in the dreamer's company she is comically embarrassed (5093–94). While she rebukes the dreamer for his tardiness in taking a new lady to replace the dead one, her concern is not simply that he observe her law, but rather that he fulfil his own potential as a man, looking positively forwards to a future rather than backwards to the lost past. And her anxiety that his current contemplative existence is 'ageyne nature' (49–45) is not simply a demonstration of her commitment to concupiscence, since it is qualified by her recommendation that the new service of love which he proceeds to undertake should be steadfast and loyal (5165–6). While we can't be certain that Charles has drawn on Chaucer for all these features of his Venus, he has clearly synthesized details from a variety of sources and produced a new figure with notable Chaucerian resonances.

The interview between Venus and the dreamer proceeds, *Book of the Duchess*-style, with a long passage of recollection of the dead lady. Even here, echoes of the *Parliament* intrude into the dreamer's memories of his state as a lover:

> And with this word she made myn hert to bold
> And with this word allas she made me cold (4837–8)

---

[25] See Guy de Téravent, *Attributs et symboles dans l'art profane, 1450–1600*, 2 vols. (Geneva, 1958) I 95–97, and Otto Schmitt, *Reallexicon zur deutschen Kunstgeschichte*, 7 vols. (Stuttgart and Munich, 1937–81), VI 267–322 (included here are some reproductions of scenes concerning love where the owl represents chastity). Slightly later examples of Venus taking over the attributes of Minerva, and *vice versa*, are discussed by R. Wittkower, 'Transformations of Minerva in Renaissance Imagery', *Allegory and the Migration of Symbols* (London, 1977), pp. 129–42.

[26] French versions of the story which may have been known to Charles are offered in Machaut's *Dit de la fonteinne amoureuse* and *Confort d'ami*, and in Froissart's *Espinette amoureuse*. On the attributes, see Ehrhart, *Judgement of Paris*, pp. 24–25. In the translation of *Les Echecs amoureux* attributed to Lydgate, Minerva's owl is replaced by swans: E. Sieper, ed., *Lydgate's Reason and Sensuality*, 2 vols, EETS ES 84, 89 (1901–3), II: 897–2700.

is very close to the *Parliament*-dreamer's response to the twin inscriptions over the gate to the garden of love:

> ... with that oon encresede ay my fere
> And with that other gan myn herte bolde;
> That oon me hette, that other dide me colde   (143–5).

Venus's advice to the dreamer concludes with an enigmatic remark about his future:

> For when ye se that / that ye nevir saw
> It may wel happe yow thynke ye neuer thought   (4962–3),

which in the context of a discussion about loyalty between lovers brings to mind the asseveration which Criseyde makes to Diomede early on in Book V of *Troilus and Criseyde*:

> Peraventure so it happen may
> That whan I se that nevere yit I say
> Than wol I werke that I nevere wroughte!   (V. 991–3).

The implied analogy between the dreamer and Criseyde is not altogether out of place, since both are about to take on a new lover in place of an old one. Invocation of Criseyde's role in Chaucer's poem as a metonym for Fortune is also not irrelevant, since the dreamer in Charles's poem now moves on to confront the goddess Fortune herself.

Just as he was unable to recognize Venus, so he seems comically incapable of interpreting the many clues in Fortune's dress and appearance about her identity. This Fortune is drawn in a chariot,[27] and she wears a jewelled, colour-changing surcoat under a rainbow-tinted mantel. Her clothing is ornamented with moons and dice, her crown devised in wavy patterns, and her face ever-changing: 'sumwhil she lowrid sore / And even as soune she lokid glad' (5038–39). Her wheel carries the inscription 'I shal rayne / y rayne / y haue raynyd // And y owt-rayne' (5044–5), an unusual detail in English depictions of Fortune,[28] which here intensifies the focus of the dream on the onward movement of time, and suggests positive aspects of 'Fortunes stabilnes' which were not apparent before the dream as the narrator composed his 'complaint' on what seemed Fortune's fixed and unchanging malevolence.

Among the figures variously poised and clambering on the wheel he sees what appears at first to be his lost object of his desire, but Venus bluntly puts him right, with another comic interchange and a lesson on Fortune. He is by

---

[27] Possibly through some analogy with the iconographic tradition of triumphs; see D.D. Carnicelli, *Lord Morley's Tryumphes of Fraunces Petrarcke* (Harvard, 1971), pp. 38–54.

[28] Howard R. Patch, *The Goddess Fortuna in Medieval Literature* (Harvard, 1927, repr. London, 1967), pp. 164–67.

this stage ready to embark on a new period of 'service', and Venus's 'kercher of plesaunce' comes at last into its own as a means of aerial transport to the new lady (5170–71). Inevitably, and perhaps in a manner familiar from Book II of *The House of Fame*, the shock of the sudden dream transposition wakes him up:

> And so dredles hir kercher thus y took
> And as me thought she bare me vp so hie
> That even for fere to falle / therwith y quok
> And gan o lady venus mercy cry
> So lowde that it awook me verily
> And fond my silf wher as y was downe layd ...   (5184–89).

What immediately follows this dream episode, though, is very unlike any of Chaucer's dream poems. Charles's dreamer wakes, astonished, to find a piece of fabric in his hand which he carefully stows away as 'remembraunce' of his dream. It is an extraordinary device for linking the dream and waking worlds while at the same time announcing the fictiveness of both. Walking disconsolately back home, and drawn unwillingly into a game of 'post and pillar' with some of his friends, the narrator then encounters no other but the new lady of the dream, and is able to initiate with her a fresh relationship which inspires a new series of *ballades*.

Chaucer too is interested in a nexus of ideas concerning memory, imagination, and 'art poetical' which the dream form can so effectively foreground, and in the ways in which the imaginative explorations permitted in dreams can constitute material for fresh books.[29] For the narrator of *The Parliament of Fowls*, who is promised by Africanus, his dream-guide, 'matere of to write' (168), his own dream, retrospectively turned into a poem, joins the ranks of 'othere bokes' which distil 'newe science' from ancient subjects. And for the narrator of *The Book of the Duchess*, the process of dreaming is tersely expressed as analagous to the process of poetic composition: having enshrined the dream in a poem, he elides the dreaming and writing activities in the concluding phrase 'this was my sweven; now hit ys doon' (1334). In a rather different way, the dream of *The Prologue to the Legend of Good Women* serves, in the form of the penance to which the dreamer is directed by the God of Love, to generate a text. Interestingly, though, Chaucer's experiments with metafictional effects which can serve to emphasize the connections between dreams and texts are comparatively restrained, and the ostensible 'realism' of the frameworks to his dream poems has often been

---

[29] Piero Boitani, 'Old Books brought to life in dreams: the *Book of the Duchess*; the *House of Fame*; the *Parliament of Fowls*', in *The Cambridge Chaucer Companion*, ed. Jill Mann and Piero Boitani (Cambridge, 1986), pp. 39–57; J.A. Burrow, 'The Poet and the Book', in *Genres, Themes, and Images. The J.A.W. Bennett Memorial Lectures, Perugia 1986*, eds. P. Boitani and Anna Torti (Tübingen, 1988), pp. 230–45.

noted.[30] Apart from what is possibly the subversive gesture of anti-closure in *The House of Fame* (and beyond the autobiographical or pseudo-autobiographical linkings of dreamers and narrators), there is in his dream poems none of the flamboyant interpenetration of dreaming and waking worlds which is so distinctive a characteristic of the *dits* of, for example, Machaut.

Charles's strategy of having the dreamer retain his piece of 'kercher' as a souvenir of the dream does not, then, seem something which immediately invites connection to a Chaucerian precedent. It has more in common with fourteenth-and fifteenth-century French *dits*, or with the structure of works like Gower's *Confessio Amantis* or Lydgate's *Temple of Glass*.[31] In the context of writing in England in the fifteenth century, it is notably similar to the device which links dream and waking worlds in *The Kingis Quair*, a poem to which it is also comparable on other grounds.[32] Here, as in Charles's 'book', the dream episode is only one part of a more complex structure, which begins with the narrator reading Boethius's *De consolatione philosophiae* and feeling impelled by it to recount his own history of capture and imprisonment. He draws from his own case a reversal of the pattern of Boethius's experience, since imprisonment for him was followed by release, marriage, and a sense of the benevolent potential of Fortune. His dream, in which he receives instruction about virtuously directed earthly love, is technically located in the past, as part of his prison history, but it leads effectively into the present of the poem's conclusion as the narrator finds in love the means, both metaphorically and literally, to re-enter the world and to reassert a social identity. One of the strategies by which this elision of past and present is effected is precisely the interpenetration of dreaming and waking worlds: on surfacing from sleep, the narrator is visited at his prison window by a turtle-dove (Venus's bird, presumably) with a spray of pinks inscribed with messages of hope – exactly the kind of 'remembraunce' which, in the form of the piece of 'kercher', is granted to Charles's dreamer-narrator.

There are several points of overlap between Charles's sequence of English poems and *The Kingis Quair*, not least the fact that the author of the *Quair*, who would eventually become King James I of Scotland, was like Charles a long-term English prisoner. Both authors exploit a range of metaphorical associations of imprisonment, and both draw into their writing, to a greater or lesser extent, the patterns of their own histories.[33] There are several parallels

---

30 As, for example, by Constance B. Hieatt, *The Realism of Dream Visions* (The Hague, 1967), pp. 74–88.
31 G.C. Macaulay, ed., *The English Works of John Gower*, 2 vols., EETS ES 81, 82 (1901, 1902); J. Schick, ed., *Lydgate's Temple of Glas*, EETS ES 60 (1891).
32 John Norton-Smith, ed., *The Kingis Quair* (2nd edn, Leiden, 1981).
33 For biographical details, see most recently Michael Brown, *James I* (Edinburgh, 1994). The similarities in the two 'books' are discussed by Bennett, 'A King's Quire', and Diane R. Marks, 'Poems from Prison: James I of Scotland and Charles of Orleans', *Fifteenth-Century Studies* 15 (1989) 245–58. For the significance of the state of

in the dream episodes included in their works. Charles's two dreams, in their different ways, deal with the advance of time over the trajectory of an individual life; the second, with its visions of a notably virtuous Venus and of Fortune, instructs the dreamer about the beneficent possibilities of change. The *Quair*, too, stresses the positive aspects of time and change, and its dream episode, like the so-called 'Love's Renewal', offers instruction from Venus, Minerva, and Fortune. It comes to seem most plausible that Charles should have learned both from Chaucer and simultaneously from those of his fifteenth-century readers who, in J.A.W. Bennett's terms, 'had drunk in Chaucer's poetry to the point of inebriety'.[34]

It would be satisfying here to be able to adduce evidence for the acquaintance of Charles of Orleans and the future James I during their respective periods of imprisonment, and for circulation of the *Quair* in forms in which it would have been available to Charles. There is, of course, very little to go on. For a short period in 1415, immediately after Charles's capture post-Agincourt, James was evidently kept with the recent prisoners of war,[35] but it seems improbable that his English would at this stage have been good enough to permit much in the way of discussions of creative practice. No contact after this period is recorded, although, having established an acquaintance, the two prisoners presumably remained informed about each others' movements and progress. Early circulation of the *Quair* is still harder to document, since it survives in only one manuscript, copied in Scotland possibly as late as c.1500, which offers no information about the form or forms in which the text had been preserved.[36]

---

imprisonment in Charles's French poems, see Daniel Poirion, *Le Poète et le prince: l'évolution du lyrisme courtois de Guillaume de Machaut à Charles d'Orléans* (Paris, 1965), pp. 271–309, and in the English poems, A.C. Spearing, 'Prison, Writing, Absence: Representing the Subject in the English Poems of Charles d'Orléans', *Modern Language Quarterly* 53 (1992) 83–99. The subject is treated more generally by Karl Heinz Göller, 'The Metaphorical Prison as an Exegetical Image of Man', *Fifteenth-Century Studies* 17 (1990) 121–45, and in terms of the Boethian associations of *The Kingis Quair*, by Michael D. Cherniss, *Boethian Apocalypse: Studies in Middle English Vision Poetry* (Norman, OK, 1987), pp. 193–210, and Julia Boffey, 'Chaucerian Prisoners', in *Chaucer and Fifteenth-Century Poetry*, ed. Julia Boffey and Janet Cowen (London, 1991), pp. 84–102.

34 J.A.W. Bennett, *The Parlement of Foules: An Interpretation* (2nd edn, Oxford, 1965), p. 59.
35 Brown, *James I*, p. 21.
36 Oxford, Bodleian Library MS Arch. Selden. B. 24, forthcoming in facsimile, intro. Julia Boffey and A.S.G. Edwards (Cambridge, 1996). In the absence of precise chronological details, it is difficult to establish whether the composition of the *Quair* preceded that of Charles's vision of 'Love's Renewal', or *vice versa*. If, as has been argued on the basis of James I's possible allusions to the Deguileville translation attributed to Lydgate, the *Quair* is to be dated as late as the 1430s, then it may in fact be the later of the two. I am indebted for advice on this point to Dr. Alessandra Petrina, who most kindly allowed me to consult her doctoral thesis, 'The Kingis Quair of James I of Scotland', University of Venice, 1995.

The vagaries of manuscript survival in England at this period, particularly in relation to shortish texts in the vernacular, which may have circulated in fragile unbound gatherings, make for general difficulties in reconstructing the potential library of formative English texts which may have been available to Charles during his detainment, and obscure our sense of his access to poems such as *The Complaint of the Black Knight* or *The Temple of Glass* just as to Chaucer's dream poems. Nowhere in the records of the books which passed through Charles's hands is there anything as gratifying as a reference to these poems, or to a collection which might have included such works. But the famous inscriptions registered by and for Charles's brother, John of Angoulême, in the copy of *The Canterbury Tales* which is now Paris, BN MS fonds anglais 39, seem virtually conclusive testimony to the likelihood that manuscripts of Chaucer's writings came Charles's way.[37] John of Angoulême was an English prisoner for even longer than Charles, taken as a hostage in 1412 and released five years after his brother in 1445.[38] Although the possibilities of meetings between the brothers were apparently rare, they were in touch by letter and messenger for much of their shared time in England, and the messengers may have carried commodities such as books as well as letters.[39] John at some stage made the acquaintance of a scribe named Duxworth who copied the *Canterbury Tales* manuscript and worked on other projects for him: part of the Latin *Dialogue of St Anselm*, now BN MS Lat. 3436, was begun by Duxworth and completed by John, a more than competent scribe, who also copied part of a commentary on Boethius's *De consolatione*.[40] He was himself responsible for copying a table of contents for *The Canterbury Tales* and making many corrections to the text, although the famous annotations – at the end of 'The Squire's Tale', 'Ista fabula est absurda in terminis . . .', or of 'The Monk's Tale', 'non plus de ista fabula quia est valde dolorosa' – are in Duxworth's hand, perhaps taken down at John's dictation. If John and Duxworth could find Chaucerian exemplars, there is every reason to suppose that Charles could as well.

Charles's possible knowledge of Chaucer's dream visions – even if, as we have seen, it was in part a knowledge acquired at one remove – is in fact important testimony to their early circulation, and a corrective to the evidence

---

[37] Martin Michael Crow, 'John of Angoulême and his Chaucer Manuscript', *Speculum* 17 (1942) 86–99, and Paul Strohm, 'Jean of Angoulême: a Fifteenth-Century Reader of Chaucer', *Neuphilologische Mitteilungen* 72 (1971) 69–76. For a description of the manuscript, see John M. Manly and Edith Rickert, *The Text of The Canterbury Tales*, 8 vols. (Chicago, 1940), I: 399–405.

[38] Gustave Dupont-Ferrier, 'La Captivité de Jean d'Orléans, Comte d'Angoulême (1412–1445)', *Revue Historique* 62 (1896) 42–74.

[39] McLeod, *Charles of Orleans*, pp. 347–50, is sceptical about the speculations of Lucy de Angulo, 'Charles and Jean d'Orléans: an attempt to trace the contacts between them during their captivity in England', in *Miscellanea di studi e ricerche sul quattrocento francese*, ed. Franco Simone (Turin, 1967), pp. 61–92.

[40] Crow, 'John of Angoulême'.

of the surviving manuscripts, which mostly postdate the mid fifteenth century. Clanvowe apparently knew *The Parliament of Fowls* and Usk *The House of Fame* before the end of the fourteenth century, but the patterns of manuscript survival bear no witness to their access to these texts, which may indeed (especially in Clanvowe's case) have involved personal contact with Chaucer.[41] Of the provenance of Cambridge, University Library MS Gg. 4. 27, the earliest Chaucer anthology, which includes *The Parliament of Fowls* and *The Legend of Good Women* alongside *Troilus and Criseyde* and *The Canterbury Tales*, little is known, although the suggested original milieu of a gentry household, possibly in East Anglia, might be a context similar to that in which Charles's contact with the poems took place.[42] One notable feature which MS Gg. 4. 27 has in common with several of the mid-and later fifteenth-century manuscripts which include the dream visions is its consciousness of things French. In Ms Gg. 4. 27 the *Legend* and the *Parliament* are copied with an anonymous text, now known as *The Parliament of Birds*, in which each stanza concludes with a line of French.[43] In manuscripts of the so-called textually related 'Oxford group', which includes Bodleian Library MS Fairfax 16, the dream visions are collected with Hoccleve's translation of Christine de Pizan's *Epistre de Cupide*, and Richard Roos's translation of Alain Chartier's *La Belle Dame sans merci*;[44] to these was added, in the later MS Longleat 258, *The Eye and the Heart*, a translation of a poem by Michault Taillevent.[45]

Not a lot is known about the owners of these early manuscripts of Chaucer's shorter poems, although it is clear that by the second half of the fifteenth century they included both metropolitan readers and members of provincial gentry families.[46] Charles himself, earlier in the century, had

---

41 V.J. Scattergood, ed., *The Works of Sir John Clanvowe* (Cambridge, 1975), pp. 12–14; Walter W. Skeat, ed., *Chaucerian and Other Pieces . . . A Supplement to the Complete Works of Geoffrey Chaucer (Oxford, in six volumes, 1894)* (Oxford, 1897), pp. xxvi–vii.

42 M.B. Parkes and R. Beadle, introductions, *Geoffrey Chaucer: Poetical Works. A Facsimile of Cambridge, University Library MS Gg. 4. 27*, 3 vols. (Cambridge, 1979–80), III: 63–65.

43 Eleanor Prescott Hammond, 'A Parliament of Birds', *Journal of English and Germanic Philology* 7 (1907–8) 105–9.

44 For some other manuscripts in the group, see Pamela Robinson, intro., *MS Tanner 346: A Facsimile*, and *MS Bodley 638: A Facsimile* (Norman, OK, 1980). The texts are edited by Thelma S. Fenster and Mary Carpenter Erler, eds., *Poems of Cupid, God of Love* (Leiden, 1990), pp. 29–75, and Skeat, ed., pp. 217–32, pp. 299–326.

45 Eleanor Prescott Hammond, 'MS Longleat 258 – A Chaucerian Codex', *Modern Language Notes* 20 (1905) 77–79, and 'The Eye and the Heart', *Anglia* 34 (1911) 235–65.

46 Metropolitan provenances are likely for MS Fairfax 16 (Norton-Smith, intro.); Trinity College, Cambridge, MS R. 3. 19 (Bradford Y. Fletcher, intro., *Manuscript Trinity R. 3. 19: A Facsimile* (Norman, OK, 1987), pp. xxix–xxx), and St John's College, Oxford, MS 57, which includes among its contents a London chronicle. From a

contacts in both these circles, since he stayed variously in provincial households and in the London residences of his different guardians. From these latter milieux he was presumably granted access to the spiritual advisors and religious communities which seem to have been influential on some of his reading and book-buying habits.[47] What is known of the history of Cambridge, Magdalene College MS Pepys 2006, a compilation of two Chaucer anthologies, which includes the dream visions, suggests the fluid inter-penetration of milieux which could have brought a collection of this sort to his attention. Its second section bears the names of William Fetyplace, merchant of London (perhaps the son of John Fetplace, a London draper), and of John Kiriel, of a family connected with Edmund Beaufort, Earl of Somerset, and with the Stourtons and Cobhams: all of these last three families in one way or another had come into contact with Charles in the years of his imprisonment.[48]

Some of Charles's guardians, like John's, were interested in books and literary matters, and could have been his sources of Chaucer manuscripts. The will of Sir Thomas Comberworth, of Bolingbroke in Lincolnshire, to whose charge Charles was transferred in 1422, records, among several references to books, the bequest of a copy of *The Canterbury Tales* to his nephew's wife, Agnes Constable,[49] and Charles's transfer in 1432, via a brief period in the care of Sir John Cornwall, to William de la Pole, Duke of Suffolk, and his wife Alice Chaucer, presumably brought Chaucer manuscripts within even closer reach. Lydgate visited this household, and a copy of *The Siege of Thebes*, Lydgate's Canterbury tale (now BL Arundel MS 119), bears signs of Suffolk ownership.[50] Both Comberworth and the Suffolks, perhaps even more significantly, were apparently interested in French texts, and their translation into English versions. Comberworth's name appears in the copy of the Middle English translation of Deguileville's *Pèlerinage de l'âme* in New York Public Library MS Spenser 19, and among Alice Chaucer's recorded books were a Lydgate translation of Deguileville and some Christine de Pizan.[51]

provincial gentry context comes the Findern Manuscript, on which see H.R.L. Beadle and A.E.B. Owen, introductions, *The Findern Manuscript* (London, 1977).
[47] Gilbert Ouy, 'Recherches sur la librairie de Charles d'Orléans et de Jean d'Angoulême pendant leur captivité en Angleterre, et étude de deux manuscrits autographes de Charles d'Orléans recémment identifiés', *Comptes-rendus de l'Académie des inscriptions et belles-lettres* (1955) 273–87.
[48] A.S.G. Edwards, intro., *Manuscript Pepys 2006* (Norman, OK, 1985), and Rosamond McKitterick and Richard Beadle, *Catalogue of the Pepys Library at Magdalene College, Cambridge, Volume V: Manuscripts. Part i: Medieval* (Cambridge, 1992), p. 43.
[49] Andrew Clark, ed., *Lincoln Diocesan Documents, 1450–1544*, EETS OS 149 (1914), pp. 44–57; see also Manly and Rickert, *The Text of the Canterbury Tales*, I: 413–14, 608–9.
[50] Carol M. Meale, ' "... alle the bokes that I haue of latyn, englisch, and frensch": laywomen and their books in late medieval England', in *Women and Literature in Britain, 1150–1500*, ed. Carol M. Meale (Cambridge, 1993), pp. 128–58 (pp. 134–35).
[51] Rosemarie Potz McGerr, ed., *The Pilgrimage of the Soul: A Critical Edition of the*

The copious evidence which remains about Charles's library, mostly left behind in France, demonstrates just how closely some of his interests must have matched those of his English contacts.[52] This library was extensive, and included books inherited by Charles from his father Louis d'Orléans (who knew writers such as Deschamps, from whom in 1398 he purchased the three volumes of Deguileville's *Pèlerinages*),[53] and from his mother Valentina Visconti, a member of the famous family whose library at Pavia was probably known to Chaucer:[54] works numbered here include *Le Roman de la Rose* and a collection of Deschamps' poems. In an inventory of the books at the family castle of Blois taken in 1417 are a number of texts of some significance to an understanding of dream poems and vision literature: the *Pèlerinage de la vie humaine*; Macrobius; four copies of Boethius, variously in French and Latin, with a commentary. Also listed are works connected with Froissart (*Le Dit royal*; *Meliador*).[55] Charles's available reading in this area virtually duplicated that of Chaucer and his early fifteenth-century successors: hallowed 'classics' of the vision literature, such as Boethius and Macrobius; seminal French poems like *Le Roman de la Rose*; more recent French *dits*.

Charles's concern to secure inventories of his books, and his negotiations over their sale and purchase, which seem to have continued virtually throughout his period of detainment, give some idea of the intense activity during this period in the trafficking of manuscripts between England and France. Manuscripts changed hands on a vast scale, as with John of Bedford's acquisition of the Louvre library after Charles VI's death in 1422,[56] and in humbler ways, as veterans of the French wars came home with books acquired during their campaigns.[57] While most of the books came from France to England, the traffic also operated in the reverse direction. In 1396 Louis d'Orléans ordered the payment of 60 écus to a Parisian grocer for a copy of *Le Roman de la Rose* and another book containing a version of

---

Middle English Dream Vision, Volume 1 (New York, 1990), pp. lxxx–lxxxiv; Meale, ' "... alle the bokes" '.

[52] For a general overview of Charles's acquisition and consultation of books, see Pierre Champion, *La Librairie de Charles d'Orléans* (Paris, 1910).

[53] Léopold Delisle, *Le Cabinet des manuscrits de la Bibliothèque Impériale*, 3 vols. (Paris, 1868–81), I 102.

[54] W.E. Coleman, 'Chaucer, the *Teseida* and the Visconti Library at Pavia: a Hypothesis', *Medium Aevum* 51 (1982) 92–101.

[55] Delisle, *Le Cabinet des Manuscrits*, I 105–8.

[56] Jenny Stratford, *The Bedford Inventories: The Worldly Goods of John, Duke of Bedford, Regent of France (1389–1435)* (London, 1993), pp. 95–96.

[57] See, for example, Westminster Abbey MS 21: Julia Boffey, 'English Dream Poems of the Fifteenth Century and their French Connections', in *Literary Aspects of Courtly Culture: Selected Papers from the Seventh Triennial Congress of the International Courtly Literature Society, University of Massachusetts, Amherst, USA, 27 July – 1 August, 1992*, ed. Donald Maddox and Sara Sturm-Maddox (Cambridge, 1994), pp. 113–21.

Brunetto Latini's *Il Tesoretto*, 'aux armes du vieux duc de Lancastre'.[58] A vast eleven-volume French translation of the Bible, whose manufacture was begun in France in the 1350s and and continued under Louis d'Orléans and later Charles, ended up in the hands of John of Bedford, and Charles's brother, John of Angoulême, bought third-hand in London in 1441 one of the Louvre manuscripts which had passed into Bedford's hands.[59] These examples are not all volumes of secular poetry, admittedly, but they illustrate the routes by which books could move back and forth in this war-torn but culturally homogeneous community of readers.

Much information about the Anglo-French culture of this period remains to be uncovered in the texts of Charles's poems and the physical forms in which they have survived. It seems likely, for example, that there are connections with Alain Chartier's influential poem *La Belle Dame sans Merci*, whether as a result of Charles's knowledge of the French text, which dates from 1424, or because the later English translator of the work, probably Sir Richard Roos, had acquired something of Charles's idiom.[60] French texts such as this were to remain desirable for many years, and the impulse to accommodate them into a 'Chaucerian' tradition of English writing was to remain powerful. Thynne's additions to his printed collection of Chaucer's works, and the incorporation into British Library MS 17492, in the 1530s, of extracts from Hoccleve's translation of Christine de Pizan's *Letter of Cupid*, alongside another from the translation of *La Belle Dame sans Merci*, suggest that the interest endured.[61] Late fifteenth-century interest in Charles's French poems, probably copied in BL MS Royal 16. F. ii as part of a presentation volume for Edward IV, and updated after his death with illumination and further texts appropriate to the tastes of Henry VII's sons, highlights the centrality of Anglo-French political and cultural relations, and the complex ways in which they might be combined, over a lengthy period.[62]

---

58 Delisle, *Le Cabinet des Manuscrits*, I 102. See also François Avril and Patricia Danz Stirnemann, *Manuscrits enluminés d'origine insulaire, viie–xxe siècle* (Paris, 1987), pp. 149–52 (further discussion of manuscripts acquired in England by Charles and John is to be found on pp. 171–84).
59 Stratford, *The Bedford Inventories*, pp. 336–37, 96.
60 Steele and Day, eds., p. xix, and Ethel Seaton, *Sir Richard Roos; Lancastrian Poet* (London, 1961).
61 See W.W. Skeat, intro., *Thynne's Chaucer* (London, 1905); E. Seaton, 'The Devonshire Manuscript and its Medieval Fragments', *Review of English Studies* NS 7 (1956) 55–56, identified the extract from Roos's translation (Skeat, ed., 717–24), beginning 'O marble herte and yet more harde, perde, / Wych mercy may not perce for no labor . . .', in BL MS Addit. 17492. It seems quite closely related to 5516 in MS Harley 682: (Steele and Day, eds., p. 184): 'O marbil hert more hard if harder be . . .'.
62 Backhouse, 'Founders of the Royal Library'.

THE FRIAR AS CRITIC: BOKENHAM READS CHAUCER

SHEILA DELANY

A collection of female saints' lives seems a thoroughly obvious idea to us now, especially for the high Middle Ages, when hagiography ranked high among popular genres. Nonetheless no one seems to have had this idea before the middle of the fifteenth century, when the Cambridge-educated Augustinian friar Osbern Bokenham compiled his verse collection of thirteen female lives, the *Legends of Holy Women*.[1] Nor would anyone think of it again in England until nearly two centuries later, when an anonymous author compiled a prose collection of women saints' lives, about 1610.[2] The surprising rarity of the phenomenon invites investigation.

In the Introduction to my translation of Bokenham's legendary, and in my longer study, *Impolitic Bodies*, I've proposed that Bokenham's unique authorial choice had primarily a political motivation.[3] Its array of charismatic holy women was meant to validate the royal claim of Bokenham's patron Richard duke of York, lord of the honour of Clare (Suffolk), where Bokenham lived. York's claim to the throne was considered invalid by some because it came from Edward III through women at two points, while the Lancastrian claim was in a completely male lineage. Thus the nature and capacities of women – particularly their ability to rule and to transmit rule – was a minor but significant theme in propaganda surrounding the English dynastic conflicts of mid-century: the so-called Wars of the Roses.[4] A Lancastrian

---

[1] *Legendys of Hooly Wummen*, ed. Mary Serjeantson, EETS OS 206 (1938). The unique ms. – BL Arundel 327 – is untitled; Serjeantson supplied the title from a line in the text. There is also a fragment – the opening lines of the life of Dorothy – on the last leaf of BL Add. 36983, a miscellany. The fragment shows minor variants from the Arundel ms. Its existence suggests the circulation of separate legends, at least of those which the author says were composed before 1445 (*LHW* 5040–46). In my quotations, I have normalized thorn and yogh to modern equivalents; orthography is mixed in the manuscript.

[2] *The Lives of Women Saints of our Contrie of England*, ed. Carl Horstmann, EETS OS 86 (1896, repr. New York: Kraus, 1973).

[3] *A Legend of Holy Women*, trans. S. Delany (Notre Dame, 1992); *Impolitic Bodies: Poetry, Saints and Society in Fifteenth Century England* (Oxford, 1997).

[4] In fact the question of women's ability to transmit rule had already been on the agenda for over a century. It was at the heart of the dynastic/reproductive politics of the Hundred Years War, for the English claim to the French throne rested on the descent of

propagandist (like Sir John Fortescue) would depreciate the capacities of women, while a Yorkist – as Bokenham ardently was – would want to affirm their qualities of leadership.

Yet if the political motive was basic to Bokenham's project, still that project was overdetermined, for other cultural factors can be brought into play as partial influences on the first English all-female legendary. One might cite the importance of women as readers, owners and patrons of literature in fifteenth- century England, roles now being meticulously documented by Carol Meale, Felicity Riddy, Jocelyn Wogan-Browne and others.[5] One might refer to Catholic liturgy, with its separate lists of male and female saints concluding the Holy Week litanies. Similarly, early Latin legendaries often classified lives according to the subject's sex, a taxonomic convention followed by the Anglo-Saxon scholar Aldhelm in dividing his treatise *De virginitate* into separate sections of male and female virgins. In 1405, Christine de Pizan compiled a set of women saints' legends to conclude her otherwise secular *consolatio, Le livre de la cité des dames*.

The textual model I want to focus on today is none of these, for although Osbern Bokenham probably knew all of the partial antecedents I've just mentioned, he imitated none of them. Instead he found a structural model in a courtly poem by a moderately educated English layman of the previous generation. This poem was a well-known and much-respected collection of lives of several women from classical history, legend and myth. Despite its classical subject matter, this poem associated itself with hagiography through its title, yet it was not hagiography but a parody of that genre. I refer to Geoffrey Chaucer's *Legend of Good Women* (1386), which borrows the title of a saint's life – 'legend' – as well as its great theme: suffering. Elsewhere I have shown that Bokenham appropriated Chaucer's *Legend* in a tale-by-tale sequential alignment of his first ten saints with the female figures in Chaucer's *Legend* starting with Chaucer's daisy and his Alceste, and proceeding in order through Chaucer's nine legends.[6] Obviously the friar knew Chaucer's text well. He may have had it on loan from a patron or friend among the local Suffolk gentry, nobility or townspeople, or it may have been among the privately owned books in his or another religious house, perhaps even his own property.[7] It is probably safe to say that Bokenham had the

Edward III from French royalty through his mother the French princess Isabel. See *Impolitic Bodies*, Chapter 7.

[5] See various essays in C. Meale, ed., *Women and Literature in Britain, 1150–1550* (Cambridge, 1993); Jeremy Griffiths, ed., *Book Production and Publishing in Britain, 1375–1475* (Cambridge, 1989); A.J. Minnis, ed., *Late-Medieval Religious Texts and Their Transmission* (Cambridge, 1994).

[6] For more detailed argument, see Introduction to *Legends* translation, or *Impolitic Bodies*, Chapter 2. The only one of Chaucer's ladies to whom I find no parallel in Bokenham's legendary is Phyllis. It is possible that the manuscript Bokenham saw did not include Phyllis, or that he did not find in the story a salient point of parallel.

[7] Bokenham names several women patrons from the local gentry and nobility: Agnes

F-text of the *Legend*'s Prologue in hand, for he uses a phrase that appears in F but not in G,[8] and the hyperbolic adoration of the daisy that I believe is a target of his critique (see below) also appears in F but not in G.

Bokenham's use of Chaucer's *Legend* as a guide in choosing and arranging his own set of good women is not the only act of homage the friar-poet performed. Like many other writers of the fifteenth century, he imitated Chaucerian verse forms, especially the *Troilus* stanza and the *Monk's Tale* stanza. And, like others, he invoked the poetic triumvirate of Chaucer, Gower and Lydgate as a peak of attainment against which he himself must fall short.[9] As well, there is verbal borrowing. For instance, when Bokenham expresses the wish to 'forge and fyle' his rhetoric (*LHW* 408), he imitates Chaucer's Cupid who in the *Parliament of Fowls* is seen to 'forge and fyle' (212) his arrows. Bokenham's Margaret has 'bent browes blake' (*LHW* 450), just as Chaucer's young Alison has 'browes ... bent and blake' (*MilT* 3245–6). For Bokenham's Agnes, Jesus is 'To me ... a wal impenetrabyle' (*LHW* 4327), much as for Chaucer's Criseyde, Troilus is 'to hire a wal/ Of steil' (*TC* 3.479–80). In the legend of Cecelia, Bokenham's odd term 'corniculer' (*LHW* 7990) for the officer Maximus also occurs in Chaucer's *Second Nun's Tale* (369). In Bokenham's version of Lucy, the Sicilian pilgrims who travel to Agatha's shrine are evoked with a syntax and a vocabulary that can only recall their more famous Chaucerian prototypes:

> Whan thorgh the provynce ...
> The gloryous fame dyvulged was
> Of the blyssyd virgyn seynt Agas ...
> Whom for to seken wyth an holy entent
> On hyr festful day mych peple went
> From every plage of the seyd Cecyle,
> And specyally from Syracuse ...   (*LHW*, 9019–28)

> Whan that Aprill, etc ...
> Thanne longen folk to goon on pilgrimages, ...
> And specially from every shires end
> Of Engelond to Caunterbury they wende,
> The hooly blisful martir for to seke ...
>   (*CT, General Prologue*, 1–17)

Flegge, Isabel Hunt, Katherine Clapton Denston, Katherine Howard, Elizabeth Vere, and Isabel Bourchier. He in turn is mentioned in the 1463 will of John Baret, a wealthy merchant of Bury. See *Impolitic Bodies*, Chapter 1. The right to a certain amount of private property was among the privileges enjoyed by masters of theology such as Bokenham was. The lending of books among religious houses, and between layfolk and religious, is well documented.

[8] The phrase is 'yive feyth & ful credence' (*LHW* 7875); cf. Chaucer's 'yive ... feyth and ful credence' (*LGW* F, 31).

[9] *LHW* lines 417, 1404, 4058 and 10531. The 'Galfryd of England' mentioned in 86 and 411 is not Chaucer (as Serjeantson erroneously assumed) but Geoffroi de Vinsauf, author of the influential rhetoric *Poetria Nova*.

The long 'when'-clause, the geographical specifications, the strategy of narrowing focus, the words 'seek', 'specially from' and 'from every' – these constitute the distinctive and memorable rhetoric of the opening lines to Chaucer's *Canterbury Tales*. No fifteenth-century reader could have missed the open and deliberate intertextuality here.

However, not everything this attentive reader of Chaucer had to say about his famous precursor can have been good. The pious friar had serious reservations about much of the verse of his day, including the Chaucerian poetry that inspired it. For one thing, Chaucer had little good to say about ecclesiastical personnel or the communal life. In particular, his scandalously scatalogical treatment of friars in the *Summoner's Prologue and Tale* could scarcely sit well with a Cambridge-trained Friar Hermit, nor could Chaucer's portrait of the venery-loving monk and vain prioress, corrupt pardoner, or randy Cambridge clerks (as opposed to a virtuous Oxford one). Even today, the chronicler of Augustinian history in England, Father Roth, is able to write this about the baneful effects of Chaucer and others:

> Too little emphasis . . . is put on the tremendous harm done by the enemies of monasticism, Wyclif and his Lollards, Langland, Chaucer and their circles. By conscious exaggeration and distortion of existing faults and weaknesses common to all human beings, they created an ugly caricature of religious men and women, and consequently an aversion for the religious life, thus causing a severe dwindling of vocations. We have seen the same forces at work in our own day, for example in Nazi Germany, and it is enlightening to notice that their purpose and methods were the same.[10]

There is, however, a more deep-seated problem with Chaucer and Chaucerians than anti-clerical satire. Chaucer was the prototype in England of what I am calling the 'classicizing courtier'. Classical poetry had rhetorical conventions that expressed its ethical or moral values; so did courtly lyric and romance. French poetry, Chaucer's poetry, and fifteenth-century ephebes combined the two systems. I want to argue that this heterogeneous poetics of the classicizing courtier is what Bokenham targets in his legendary, seeing it as antithetical to the proper Christian poetics so forcefully delineated in Augustine's *De doctrina christiana*. My definition should make it clear that the offending poet need not be actually a courtier nor anti-clerical. Hence we might cite Deschamps, Machaut, and Charles of Orleans, but also Gower, Usk, Lydgate, and various anonymous English writers as contributors, in varying degrees, to the tradition of a classicizing courtly poetic. Bokenham counters this tradition both implicitly by his own example, and in explicit commentary (though without naming names). In some places he emphasizes the classicizing component, in others the courtly. A closer look at Bokenham's legendary and Chaucer's *Legend* will illustrate the friar's indirect method.

---

[10] Francis Roth, *The English Austin Friars*, 2 vols. (New York, 1961), I: 84–5.

Both works open with a 'marguerite' as object of the Narrator's personal devotion, but while Chaucer's 'marguerite' is a daisy, Bokenham's is St Margaret.[11] That contrast already carries the friar's point, but it doesn't stop there. Here is the language in which Chaucer invokes his inanimate 'marguerite' as muse, mistress, saint and even deity, switching from third to second person in the intensity of his emotion:

> She is the clernesse and the verray lyght
> That in this derke world me wynt and ledeth.
> The hert in-with my sorwfull brest yow dredeth
> And loveth so sore that ye ben verrayly
> The maistresse of my wit, and nothing I.
> My word, my werk ys knyt so in youre bond
> That, as an harpe obeieth to the hond
> And maketh it soune after his fyngerynge,
> Ryght so mowe ye oute of myn herte bringe
> Swich vois, ryght as yow lyst, to laughe or pleyne.
> Be ye my gide and lady sovereyne!
> As to myn erthly god to yow I calle,
> Bothe in this werk and in my sorwes alle.   (F, 84–96)

Later, Eros calls the daisy his 'relyke' (F 321). Thus the Chaucerian daisy elicits reverence and passion so grossly disproportionate as to approach blasphemy. Behind Chaucer's hyperbole stands the work of Machaut, Deschamps and Froissart. It is perhaps from Deschamp's *Lai de franchise* that Chaucer derived the most offensive phrase in the passage cited – 'erthly god' – for Deschamps refers to his daisy as 'la déesse mondaine' and had called Chaucer himself 'd'amours mondains Dieux en Albie'. Deschamps also calls Machaut 'mondains dieux d'armonie', while Machaut promises to worship his lady 'comme dieu terrien'.[12] This common French courtly locution would surely offend a pious orthodox friar. Yet it remains only the tip of the ideological iceberg, for it is merely one symptom of a classicizing spirit popular in the fifteenth century but already blatant in Chaucer's *Legend*. There, devotion to classical sources is even more troublesome than in other late medieval works. This is because Chaucer's poem ostensibly praises ten women so true in love that half of them commit the deadly sin of suicide, and nowhere does the author condemn their act.

Bokenham offers something formally similar but ideologically opposite. He offers a gallery of portraits of women who died for the right reason: not in

---

11   On the equivalence of daisy, pearl and saint by way of shared name, see James Wimsatt, ed., *The Marguerite Poetry of Guillaume de Machaut* (Chapel Hill, 1970) especially 'Dit de la fleur de lis et fe la marguerite'; also Lydgate, 'Margarete' (about 1430), in *Lydgate's Minor Poems*, Part 1, ed. H. MacCracken, EETS ES 107 (1910).
12   See J.L. Lowes, 'The Prologue to the *Legend of Good Women* as related to the French Marguerite Poems and the *Filostrato*', *PMLA* 19 (1904) 593–683; cf. pp. 620–21.

despair but in faith and hope; not for erotic passion but for *caritas*. Thus he reasserts the proper duty of the Christian poet. This paradoxical technique is Bokenham's method throughout his legendary. His saints are lined up with Chaucer's love-lorn ladies, precisely for the contrast. If Chaucer parodies hagiography, Bokenham parodies Chaucer in order to restore the original paradigm, real hagiography, and cleanse it of its courtly-classical accretions. I'll briefly trace this method through the rest of Bokenham's first ten lives, taking his and Chaucer's figures in order of their textual appearance. Then I will turn to other aspects of the friar's critique.

After the daisy, the next object of Chaucerian devotion in the *Legend* is Alceste, companion to the god of erotic love; her fame came from her descent to the underworld in place of her husband. Bokenham's second life is of St Anne, grandmother of Jesus who is god of spiritual love. Anne's daughter is evoked here as 'empress of hell', a reference to the legend of Mary's descent to the underworld; Persephone, who went to Hades, is also mentioned. The point of contact is this image.

Chaucer's Cleopatra is lined up with, or against, Bokenham's Christine. Both women are associated with three Roman rulers – lovers in one case, persecutors in the other. Both are exposed to snakes, which kill Cleopatra but worship Christine. Both participate in a major sea-scene: the battle of Actium, a miracle of walking on water.

Chaucer's Thisbe narrates the engagement of a young couple, offspring of feuding parents; circumstances prevent the marriage, but the couple meet away from home and are killed. The same structural outline constitutes the plot of Bokenham's fourth legend, that of St Ursula.

Next, Chaucer's tale of Dido focuses on the bed as key image and *locus dramatis*. Repeating the image is Bokenham's tale of St Faith, who is tortured on a grill or 'bed of brass' (*LHW* 3715) – the bed is one of her emblems – and roasted. The cave in which Dido and Aeneas first make love becomes the cave in which the Christian refugee Caprasius hides. The famous rainstorm that forces the classical couple into their cave has its antithetical analogue in the miracles of water performed by Caprasius once he exits the cave. Aeneas abandons his lady, but Caprasius seeks his out in order to share her ordeal.

Chaucer's double legend of Hypsipyle and Medea is matched by Bokenham's version of Agnes and her devotée Constantia. The Chaucerian lover, Jason, is associated with great personal wealth and a treasure hunt; Agnes boasts of her lover, Jesus, and his immense wealth surpassing that of any other suitor.

Both Chaucer's Lucrece and Bokenham's Dorothy are Roman, and feet figure prominently in their suffering: Lucrece modestly remembers to cover her feet as she falls, and Dorothy is hung upside down by the feet. It is significant too that Augustine used the story of Lucretia to polemicize against the classical custom of committing suicide to preserve honour (*City of God* 1.16–27). He denounced the Roman matron's pride, contrasting it with the humility of Christian women who prefer to suffer rape or martyrdom rather than take their own lives in despair. Quite possibly Bokenham's contrastive strategy is indebted to the authoritative example of the founder of his order.

Chaucer's Ariadne opens in Athens; Bokenham's Magdalene opens with an extended reference to Athena. In Ariadne's story, thread is the means by which the heroine assists her lover, Theseus, out of the labyrinth. In Bokenham's Magdalene material, Athena appears as goddess of weaving, and the author makes much of the brilliant clothing of his patron's children whom he observes at a social occasion. Again, a shared image is the link.

Chaucer's Philomela is about speech, silence, and a tongueless heroine. Bokenham's Katherine foregrounds the heroine's public debate with fifty male scholars; its climax is the utter silence to which she reduces them; and the enraged emperor baits his scholars with the question, 'Be ye tunglees?' (*LHW* 6807).[13]

Both Chaucer's Hypermnestra and Bokenham's Cecelia are young brides with a secret from their groom. The secret proceeds from a male authority figure who intervenes in the wedding night in a way harmful to the groom; in one case this is the bride's father, in the other, Jesus. In both cases, the secret is revealed and it reconciles the couple, though not to a conventional marriage in either case. Here, structure rather than imagery is the common thread.

The pattern, then, is that of a shift from literal to metaphorical levels of meaning, from physical to spiritual, from erotic to religious. This movement defines the revisionary thrust of Bokenham's moral critique of Chaucer's courtly-classical mock legendary.

Revision is not, however, the clever friar's only technique of criticism. He has his own poetic credo, with methods both ironic and earnest of making it known. It is in the Prolocutory to his Magdalene that he chose to launch his manifesto.

The legend of Mary Magdalene may be considered the most important in Bokenham's set of thirteen. It is the longest; it is the only one with three parts rather than two (a Prolocutory in addition to the usual Prologue and Life); it was commissioned by the poet's most distinguished patron, the royally descended Isabel Bourchier, Countess of Eu and sister to Richard duke of York. The Magdalene is not numerically central, coming eighth rather than seventh in the set of thirteen, but it does straddle the mid-point of the work as a whole. Mary herself is distinctive among saints because of her scriptural presence and her prolonged association with the adult Jesus.

Given the special features of the Magdalene story, it is clear that Bokenham constructed a special setting for his poetic credo. That credo irradiates the text from the centre outward, like a virtuous gem set in a ring –

---

[13] Bokenham may have found the image in the Middle English *Seinte Katherine* (line 465). It is unusual, not appearing in versions of Katherine by Clémence of Barking or John Capgrave, or in Voragine's *Legenda Aurea*. That Bokenham chose to use or retain it suggests his intention of connecting his version with Chaucer's *Legend* by way of a shared key image.

or like the powerful curative relic contained in a shrine. Here Bokenham addresses most forcefully the key issues of his aesthetic; here he administers doctrinal truth as antidote to a potentially dangerous poetics. To this point we have considered an indirect critique accomplished by the alignment of real saints with Chaucer's mock saints; in the Magdalene Prolocutory the poet is more explicit about the issues at stake.

The Magdalene material opens with a burst of classical and rhetorical erudition. It is an astronomical statement of the date on which the life was commissioned, but so elaborately aureate in diction and imagery that it can only be called burlesque:

> What phebus (wych nowher is mansonarye
> Stedefastly, but ych day doth varye
> Hys herberwe among þe syngnys twelve,
> As the fyrste mever ordeynyd hym-selve)
> Descendyd was in hys cours adoun
> To the lowest part by cyrcymvolucyoun
> Of the Zodyac cercle, Caprycorn I mene,
> Wher of heythe degrees he hath but fyftene,
> And hys retur had sumwhat bygunne.
> By wych oo degre oonly he had wunne
> In clymbyng, & drow towerd Agnarye . . .   (*LHW* 4985–95)

After ten lines of this grandiloquent bombast, the author interrupts his own flight of rhetoric:

> But in thys mater what shul I lenger tarye?
> I mene pleynly up-on that festful eve
> In wych, as alle crystene men byleve,
> Thre kyngys her dylygence dede applye
> With thre yiftys newe-born to gloryfye
> Cryst, aftyr hys byrthe the threttende day . . .   (*LHW* 4996–5001)

Thus the poet reformulates the date in terms of its Christian meaning. This move from overblown rhetoric to plain language, and from classical erudition to Christian doctrine, encapsulates the doctrinal point that Bokenham makes elsewhere in his legendary, and that his master Augustine elaborates in *De doctrina christiana*.

We now learn the reason for this careful specification of date in two dialects, that of astronomy and that of faith: Twelfth Night, 1445 is the occasion when the poet attended a celebration at Clare Castle sponsored by his patron's sister, Isabel lady Bourchier. The Prolocutory accordingly moves into a genealogy of Lady Isabel and her brother Richard duke of York, then into a short sketch of the gay scene of guests dancing in their gaily coloured finery. Bokenham's rhetoric here takes us to the heart of his aesthetic and moral concerns. No flowered meadow, he writes, could be more brightly coloured than the dancers' clothing, for

> as it semyd me
> Mynerve hyr-self, wych hath the sovereynte
> Of gay texture, as declareth Ovyde,
> Wyth al hire wyt ne coude provyde
> More goodly aray thow she dede enclos
> Wyth-inne oo web al methamorphosyos. (5029–34)

This little classical reference, however, harbours an important doctrinal statement. Let's look more closely at it.

Athena appears here as artist. The word 'texture', with its double history as woven and verbal fabrication (textile/text) prepares us for a statement about art, and indeed the passage about Minerva continues the manifesto already begun in the Prolocutory's opening movement. Bokenham's citation of *Metamorphoses* refers to Ovid's story of the presumptuous mortal, Arachne, who challenged the goddess's supremacy in weaving. A contest takes place, which Athena wins – not by skill but by force, for in anger she destroys Arachne's masterpiece and, when Arachne commits suicide by hanging herself, transforms her into a spider (*Met.* 6, 1–145). The story thus works first as an exemplum of foolhardy human pride, particularly as expressed in art. Bokenham goes on to add that the brilliancy at Lady Bourchier's is such that not even Minerva could surpass it, even if she wove all of Ovid's text into a single pictorial fabric. In this instance art fails, unable to compete with life. This is the dual position from which Bokenham's legendary mounts its (always implicit) critique of Chaucer: that artists must be always conscious of the power of deity, and that life is the test of art.

After the Minerva passage, Bokenham relates Lady Isabel's commissioning of the life of Magdalene. Before writing, however, he must follow the advice of Plato, in *Timaeus*, for there Plato recommends prayer as a fitting beginning to any work (5118–33). This choice of text is especially interesting because *Timaeus* had figured large in philosophical controversies of the high Middle Ages. Its version of creation is blatantly opposed to that of Holy Writ, a juxtaposition that agonized many Christian philosophers over the preceding three centuries as they sought to confront the problem of opposed and mutually exclusive authoritative texts: classical philosophers versus Scripture, eternity of the cosmos versus a magical moment of creation, rationalism versus faith in Scripture.[14]

---

[14] Interest in this complex of questions remained lively in Bokenham's day. Every Austin was obliged to read all the work of the great Augustinian scholar Giles of Rome, who had participated in the controversy surrounding the 1277 condemnation of rationalist and other philosophical propositions at Paris. Giles's anti-rationalist treatise *De erroribus philosophorum*, which targets the 'nothing from nothing' principle as the seminal error, was held in the Clare Priory library, at least in 1318: see Christopher Harper-Bill, ed., *The Cartulary of the Augustinian Friars of Clare* (Woodbridge, 1991). The problem of rationalism had erupted again in the fourteenth century in the work of William of Ockham and his numerous followers at various European

For Bokenham, however, it is not a problem. Serenely he observes that if pagans were capable of such piety as Plato displays, how much more ought we Christians to do (5134–9). He is quite willing, therefore, to follow Plato's advice about prayer, and produces a sermon on creation, the fall, and redemption (5143–5213). It is an exemplary lesson in the proper use of classical learning as stimulus to Christian devotion, not as substitute for it. Though Bokenham does not quote St Paul's famous dictum 'All that is written is written for our learning' (Romans 15:4), his method effectively illustrates it. Even more to the point for my purpose is Augustine's elaboration on this Pauline statement, in *De doctrina christiana* 2.40: the interpretation of 'despoiling Egyptian gold' which, as Beryl Smalley comments, 'really boils down to the proviso that a Christian, when studying the classics, must remember that he is a Christian'.[15]

Like any proper ideologue, Bokenham is not content merely to display the right, he must also correct the wrong. In Augustinian terms, 'The defender of right faith and the enemy of error should both teach the good and extirpate the evil' (*DDC* 4.4.6). Bokenham's prayerful sermon therefore modulates into a polemic against, first, the abuse of classicism and then the abuse of courtly rhetoric, for these aesthetic practices are contrary to the moral principles just enunciated. Regarding classicism, the poet writes:

> Where-fore, lord, to the alone I crye
> Wych welle are of mercy & of pyte,
> And neythyr to Clyo nor to Melpomene,
> Nere to noon othir of the musys nyne,
> Ner to Pallas Mynerve, ner Lucyne,
> Ner to Apollo, wych, as old poetys seye,
> Of wysdam beryth both lok & keye,
> Of gay speche eek & of eloquncye;
> But alle them wyttyrly I denye,
> As evere crystene man owyth to do,
> And the oonly, lord, I fle on-to . . .   (5214–24)

Bokenham was not the only or the first writer to make such a declaration: Gower, Lydgate, John Walton and John Hardyng offer instances of the trope.[16] Yet if the protestation of exclusive religious loyalty has a somewhat formulaic

---

universities; again an Augustinian scholar and administrator, Gregory of Rimini, rose to the occasion with lengthy refutation. Lastly, as long as university students and teachers continued to comment Aristotle's *Physics*, the ancient Greek cosmological theory (also represented in Plato) would remain an issue.

15 Beryl Smalley, *English Friars and Antiquity in the Early Fourteenth Century* (New York, 1960), p. 40.

16 See, e.g., Gower, *Vox Clamantis* 2.96 (Prol.); Walton's Boethius translation (Ed. Mark Science, EETS OS 170, 1927), stanzas 6–8; Lydgate, 'St. Alban', 1–27; Hardyng's verse Chronicle in both versions: BL Lansdowne 204, f. 9; Henry Ellis (London, 1812), 31.

character, this should not vitiate the sincerity of our poet, nor detract from his distinctive project, for the sentiment is integrated into his work at every level. Further, if the topos meant anything in the late Middle Ages it is because some classicizing writers did invoke paganism too liberally for the taste of those with more austere sensibilities, thus provoking once again the confrontation with its greatest intellectual rival that characterizes Christian history from the start. An anonymous classicizing clergyman of the late fourteenth or early fifteenth century drily records his own encounter with rigorism:

> I rede in haly wryte, I sey noght at I red in ovidie, noyther in oras. Vor the last tyme that I was her ich was blamyd of som men word, be-cause that I began my sermon wyt a poysy. And ter-vorn, I say that I red in haly wryt, in the secund book of haly wryt, that I suppoise be sufficiant inowgh of autoritee, that wen the childyr of that Israel wer in the land of Egipt...[17]

Chaucer is an obvious candidate for reproach here, perhaps *the* obvious candidate for reproach. Though the classical invocation was used by all and sundry in Bokenham's time, nonetheless it was Chaucer who effectively introduced it into English literature. The classical deities he invokes at some length include Clio (*TC* 3), other muses (ibid. and *HF* 2), Apollo (*HF* 3), Mars and Polyhymnia ('Anelida'). In the matter of invocations and muses, Chaucer shares the spotlight with many, among them Thomas Usk, whose prologue to *The Testament of Love* invokes Aristotle and David; or Charles of Orleans, prisoner of war in England between 1415 and 1440, who in various lyrics calls on Cupid, Venus, Fortune, Danger, Death, Clotho, Lachesis and Atropos. Lydgate begs Mars, Othea, Clio and Calliope for their 'grace' (*Troy Book*, Prol. 1–62) and elsewhere invokes Niobe ('Complaint of the Black Knight') and Lucina ('On the Departing of Thomas Chaucer'). Even in his 'Exposition of the Pater Noster' Lydgate displays ambivalence: hope 'doth my brydel leede/ Toward Pernaso, to fynde there som muse' (15–16), though once arrived there the poet dares not call on Euterpe but hopes to find sufficiency in Jesus. More problematic is Lydgate's classicizing hagiography, the *Life of St Alban and St Amphibel* in which he manages 'to introduce the humanistic world of antiquity into the religious sphere, to sing the praises of Christ as Orpheus, Hercules and Achilles, to make the Romans and Trojans progenitors of the Saints, or to invoke the Muses in a religious legend'.[18] Elsewhere, Lydgate advises the reader to 'Lat Pale Aurora condute yow and dresse/To holy churche, of Cryste to have a syght' ('On the Mass', 23–4). That Lydgate himself felt the tension between his two referential systems is

---

[17] *Three Middle English Sermons From the Worcester Chapter Manuscript F. 10* ed. D. M. Grisdale (Leeds, 1939), p. 22.

[18] Walter Schirmer, *John Lydgate: A Study in the Culture of the XVth Century* (London, 1962), p. 116.

suggested in his 'Misericordias Domini' in which he ostentatiously bids farewell to classical subject matters before embracing 'hooly writ' as a preferred source of poetic material.

What then is to be the use of classicism for the Christian poet? As Smalley remarks of her 'friar doctors', 'The answer is that it was a matter of where to draw the line' (*English Friars*, p. 40). While a certain flexibility or compromise is inevitable, it seems clear that in various places both Chaucer and Lydgate can be said to have crossed the line.

After dealing with the matter of invocations as symptomatic of overenthusiastic classicism, Bokenham takes on the question of courtly style, particularly as manifested in the courtly love-lyric. He will pray only to God, he says,

> Not desyryng to have swych eloquence
> As sum curyals han, ner swych asperence
> In uttryng of here subtyl conceytys,
> In wych oft tyme ful greth dysceyt is,
> And specyally for there ladyis sake
> They baladys or amalettys lyst to make,
> In wych to sorwyn & wepyn thei feyn
> As thow thee prongys of deth dede streyn
> Here hert-root, al-be thei fer thens;
> Yet no-for-than is here centens
> So craftyd up, & wyth langwage so gay
> Uttryd, that I trowe the monyth of may
> Nevere fresshere enbelshyd the soyl wyth flours
> Than is her wrytyng wyth colours
> Of rethorycal speche both to & fro. (*LHW* 5225–39)

The issue here is the abuse of eloquence, or the ethics of composition, or the abuse of signs. The test case chosen here is the courtly love lyric, which fails the ethical test more disastrously the more successful it is in achieving the poet's erotic desire; for, like any of the world's goods, language can be enjoyed, used or abused, as Augustine reminds us in *De doctrina christiana* (e.g., 1.4 or 4.5).

Besides seduction, another way in which courtly lyric or romance abuses the linguistic sign is in its development of a language of the religion of love. With its vocabulary of service, devotion, grace, passion, divinity, saints, judgement, bliss and so on, this poetic language represents a perversion of devotional language to erotic ends. In Augustinian terms, it is the language of *caritas* turned to the aims of *cupiditas*, the referentiality of its signs not only ambiguous but deliberately misleading.

Egregious in this respect are two in the revered trio of famous English authors: Geoffrey Chaucer and John Gower. I have briefly discussed Chaucer's *Legend* above for its potential to offend the religiously minded. His *Troilus* displays a continuous stream of parodic references that turn the language of orthodox religion to the uses of eroticism. These culminate in an ineffably vulgar statement by the Narrator when, after the first consummation by his principals, he comments on the happy conclusion of the good-natured tiff between Pandarus and Criseyde: 'What! God foryaf his deth, and she al so/ Foryaf, and with here uncle gan to pleye' (3.1577–78).[19] Even if one believes, as I do, that Chaucer meant, in both *Troilus* and the *Legend*, to expose the religion of love for its bad taste and bad judgement, nonetheless it isn't hard to understand how a moralistically inclined reader such as the Austin friar might hesitate to grant the separation of author, narrator and character that such an interpretation requires.

Gower's *Confessio Amantis* parodies the institution of confession. Though it does convey a good deal of perfectly conventional morality, nonetheless the priest and 'holy fadir' to whom Amans confesses is Genius, Venus's 'oghne Clerk'. Genius is thus, like his mistress, committed to the realm of nature, according to whose principles he is shriven and pardoned.

Of course any number of minor texts might be quite as offensive, especially to a member of the clergy. One such piece is the so-called 'Lover's Mass' or 'Venus's Mass', a blatant liturgical parody. The poem was published, about 1450, in the beautifully produced anthology of Chaucerian and other works known to us as MS. Fairfax 16; doubtless it circulated independently for some time before its incorporation into the Fairfax edition, as did most of the other material in the manuscript.[20] With its detailed erotic revision of the Catholic mass and its extremely sexualized vocabulary, the poem could scarcely be better calculated to offend a priest.

At the end of his Magdalene Prolocutory, Bokenham reverts to the modesty topos, admitting that it would be foolish for him to aspire to an eloquence appropriate neither to his age nor his 'degree' (5245: social position). His prayer ends, therefore, with a humble request:

> That I kunnyng may han suffycyently
> To serven the devocyoun of my lady
> Aftyr hyr entent, that is to seyne,
> That I may translate in wurdes pleyne
> In-to oure langwage oute of latyn
> The lyf of blyssyd Mare Mawdelyn. (5249–54)

This restores to its original function the language of religious devotion, cleansing the linguistic signs of their social-erotic accretion. To serve a lady is to attend 'To hyr goostly confourth' (5255) and therefore to the spiritual comfort of a larger audience, 'them generally wych it redyn shal' (5256).

---

[19] For a detailed analysis of this view of *Troilus*, see my 'Techniques of Alienation in *Troilus and Criseyde*', in *The Uses of Criticism*, ed. A. P. Foulkes (Bern/Frankfurt, 1976) and reprinted in *Chaucer's Troilus and Criseyde: Current Essays in Criticism*, ed. R.A. Shoaf (Binghamton, 1992).

[20] Printed in Eleanor Hammond, 'The Lover's Mass', *JEGP* 7 (1907–8) 95–104; see also *Bodleian Library MS Fairfax 16. A Facsimile*, ed. John Norton-Smith (London, 1979).

The critique levelled by the Austin friar at his great predecessor is hard to miss, I think, though it remains indirect. It had to, for several reasons. Perhaps most obvious to us is that Chaucer was already revered as a great poet, indeed, as the great English poet of all time. This evaluation is not without its politics, and there is a worldly and political register – not merely an aesthetic one – of tactical considerations for the fifteenth-century scholar or poet who would criticize Chaucer. The Chaucers were doing very well in Bokenham's day, for the Ricardian poet was father and grandfather to some very considerable people in fifteenth-century England; they in turn were related to and allied with some of the most powerful individuals in the realm. The poet's son Thomas, who died in 1434, was a substantial landowner, high-level civil servant and parliamentarian who made his fortune partly through the sale of wine to the army. He was also related by blood and by marriage to nobility and king's councillors. Thomas's daughter Alice achieved even more brilliant social status through her advantageous marriages. Her third, last and most notorious spouse was William de la Pole, earl and duke of Suffolk – Bokenham's neighbourhood. Suffolk would eventually become one of the most hated men in England, widely perceived as the councillor responsible for England's losses to France. While Bokenham wrote his legendary, though, Suffolk was still in favour as the king's chief minister and confidant of the queen.

In the late 40s, then, to criticize Chaucer was to criticize the near ancestor of extremely family-conscious people who were in a position to do something about their displeasure. I don't mean that Bokenham's head would necessarily roll as a penalty for tactless literary criticism, though it was a time when heads did roll, sometimes for sharp remarks interpreted as subversive or treasonous. Nevertheless I think that other consequences of tactlessness would be more likely here: fewer political favours for Augustinians; fewer land bequests to Clare or to other Austin houses by friends or would-be friends of the offended parties; a tax imposed here and there, a liberty interfered with, and so on. Given the Augustinians' pro-Yorkist tendency, and particularly the Yorkist patronage and partisanship at Clare, it was wise to be careful.

A similar sense of tactical caution would apply to any critique of Lydgate, who was a protegé of the king's uncle Duke Humphrey of Gloucester and a propagandist for the Lancastrian regime. Lydgate was a fairly significant person because of his commissions and connections, so that with regard to him as well as to Chaucer, the network of political affiliation dictated a discreetly indirect approach.

In concluding, I'd like to relate Osbern Bokenham's work to broader European perspectives that help to contextualize his ambivalent take on Chaucer. My title repeats that of a book by Judson B. Allen,[21] but it designates neither

---

[21] *The Friar as Critic* (Nashville, 1971).

the same friar nor the same criticism as are studied in that book. Allen was concerned with exegesis; his focus was what Beryl Smalley called 'the classicising group' of friars: several English Franciscans and Dominicans who, during the fourteenth century, applied to classical literature the same exegetical methods they used on Scripture. The critique performed by Bokenham has rather to do with the production of vernacular poetry and with the literary ethics of the Christian poet.

Thus Bokenham occupied an interval between English humanisms: one clerical and already defunct, the other mainly secular and still to be born. His Janus-like cultural position is epitomized in the translation of a late Latin encomium – the *De consulatu Stiliconis* – which is probably his work. On one hand, this was the first Claudian translation into any vernacular; on the other, the proto-humanist thrust of the project is offset by its arch-medieval allegorization into an encouraging exemplum for Richard duke of York.[22] Classicism was still a challenge, and its problematic was much in evidence during the first half of the fifteenth century. This was particularly the case at Rome and Florence, the two cities with which Augustinians had special institutional connections and to which they often travelled as students, pilgrims, petitioners, observers or participants in councils, and administrators. Reciprocally, Clare Priory would have entertained a steady flow of visitors, for it was one of seven English houses designated as vacation destinations for foreign Austin friars. Bokenham was in Italy at least twice, and some English Austins attended the *studium generale* at Florence. Opportunities for intellectual exchange were thus plentiful.

One Florentine humanist school centered on Luigi Marsigli (d.1394), an Augustinian friar at the convent of Santo Spirito and a leading light of the Florentine humanist avant-garde. Marsigli's disciples Roberto de' Rossi, a translator of Aristotle and other Greek authors, and Niccolò Niccoli (d.1437) were well known in the first half of the fifteenth century; there is no reason why an English traveller could not have brought back Rossi's translations to his own priory library. Quattrocento humanists and their critics disputed questions such as the role of pagan literature in Christian education, the salvation of virtuous pagans, the relative weight of classical and Christian authorities, and the threat of polytheism. Francesco da Fiano's invective *Contra Oblocutores et Detractores Poetarum* reported that 'In the presence of the Pope, an orator had delivered an address that drew heavily on pagan poets and this had caused resentment among many members of the Curia'.[23] The

---

22 The translation was edited by Ewald Flügel in 'Eine Mittelenglische Claudian-Setzung (1445)', *Anglia* 28 (1905), pp. 255–99 and 421–38. The Claudian scholar Alan Cameron believes it is the first translation of Claudian into any vernacular: *Claudian. Poetry and Propaganda at the Court of Honorius* (Oxford, 1970), p. 429. For a discussion of the allegory, see *Impolitic Bodies*, Chapter 7, or my 'Bokenham's Claudian as Yorkist Propaganda', *Journal of Medieval History*, 1996.

23 Hans Baron, *The Crisis of the Early Italian Renaissance* (1955; rev. ed. Princeton,

Invettivo of Cino Rinuccini, on the other hand, attacked the demoralizing aspects of classicism, especially its ability to undermine civic spirit and family commitment.

The English friar's polemic against overclassicizing poets is more muted than that of his Italian contemporaries; as we have seen, it had to be. Yet it does participate in the current of ideas associated with the early Italian Renaissance.

In *The Anxiety of Influence*, Harold Bloom wrote that in the ages before Shakespeare, the influential author 'moved his ephebe only to love and emulation and not to anxiety'. It is easy to recognize the naiveté, perhaps the wishful thinking, of this estimate. Nonetheless, it is rare to find a negative critique of Chaucer during the fifteenth century. If we grant that a negative critique of Chaucer is indeed what Bokenham gives us, then we must recognize it as a minority report, unmatched until the last years of the century, when the Scots poet Robert Henryson's *Testament of Cresseid* would challenge narrative authority with its famous 'Quha wait gif all that Chauceir wrait was trew?', or until early in the following century when, also in Scotland, Gavin Douglas would reproach Chaucer for exactly the opposite fault Bokenham does, though in the same work, the *Legend of Good Women*. Douglas blames Chaucer for not remaining true enough to Virgil, whose light Chaucer professed to follow in retelling the Dido story in his *Legend*. What was too much classicism for Bokenham became too little for Douglas (see *Eneydos*, written in 1513).

In Bokenham's mid-century legendary, then, we witness an act of literary reception in which an English reader subtly constructs his literary past – but not in a shape resembling that imposed by most other writing readers whether scribes, editors, commentators, or poets. The reinvention analysed here was not performed by someone who was, or even aspired to be, a member of what Seth Lerer calls the *familia Chauceriana*.[24] Indeed, Bokenham's version of the precursor would almost inevitably be doomed to marginality as long as the 'star-maker machinery' of the Chaucer-Lancastrian establishment remained in place, or its legacy culturally dominant in a consensus only now starting to be deconstructed.

In defining the terms in which a moral-theological critique of Chaucer could be made, Bokenham may strike us as odd in another way. For this is, after all, precisely the sort of critique that Chaucer tried to pre-empt in his Retraction to the *Canterbury Tales* and, earlier, in the so-called 'epilogue' to *Troilus* – the two places where Chaucer seems to try to establish, in his own voice, his ideological *bona fides*. Moreover we have learned, through the

---

1966), p. 301. Also see Baron, *Humanistic and Political Literature in Florence and Venice* (Cambridge, Mass.,), Chap. 1.

[24] Seth Lerer, *Chaucer and His Readers. Imagining the Author in Late-Medieval England* (Princeton, 1993), p. 18.

work of D. W. Robertson and others, to integrate with other facets of Chaucer's sensibility the strong Augustinian current in his work.[25] Why does the Austin friar ignore or minimize this current rather than emphasize and celebrate it?

One reason is surely that the *Legend of Good Women* – the text which Bokenham used as structural model – is not one in which this current is readily discernible, cloaked as it is in a rhetorical veil of dream-vision, wordplay and irony. Whatever its kernel of truth, its shell could only give offense to such as Osbern, not least in presenting itself as a parody of the saint's legend. At another level, though, perhaps it is Harold Bloom who helps us to understand the phenomenon, for we might look at Bokenham's approach to Chaucer as a 'creative misprision' enabling him to distinguish himself from a precursor whose influence dominated the fifteenth century. However we explain it, Bokenham's legendary stands as evidence that veneration may oppose as well as imitate, indeed it may do both in a single act.

---

[25] For a more recent study than Robertson's *A Preface to Chaucer* (Princeton, 1969), see my *The Naked Text. Chaucer's Legend of Good Women* (Berkeley, 1994).

READING WOMEN'S CULTURE IN FIFTEENTH-CENTURY ENGLAND: THE CASE OF ALICE CHAUCER

CAROL M. MEALE

For Christine de Pizan, the initiatory stages of the revisionist project she engaged with in her re-writing of history from a woman's perspective, the book known as *La Cité des Dames*, completed in 1405, involved her in a mental struggle generated by what in modern critical terminology has come to be known as the anxiety of influence.[1] Surrounded in her room by male-authored texts, which she herself had been trained to regard as authoritative, she recounts how she found the largely hostile, and frequently overtly misogynistic, representation of women in their pages to be directly at odds with her own lived experience of women.[2] The book which resulted from her deliberations – cast in the form of an allegory in which, with the help of the female personifications of Raison, Droiture (Rectitude) and Justice, she simultaneously constructed a defence of women, and an analysis of their contributions, both past and present, to secular and religious life and thought – acts as a testimony to her belief that women not only brought their influence to bear on historical events, but also that they had a specific culture of their own. It is Christine's struggle to come to terms with the dominant value system of her age, and to define a role for women within this system,[3] that I

I should like to thank John Marshall for his inspiration and practical help in the writing of this paper.

[1] There is no modern accessible French edition of Christine's text. I have used the translation by Earl Jeffrey Richards, *The Book of the City of Ladies* (London, 1983). Harold Bloom's influential book *The Anxiety of Influence* (New York, 1973) was first used as an analytical tool by which to read Christine by Sheila Delany, 'Rewriting Woman Good: Gender and the Anxiety of Influence in Two Late-Medieval Texts', in *Chaucer in the Eighties*, ed. by Julian N. Wasserman and Robert J. Blanch (Syracuse, N.Y., 1986), pp. 75–92.

[2] *City of Ladies*, ed. by Richards, pp. 3–5.

[3] My view of Christine, and her relation to prevailing ideologies, differs markedly from that of Sheila Delany, ' "Mothers to Think Back Through": Who Are They? The Ambiguous Example of Christine de Pizan', in *Medieval Texts and Contemporary Readers*, ed. by Laurie A. Finke and Martin B. Schichtman (Ithaca, 1987), pp. 177–97, but cf. Maureen Quilligan, *The Allegory of Female Authority: Christine de Pizan's Cité des Dames* (Ithaca and London, 1991), for a reading which allows for Christine's consensual and essentially non-radical political stance.

have used as a central metaphor in thinking about both the subject of this paper – Alice Chaucer, who is one of the earliest known owners of Christine's text – and about my own enterprise in attempting to locate Alice within the cultural constructs of late-medieval England. There is, for example, a deliberate play on words in the title I have chosen, in the ambiguity of the formulation 'reading women's culture', for in addition to its explicit engagement with the issue of women's access to books, to the written word, it raises the question of how we, at a considerable historical remove, in turn 'read' the evidence which may be recovered about women's activities as the patrons and owners of literary texts. And I am alert to my own agenda, as a literary historian, and as a woman, of the delicacy with which it is necessary to handle the materials with which I am dealing: the attempt to define the culture of medieval women may itself prove to be a pursuit of the chimerical, in that it may not be possible to distinguish between female and male, feminine and masculine, within socially-constructed patterns of cultural expectation and aspiration. But, giving all due allowance to the inevitable constraints which surround such an enquiry, the project to which I am committed must extend beyond the archaeological – if I may so define the act of recovery and interpretation of evidence – to engage with the broader issue of the silencing of women's voices within both the medieval and the modern periods.

Alice Chaucer, the primary focus of my explorations in this paper has, in many ways, come to symbolize for me this process of silencing. (Plate 1) Although politically active in her lifetime, alternately characterized as a figure of fear and loathing, or as a powerfully political advocate, depending on the political affiliations of those who wrote about her (in 1462, for example, Margaret Paston wrote that the people in East Anglia 'love not in no wyse the Dwke of Sowthfolk nor hys moder', whilst twelve years later Sir Richard Harcourt, a member of her Oxfordshire-based affinity, described her 'as owr owne good lady, my lady of Suffold'),[4] there remains a tendency amongst historians of the fifteenth century to categorize her according to the various social roles – as daughter and heiress; as wife to the powerful but ultimately doomed duke of Suffolk, William de la Pole; and subsequently as widow, and mother to a potential claimant to the throne of England – which would be easily recognizable to the writers of medieval handbooks on the theory of social organization.[5] What I should like to attempt is to break through this

---

[4] For the Paston quotation see *Paston Letters and Papers of the Fifteenth Century*, 2 vols., ed. by Norman Davis (Oxford, 1971, 1976), 1, p. 279; and for the Harcourt letter, *The Stonor Letters and Papers 1290–1483*, 2 vols., ed. by Charles Lethbridge Kingsford, Camden Society, Third Series, 29, 30 (London, 1919), 1, p. 114.

[5] A major exception to this general treatment of Alice is Carol A. Metcalfe, 'Alice Chaucer, Duchess of Suffolk, c.1404–1475', unpublished B.A. dissertation, University of Keele, 1970. I am grateful to Colin Richmond for allowing me to consult this work. See also Rowena Archer, ' "How ladies . . . who live on their manors ought to manage

system of categorization, and to see Alice Chaucer as a figure in her own right, to attempt to understand how she formulated her cultural identity: to try to assess the importance to her of networks of kinship and affinity, and – most problematic and difficult of recovery of all, particularly in the absence of a surviving testament – of friendship.[6] An agenda defined in these terms is, of course, beyond the scope of a paper such as this.[7] But I should like to begin by looking at her as a woman with a well-documented interest in books and in literature, and through this process try to define both the extent to which she was subject in her choice of reading materials to the various cultural influences operative in her lifetime, and the extent to which it is possible to hear an echo of her own voice – however faint – through the socially-determined roles which she fulfilled so conscientiously.[8]

The starting-point for my discussion is a list of books preserved in the collection of Ewelme Muniments now housed in the Bodleian Library (VII.A.47 [3]). The books formed part of a collection of items 'brought from Wingfeld [in Suffolk] to Ewelme' and received by one Robert Newell, delivery being accomplished on the 10 September of the 'vjth yere of kyng Edward þe fourth' (i.e. 1466). That these books in all probability belonged to Alice herself has not always been readily acknowledged: as recently as 1989, for example, the editor of the group of English lyrics authorship of which was for some time erroneously attributed to Alice's third husband, William de la Pole, concurred with a mid-nineteenth-century judgement that they were, properly-speaking, in the possession of Alice's son John, as William's heir.[9] It

---

their households and estates"': Women as Landholders and Administrators in the Later Middle Ages', in *Woman is a Worthy Wight: Women in English Society c.1200–1500*, ed. by P.J.P. Goldberg (Gloucester, 1992), pp. 149–81 (pp. 153–56).

6   The only surviving document is a grant made during Alice's lifetime (3 October 1471) to her son, John, and his wife, Elizabeth Plantaganet, of 'alle my stuffe of plate of sylver of gilte and of golde. And all my beddys of clothe of gold and of silke and of arras and of tapiserye werke. And all my tapices of arras and of tapiserye', save those pieces 'that dayly serven me'; see *A Descriptive Catalogue of Ancient Deeds in the Public Record Office*, 5 (London, 1906), A.11118, pp. 95–96.

7   I hope to deal with these issues at greater length elsewhere, for evidence of Alice's networks and relationships is extensive. The whole subject of female friendship during the medieval period is a neglected one, most evidence discussed so far relating specifically to women's spiritual friendships and support: see, e.g., Felicity Riddy, ' "Women talking about the things of God": a late medieval sub-culture', in *Women and Literature in Britain 1150–1500*, ed. by Carol M. Meale (Cambridge, 1993), pp. 104–27; but cf., on the issue of friendship in general, Philippa Maddern, ' "Best Trusted Friends": Concepts and Practices of Friendship among Fifteenth-Century Norfolk Gentry', in *England in the Fifteenth Century: Proceedings of the 1992 Harlaxton Symposium*, ed. by Nicholas Rogers (Stamford, 1994), pp. 100–117.

8   Cf. Archer, 'Women as Landholders and Administrators in the Later Middle Ages', and the references in Colin Richmond, *The Paston Family in the Fifteenth Century: The first phase* (Cambridge, 1990), *passim*.

9   See J.P.M. Jansen, *The 'Suffolk' Poems: An Edition of the Love Lyrics in Fairfax 16 attributed to William de la Pole* (Groningen, 1989), p. 15; H.A. Napier, *Historical*

is, however, clear that the movement of household and chapel goods from the Suffolk castle of Wingfield to the manor of Ewelme in Oxfordshire coincided with a move on Alice's part, after a widowhood of sixteen years, back to her family home, an inventory of 'the stoff of bedys and hangyngys of chambyrs at Ewelme', compiled in August of the same year, noting the removal there of tapestries, cushions and other furnishings from Alice's 'Inne' in London (the 'Mannor of the Rose', in Suffolk Lane, in the parish of St Laurence Poultney, Dowgate ward) as well as from Wingfield.[10] Alice's interest in, and care for, her books could scarcely be better demonstrated than her signed note (regrettably undated by year) to one of her servants, perhaps her steward, at Ewelme, which runs as follows:

> William Bylton. I grete you wele. And pray you / my good William yef my books be in myther closette // by grounde þat ye woll put them in some other place. for takyng of harme. And god kepe you. Writen // in myn Inne the xxiiij day of Ianyver. Alyce[11]

The booklist itself is characterized by its generic diversity, and follows a lengthy inventory of chapel furnishings. Of the books listed, fourteen were clearly designed for use within the chapel, rather than by Alice herself, and were lavish in their bindings.[12] These were a mass book, or missal, 'couered with white lethur. with a latoun closp' (sic) and þe oþer broken'; three antiphoners, one large one 'noted couered with white lether and clospes of laton and gilt tasseld with silk And a regestre pynne of siluer þerynne', another 'noted couered in white lether with lether with tassells of lether

---

Notices of the Parishes of Swyncombe and Ewelme in the County of Oxford (Oxford, 1858), pp. 127–28. (Not very accurate transcriptions of this list are given in Napier, pages cited, and Jansen, p. 17 n. 12; cf. the equally inaccurate account in *Historical Manuscripts Commission*, 8th Report (London, 1881), Appendix, pp. 628–29). S.W.H. Aldwell, *Wingfield, Its Church, Castle and College* (Ipswich, 1925), p. 18, on the other hand, acknowledges Alice's ownership of the books and other movable artefacts (although this transcription, too, is flawed).

10 *John Stow, A Survey of London*, 2 vols., with introduction and notes by Charles Lethbridge Kingsford (London, 1908; repr. 1971), 2, p. 322. It is possible that Alice's move from Suffolk to Oxfordshire was motivated in part by a desire to see her son exercise his due rights in the former county, although throughout her life she seems to have influenced him considerably; see J.A.F. Thomson, 'John de la Pole, Duke of Suffolk', *Speculum* 54 (1979) 528–42. An additional factor, though, may have been her identification with her family home at Ewelme: Leland, in his *Itinerary in England and Wales*, 5 vols., ed. by Lucy Toulmin Smith (vols. 1–4 repr. Carbondale, 1964; vol. 5 repr. London, 1964), 1, pt. II, p. 112, noted that William de la Pole 'for love of [Alice] and the commodite of her lands fell much to dwell in Oxfordshir and Barkshir where his wifes landes lay'.

11 Bodleian Library, Ewelme Muniments VII.A.48 (1).

12 For a discussion of contemporary examples of bindings see Mirjam M. Foot, 'English decorated bookbindings', in *Book Production and Publishing in Britain 1375–1475*, ed. by Jeremy Griffiths and Derek Pearsall (Cambridge, 1989), pp. 65–86.

closped w*ith* lato*u*n', and another 'with þe legende þ*e*rynne (i.e. a legendary) cou*e*red w*ith* white lether closped w*ith* lato*u*n' (the antiphoner providing the music for services to be read at the various canonical hours); 'ij large graill*s* cou*e*red in white lether tasselld w*ith* silk And closped w*ith* lato*u*n' (grails, or graduals, containing musical responses to the scriptural passages read); 'a boke for Rectors cou*e*red in white lether closped w*ith* lato*u*n' (perhaps either a volume of instruction relating to penitence and confession, or a book setting down the regulations for the conduct of religious services);[13] 'ij lectornall*s* cou*e*red w*ith* white lether and closped w*ith* lato*u*n' (these were books of lessons to be read during Matins); 'a collectall boke cou*e*red w*ith* white lether tasseld w*ith* grene silk closped w*ith* lato*u*n' (the basis for the book of collects being the short lessons used at all the canonical services except Matins, though it may also by this period have included a calendar, psalter [or collection of psalms], and a hymnal); 'iij p*r*ocessionall*s* ij cou*e*red w*ith* white lether, and oon w*ith* Rede lether' (processionals being volumes which contained the rubrics, texts and music used during formal processions); and 'a large boke of p*r*iked songe bounden *and* cou*e*red in Rede lether and closped w*ith* lato*u*n' (i.e. a volume of plainsong).[14] The implication to be drawn from this not inconsiderable collection of service books is that the chapel figured largely in Alice's life, both individually, and in her role as lady of the manor. Detailed information from this period on the number of chapel personnel retained by those members of the nobility who had the means to maintain a regular staff is not easy to come by, but it would seem that the singers alone employed by Alice could have numbered between three and six – although the descriptions of the service books given in the inventory would imply that polyphonic music did not play a part within her chosen performance of religious devotions, the details nevertheless suggest that music made a significant contribution to liturgical ritual and celebration.[15] We do not know

---

[13] I owe this latter suggestion to Wyndham Thomas, to whom I am most grateful for discussing Alice's chapel arrangements with me.

[14] A useful discussion of these kinds of books remains Christopher Wordsworth and Henry Littlehales, *The Old Service-Books of the English Church* (London, 1904).

[15] On contemporary church music see Nick Sandon, 'Music', chapter 7 in *The Cambridge Cultural History, Vol. 2: Medieval Britain*, gen. ed. Boris Ford (Cambridge, 1992), pp. 215–34, and Andrew Wathey, 'The Production of Books of Liturgical Polyphony', in *Book Production and Publishing in Britain*, ed. by Griffiths and Pearsall, pp. 143–61. It was, of course, only the large royal and noble chapels which could afford the expenditure involved in elaborate musical devotions and in the employment of musicians and composers with established reputations: see, e.g., *The Household of Edward IV: The Black Book and the Ordinance of 1478*, ed. by A.R. Myers (Manchester, 1959), *passim*; and Jenny Stratford, 'The Manuscripts of John, Duke of Bedford: Library and Chapel', in *England in the Fifteenth Century: Proceedings of the 1986 Harlaxton Symposium*, ed. by Daniel Williams (Woodbridge, 1987), pp. 329–50, and her edition of *The Bedford Inventories: The Worldly Goods of John, Duke of Bedford, Regent of France (1389–1435)* (London, 1993), 'General

whether the chapel personnel included children as, for example, was the case with the Suffolks' rival East Anglian magnates, the Norfolks, although it may be not be too far-fetched to assume that Alice's son, John, maintained a chapel in some style in the Suffolk castle of Wingfield.[16]

The remainder of the books, seven in all, may be designated broadly as 'literary'. The content of one of these manuscripts, 'a quare of a legende of Ragge hande', is obscure, but it was most probably a saint's life copied in what the *MED* tentatively glosses as a 'style of irregular or uneven handwriting'. The apparent informality of its format and production and its relatively simple covering (it is unique amongst Alice's books as being described as 'couered in a solipelle' – most probably a loosely-attached wrapper of animal skin) suggests that it was intended for private, and possibly portable, use.[17] The contents of the majority of the rest of the volumes may be identified with no great difficulty. The texts listed are as follows: 'a frensh boke of quaterfitȝ Emond' couered in rede lether closped with tyssu of threde and latoun'; 'a frensh boke of temps pastoure' 'conteyned diuers stories in the same couered in Rede lether bossed and clasped with latoun'; 'a frensh boke of le Citee de dames couered with rede lethere clasped with latoun newe'; 'a boke of latyn of þe morall Institucion of a prince conteynyng xxvijti chapters couered in rede lethere And clasped with rede lether'; 'a frensh boke of þe tales of philisphers couerd in black damask bosed and clasped (sic) with siluer and gilt'; and 'a boke of English in papir of þe pilgrymage translated by daune John lydgate out of frensh couered with blak lether withowte bordes'. The elaboration of the majority of the bindings of these books, plus the fact that only one – the Lydgate text – was apparently copied on paper rather than parchment, gives some indication of the value which Alice attributed to them,

---

Introduction'. On the place of the chapel within household organization in general see Kate Mertes, *The English Noble Household 1250–1600* (Oxford, 1988), esp. chapter 5, 'The Household as a Religious Community'; and Suzanne R. Westfall, *Patrons and Performance: Early Tudor Household Revels* (Oxford, 1990), esp. pp. 13–28, although the emphasis here is primarily on the possible involvement of chapel personnel in dramatic entertainments.

[16] See *The Household Books of John Howard, Duke of Norfolk, 1462–1471, 1481–1483*, with introduction by Anne Crawford (Gloucester, 1992), *passim*.

[17] I have failed to discover the term 'solipelle' in any of the standard dictionaries of medieval Latin, and it does not even occur in contemporary reference-works such as *Catholicon Anglicum . . . dated 1483*, ed. by Sidney J.H. Herrtage, Camden Society, n.s. 30 (London, 1882). But see, e.g., Michelle P. Brown, *Understanding Illuminated Manuscripts: A Guide to Technical Terms* (London, 1994), p. 38, under the entry 'Chemise Binding', and Barbara A. Shailor, *The Medieval Book: Illustrated from the Beinecke Rare Book and Manuscript Library* (Toronto, 1991), p. 66, under 'Girdle Book'. Illustrations of such bindings do, however, abound, particularly in paintings of the Flemish school: see, e.g., the book held by the Virgin at the Annunciation in The Campin Altarpiece, now in the Cloisters Collection of the Metropolitan Museum of Art in New York.

though given the care with which the actual texts seem to have been chosen, it is unlikely that they were appreciated simply as *objets d'art*.[18]

It is a plausible hypothesis, and one to which I shall return, that many of the volumes which Alice acquired and later had moved to Ewelme may be linked with particular phases in her life. The 'quaterfit₃ Emond', for instance, was a copy of a recent French prose redaction of *Renaud de Montaubon*, an early-thirteenth-century *chanson de geste* concerning Charlemagne;[19] 'le Citee de dames' was Christine de Pizan's defence of women; the Latin text of 'þe morall Institucion of a prince' was undoubtedly the mid-thirteenth-century 'De morali principis institutione' written by the Dominican friar, Vincent de Beauvais, a text which seems to have had a relatively limited circulation in England, and that principally amongst learned and intellectual circles;[20] 'þe tales of philisphers' can be identified as a copy of the *Ditz de Philisophius*, a translation made from the Latin for Charles VI of France by Guillaume de Tignonville, provost of the city of Paris in 1401 and a chamberlain to the French king;[21] and the Lydgate text must be the verse translation of Guillaume Deguileville's *Pèlerinage de la Vie Humaine*, written in 1426, as Lydgate states in his translator's prologue, at the 'comavndement' of 'my lord / Of Salysbury, the noble manly knyht' – that is, Thomas Montagu, earl of Salisbury, Alice's second husband, who was killed at the siege of Orléans in November, 1428.[22] The reference to the 'frensh boke of

---

18 See n. 22 below for further discussion of the possible significances which may be deduced from the fact that the Lydgate work survived, in Alice's collection, in a paper copy.

19 For details of various codices and an outline of the text see *Catalogue of Romances in the Department of Manuscripts in the British Museum*, 3 vols., vols. 1 and 2 ed. by H.D.L. Ward, vol. 3 ed. by J.A. Herbert (London, 1883–1910), 1, pp. 619–25; also the introduction to Caxton's printed translation, *The Right Plesaunt and Goodly Historie of the Foure Sons of Aymon*, 2 vols., ed. by Octavia Richardson, EETS, ES 44, 45 (1884, 1885), 2, esp. pp. v–vii.

20 Wilhelm Berges, *Die Fürstenspiegel des hohen und späten Mittelalters*, Schriften des Reichsinstituts für ältere deutsche Geschichtskunde (Monumenta Germaniae historica), 2 (Leipzig, 1938), no.15, pp. 306–08. See further below, pp. 98–100.

21 See the conveniently accessible account in *The Dicts and Sayings of the Philosophers*, ed. by Curt F. Bühler, EETS OS 211 (1941), esp. p. xi.

22 *The Pilgrimage of the Life of Man, englisht by John Lydgate*, ed. by F.J. Furnivall and Katharine B. Locock, EETS ES 77, 83, 92 (1899, 1901, 1904, repr. in 1 vol., 1973), p. 4, ll. 123–34. As observed above, n. 18, it is curious that Alice Chaucer's copy of this text was on paper, and was not elaborately bound: this may well imply that it was not the presentation copy. Of the extant manuscripts only one, BL MS Stowe 952, is composed of paper; approximately the last fifth of the text was copied by John Stow: see ed. cit., p. lxix. (For a slightly sceptical view as to whether Alice's book was indeed Lydgate's verse translation of the work, a scepticism which I do not share, see Richard Firth Green, 'Lydgate and Deguileville Once More', *Notes and Queries*, 223 (1978) 105–6.) There is an additional puzzle, which remains to be solved, concerning what would appear to be a presentation miniature connected with the text, now pasted into BL MS Harley 4826 (fol. 1*): this has often been reproduced, but is most

temps pastoure' is more puzzling. The description suggests initially that it may have been an early version of a work such as the *Compost et Kalendrier des Bergiers*, published in France by Antoine Vérard in 1493, and issued by him ten years later for the English market under the title of the *Kalender of Shepherdes*, an instructional text in which a Master Shepherd discourses on a variety of topics such as astrology and astronomy, the seasons of the year, and such-like.[23] An alternative identification would be that Alice's book was a copy of Jehan de Brie's *Le Vray Regime et Gouvernement des Bergers et Bergeres*, generally known by the short title of *Le Bon Berger*, a work which, although extant only in a version printed in 1541, was originally commissioned by Charles V of France in 1379.[24] But neither of these suggested identifications seems fully satisfactory, given the terms in which the text is described in Alice's booklist. There is, however, a third possibility which, given her evident interest in the work of Christine de Pizan, seems worth raising. In May 1403 Christine completed a text known to modern scholars as *Le Dit de la Pastoure*. This is a text which owes much to the contemporary vogue for the pastoral – and the central narrative recounts the love affair between a shepherdess and a nobleman which had been a standard component of works in this genre from the thirteenth century onwards.[25] But Christine, like her earlier contemporary, Jehan de Brie, gives an eminently practical account of the seasonal duties of a shepherdess (which may account for the use of the term 'temps'), and the specificity of the reference to the

---

conveniently discussed, in Margaret Rickert, *Painting in Britain in the Middle Ages*, 2nd ed. (Harmondsworth, 1965), p. 184 and plate 184. This scene, showing a monk and a kneeling pilgrim presenting a book to a man in armour, is dated by Rickert to not 'much before the middle of the fifteenth century' – that is, approximately twenty years after Salisbury's death. Furthermore, the picture is now attached to a manuscript which contains amongst other items Lydgate's *Lives of St Edmund and St Fremund*, a partial copy of his *Secreta Secretorum* and Hoccleve's *Regiment of Princes*: see M.C. Seymour, 'The Manuscripts of Hoccleve's *Regiment of Princes*', *Transactions of the Edinburgh Bibliographical Society* 4:7 (1974) 253–97, pp. 268–69. (It is also curious that the verso of the drawing now contains medical recipes in two different late-medieval hands, which might indicate that the drawing circulated independently for a while). Rickert would associate the style of the drawing with Bury St Edmunds, although this is a point which remains to be clarified (though there is a note associating the volume with the Suffolk family of Drury, in the seventeenth century, Seymour, p. 268). Whether or not this surviving drawing is a copy or adaptation of the prefatory miniature in the original presentation volume is a question which must be addressed in future research – as must Alice Chaucer's possible role in its commissioning.

23 Helen Cooper, *Pastoral: Medieval into Renaissance* (Ipswich, 1977), pp. 73, 78.
24 Elizabeth Salter, *English and International: Studies in the Literature, Art and Patronage of Medieval England*, ed. by Derek Pearsall and Nicolette Zeeman (Cambridge, 1988), pp. 283–4.
25 *Oeuvres Poetiques de Christine de Pisan*, vol. 2, ed. by Maurice Roy (Paris, 1891), pp. 223–94. See Charity C. Willard, 'Jean Bodel and Christine de Pizan, Pastoral Poets', *Marche Romane* 30 (Medievalia 80) (1980), pp. 293–300; the text is also discussed by Cooper, *Pastoral*, pp. 49, 50, 51, 57, 67, 69–70, 80–81, 106, 163, 164.

feminine 'pastoure' in the English list, as opposed to the more usual 'berger' or 'bergere', suggests to me that it may well be Christine's poem which is being referred to.

Additional, if circumstantial, support for this interpretation is that Christine's *Dit* is known to have been in circulation in England during Alice's lifetime. Westminster Abbey MS 21 was a volume produced in France, but it contains the names of Englishmen associated with Thomas, lord Scales of Middleton in Norfolk, a commander, along with Alice's second and third husbands, of the English forces in France – and, indeed, the 'Strelley' whose name occurs on fol. 5v may have been the John Strelly who was recorded as one of Bedford's *valets de chambre* in 1431.[26] The book's contents include Christine's 'livre de la pastoure', together with copies of her 'l'epistre au dieu d'amours'; a collection of *demandes d'amours*; and various other texts and lyrics, both pro-and anti-feminist, which have women as their focus.[27]

The chief characteristics of Alice's selection of titles, aside from the generic diversity which I have already referred to – romance, and works of piety and didacticism all have their place here – are its contemporaneity, and its emphasis, in particular, on what was currently fashionable amongst courtly circles in France, and amongst those of the English nobility who, for reasons of war or diplomacy, spent much of their time in that country. *The Four Sons of Aymon*, for example, was one of the French romances contained in the magnificent volume presented by John Talbot, earl of Shrewsbury, to Margaret of Anjou around the time of her marriage to Henry VI in 1444/45 (an occasion at which both William and Alice were in attendance);[28] and Christine de Pizan's *Cité des Dames*, extant in many codices, was one of the texts contained in what is now BL MS Harley 4431, a presentation copy of the writer's collected works given to the French queen, Isabeau de Bavière, a volume which, incidentally, passed into the ownership of Jacquetta of Luxembourg, second wife of John, duke of Bedford, after the latter's

---

26 See most recently, Julia Boffey, 'English Dream Poems of the Fifteenth Century and their French Connections', in *Literary Aspects of Courtly Culture*, ed. by Donald Maddox and Sara Sturm-Maddox (Cambridge, 1994), 113–21, pp. 118–20. For John Strelly see Stratford, *The Bedford Inventories*, p. 405.

27 For a full listing see Paul Meyer, 'Notice d'un recueil manuscrit des poésies françaises du XIIIe au XVe siècle, appartenant à Westminster Abbey', *Bulletin de la Societé des Anciens Textes Français* (1875), pp. 25–36; further details of manuscripts containing the text may be found in Angus J. Kennedy, *Christine de Pizan: A Bibliographical Guide* (London, 1984), pp. 69–70. The *Dit* was also one of the texts collected in BL Harley 4431, a volume of Christine's 'collected works', discussed below, which ended up in an English library in the fifteenth century.

28 The volume is described in G.F. Warner and J. Gilson, *Catalogue of the Western Manuscripts in the Old Royal and King's Collections*, 4 vols. (London, 1921), 2, pp. 177–79; *Le Rommant de Guy de Warwik et de Herolt d'Ardenne*, ed. by D.J. Conlon, University of North Carolina Studies in the Romance Languages and Literatures, 102 (Chapel Hill, 1971), pp. 16–26. See below n. 50 for Alice and William's presence in France at this time.

acquisition and disposal of the French royal library.[29] And de Tignonville's *Ditz de Philisophius* was sufficiently popular to have been the subject of several translations into English.[30] One of these is anonymous, but others have secure ascriptions: Stephen Scrope's version, for instance, dated 1450, was made for his step-father, Sir John Fastolf, steward to John, duke of Bedford, and one of his executors; (Scrope's text was later revised by another of Fastolf's secretaries, William of Worcester); and Anthony Wydville, 2nd earl Rivers and brother to Queen Elizabeth, wife of Edward IV, was inspired to make his translation after being introduced to the book by a fellow-traveller on a pilgrimage to Spain in 1473. Thirteen manuscripts in all survive of these various translations. Nor was Alice Chaucer's husband, Thomas Montagu, alone in finding the work of the Cistercian monk Deguileville of interest: a total of six manuscript copies of a prose translation – as opposed to Lydgate's verse adaptation – into English survive,[31] whilst the duke of Bedford, during the period of his regency in France, commissioned from Jean Galopes, dean of St Louis de Saulsoye, a translation into Latin of the companion text to the *Pèlerinage de la Vie Humaine* – the *Pèlerinage de l'Ame*.[32] Neither was the popularity in the late middle ages of the texts owned by Alice confined to their reproduction and circulation in manuscript, literary entrepreneurs such as Caxton and Henry Pepwell capitalizing on their evident appeal to an English reading-public. Caxton's translation of *The Four Sons of Aymon*, for example, was published at the instigation of the earl of Oxford in 1490 (apparently from the earl's own copy of the French text),[33] thirteen years after the same printer's edition of Anthony Wydville's *Dicts and Sayings of the Philosophers*;[34] and Pepwell issued Bryan Anslay's translation of Christine's *Cité* in 1521.[35]

---

[29] Jacquetta's signature is reproduced as fig. 43 in Lotte Hellinga, *Caxton in Focus: The Beginning of Printing in England* (London, 1982), p. 85. The manuscript is discussed by Sandra Hindman, 'The Composition of the Manuscript of Christine de Pizan's Collected Works in the British Library: A Reassessment', *British Library Journal* 9 (1983) 93–123, and by J.C. Laidlaw, 'Christine de Pizan – An Author's Progress', *Modern Language Review* 78 (1983) 532–50, and 'Christine de Pizan – A Publisher's Progress', *Modern Language Review* 82 (1987) 35–75.

[30] For the following details see *The Dicts and Sayings of the Philosophers*, ed. by Bühler, pp. xix–xlvi.

[31] *The Pilgrimage of the Lyfe of the Manhode*, 2 vols., ed. by Avril Henry, EETS OS 288, 292 (1985, 1988).

[32] Stratford, 'The Manuscripts of John, Duke of Bedford', p. 348.

[33] N.F. Blake, *Caxton's Own Prose* (London,1973), pp. 83–84. For full details of this and the following Caxton text see Paul Needham, *The Printer and the Pardoner: an unrecorded indulgence printed by William Caxton for the hospital of St Mary Rounceval, Charing Cross* (Washington, 1986), pp. 93, 94.

[34] Blake, *Caxton's Own Prose*, pp. 73–77.

[35] Maureen C. Curnow, '*The Boke of the Cyte of Ladyes*, an English Translation of Christine de Pisan's *Le Livre de la Citie des Dames*', *Les Bonnes Feuilles* 3 (1974) 116–37.

Having established the extent to which Alice's collection of books marks her tastes as being at one with certain of her contemporaries, however, the crucial questions arise as to when she acquired them, and whether or not the acquisitions were made on her own initiative; and whether they can, in any sense, be seen as constituting part of a specific women's culture. In respect of these questions it is fortunate that a certain amount of detail can be recovered about her life, and the circumstances which may have influenced her in her choice of reading matter. Three factors, in particular, may have had a significant role to play in this regard: her upbringing at Ewelme, where her father, Thomas Chaucer, may have been influential in introducing her to the work of Lydgate; her subsequent marriages to two English noblemen and soldiers, each of whom spent a considerable time in France, and each of whom she appears to have accompanied abroad at different times of her life; and her role as mother, and possible educator, of the heir to one of the leading peers and governors of England during the fifteenth century.

The evidence for an early acquaintance with Lydgate comes from a poem given the title 'Balade made by Lydegate at þe Departyng of Thomas Chaucyer on Ambassade *into* France' in a manuscript copied by John Shirley, one-time secretary to Richard Beauchamp, earl of Warwick, another of the English commanders contemporary with Alice's husbands, the earls of Salisbury and Suffolk.[36] Thomas Chaucer (c.1367–1434), son of the poet, fulfilled a number of roles within local and national politics.[37] Several times sheriff for the counties of Oxfordshire and Berkshire, five times Speaker of the House of Commons, and member of Henry VI's council for over three years (1424–1427), on three occasions he formed part of an English embassy sent to France to treat for peace – in 1414, 1417, and 1420. Which of these embassies offered the occasion for Lydgate's paeon of praise of Alice's father is unclear.[38] Alice herself could have been no more than ten years old when her father first visited France, but the suggestion that Lydgate became acquainted with the Chaucers during his time at Oxford, and that the circle of gentry and nobility he encountered at Ewelme formed the basis for much of the future patronage he enjoyed, has the ring of plausibility.[39] Whilst it can never be established with any certainty that Alice herself instigated Thomas Montagu's commissioning of the Deguileville translation, as has sometimes been assumed (in 1426, the year of the commission, Lydgate himself was in Paris, where he became engaged in producing literary propaganda on behalf

---

[36] *The Minor Poems of John Lydgate*, 2 vols., ed. by Henry Noble MacCracken, EETS ES 107, OS 192 (1911, 1934), 2, pp. 657–59.

[37] J.S. Roskell, Linda Clark and Carole Rawcliffe, *The History of Parliament: The House of Commons 1386–1421*, 2 (Stroud, 1992), pp. 524–32.

[38] Derek Pearsall, *John Lydgate* (London, 1970), pp. 161–63, though Walter F. Schirmer, *John Lydgate: A Study in the Culture of the XVth Century*, trans. by Ann E. Keep (London, 1961), appears to place the poem's composition in 1417 with some confidence (p. 59).

[39] Pearsall, *John Lydgate*, pp. 162–63; Schirmer, *John Lydgate*, pp. 59–61.

of the English, so Salisbury could have made his acquaintance at first-hand),[40] it is a coincidence, if no more, that Alice's second husband also demonstrated an interest in the work of the Bury poet – the earliest, and best, copy of *The Siege of Thebes*, now BL MS Arundel 119, bears Suffolk's arms and crest[41] (Plate 2) – and Alice, as countess of Suffolk (she became duchess on William de la Pole's elevation in 1448), is credited with the commissioning of Lydgate's undated poem on *The Virtues of the Mass*: the copy extant in Oxford, St John's College MS 56 contains the inscription 'Hyc incipit interpretatio misse in lingua materna secundum Iohannem litgate monachum de Buria ad rogatum domine Countesse de Suthefolchia'.[42] Alice could well have been instrumental in introducing the poet to both Salisbury and Suffolk, and in this respect the latter's copy of the *Thebes* is of some interest. The poem itself has been dated, on astronomical grounds, to 1421,[43] and its relevance to Suffolk's political concerns is evident in the concluding lines of the poem, which refer to the Treaty of Troyes, concluded between the warring countries in May, 1420. Whilst there is no incontrovertible evidence as to the date at which Arundel 119 was copied – palaeographical analysis on its own is an insufficiently refined tool to place the manuscript chronologically with any precision – it is not impossible that it could date from around 1430, in which year Alice's betrothal to Suffolk was formalized (the actual date of their marriage is not known, but it had certainly taken place by 21 May 1432, when as countess of Suffolk she was issued with robes of the Garter).[44] The manuscript itself is an intriguing document, in that it may well be an early instance of a book issued from an organized centre of manuscript production at Bury St Edmunds.[45] (Plate 3) The dialect of the scribe has recently been pinpointed as Essex,[46] but the same hand is known to have copied at least two

---

[40] Pearsall, *John Lydgate*, p. 162, makes the assumption of Alice being the instigator of the translation. On Lydgate's propagandist activities at this time see, e.g., Pearsall, pp. 166–67, Schirmer, *John Lydgate*, pp. 116–19.

[41] *Lydgate's Siege of Thebes*, ed. by Axel Erdmann, EETS ES 108 (1911), p. viii; Pearsall, *John Lydgate*, p. 162.

[42] *Minor Poems of John Lydgate*, I, ed. by MacCracken, pp. 87–115.

[43] Johnston Parr, 'Astronomical Dating for some of Lydgate's Poems', *Publications of the Modern Language Association* 67 (1952), p. 256.

[44] For the issuing of the Garter robes to Alice see the *Dictionary of National Biography*, ed. by Sidney Lee, vol. 46 (London, 1896), p. 55, and *GEC: The Complete Peerage*, vol. 12:1, ed. by Geoffrey H. White (London, 1953), p. 447, n. (a) (both references under the entries for William de la Pole). The marriage settlement, noted in *GEC*, is BL Harleian Charter 54.I.9.

[45] This, again, is a point which requires verification, but see Kathleen L. Scott, 'Lydgate's Lives of Saints Edmund and Fremund: A Newly-located Manuscript in Arundel Castle', *Viator* 13 (1982) 335–66, and Nicholas J. Rogers, 'Fitzwilliam Museum MS 3–1979: A Bury St Edmunds Book of Hours and the Origins of the Bury Style', in *England in the Fifteenth Century*, ed. by Williams, pp. 229–43.

[46] See Angus McIntosh, M.L. Samuels and Michael Benskin, *A Linguistic Atlas of Late Medieval English*, 4 vols. (Aberdeen, 1986), 1, p. 105; 3, p. 132.

other books with East Anglian connections: a copy of the *South English Legendary* now in the Takamiya collection in Japan, and a copy of Walton's verse translation of Boethius's *Consolation of Philosophy*, now in the private library of Martin Schøyen in Norway (MS 615).[47] The latter is a particularly important witness to a Bury connection, since it bears the name of Thomas Hingham, a monk of Bury, who may be the same Hingham whose name also occurs on pages of the copies of the East Anglian plays of *Mankind* and *Wisdom* in the Folger Library in Washington (MS V.a.354). Now, given that Suffolk himself appears to have been in France almost continuously during the 1420s – he was captured by Joan of Arc's forces in June 1429, and although released before March 1430, he does not appear to have been back in England for any length of time prior to his marriage to Alice[48] – it is tempting to speculate that she may have been responsible, either directly or indirectly, for the commissioning of Arundel 119.

Where the question of Alice's interest in contemporary French literature is concerned, there is sufficient evidence to suggest that it may have been acquired first-hand, during her visits to France. The earliest reference to a stay abroad is the account given by the Burgundian chronicler, Jean de Waurin, of the attempted seduction of Alice by Philip the Good, duke of Burgundy, on the occasion of the wedding of Sir John de la Trémouille, Lord of Jonvelle and the demoiselle of Rochbaron, sister of the Lord of Amboise, in Paris, in November 1424.[49] By this time, aged twenty, she had married Thomas Montagu. She returned to France for an extended visit with her third husband, William de la Pole, during the period of the negotiations over the marriage of Henry VI to Margaret of Anjou. Suffolk himself was the chief negotiator and, indeed, was Henry's proxy for the betrothal, which took place in Tours, on 24 May 1444. When William, now marquess of Suffolk, once again left England for France in November of the same year to escort Margaret to England, he was accompanied by Alice and her own entourage of women, together with several other barons and their wives, and a large number of knights, esquires and valets. The company did not reach England again until 9 April 1445.[50] It

---

[47] The scribal connections between these codices was initially pointed out by Jeremy Griffiths, who has an article forthcoming on the subject in vol. 5 of *English Manuscript Studies*. I should like to thank A.S.G. Edwards for this information. See further, Richard Beadle, 'Monk Thomas Hyngham's Hand in the Macro Manuscript', in *New Science Out of Old Books: Studies in Manuscripts and Early Printed Books in Honour of A.I. Doyle*, ed. by Richard Beadle and A.J. Piper (Aldershot, 1995), pp. 315–41.

[48] *GEC*, p. 445; and for a comprehensive account of Suffolk's career during these years see Ralph A. Griffiths, *The Reign of Henry VI* (London, 1981), *passim*.

[49] The anecdote is cited in the translation of part of the *Recueil des Croniques et Anchiennes Istories de la Grant Bretaigne, a present nommé Engleterre, par Jehan de Waurin*, ed. by William Hardy and E.L.C.P. Hardy, 3 vols. (London, Rolls Series, 1864–91), 3 (1422–31), p. 130, and is cited by Metcalfe, 'Alice Chaucer', p. 62.

[50] Griffiths, *Reign of Henry VI*, pp. 315–16; Napier, *Historical Notices of the Parishes of Swyncombe and Ewelme*, p. 61. The records compiled by one of the royal clerks in

seems quite possible that Alice acquired some of her French books during one or other of these visits. Although none of the actual copies of the books on the Ewelme list have as yet been certainly identified, there is a notable connection, in terms of production and the artistic personnel involved, between the volume of romances and other chivalric texts commissioned in France by John Talbot for Margaret of Anjou, mentioned above, and one of the only other two codices of the French text of *The Four Sons of Aymon* now extant in a British library.

Margaret's manuscript is London, British Library MS Royal 15.E.VI. It has elaborately-decorated borders and is profusely-illustrated. The copy of *The Four Sons* which I wish to compare with this codex is another, although less luxuriously-produced, book from the Royal Collection in the British Library, MS 16.G.II.[51] Although there are differences between the presentation of the two texts of *The Four Sons* (that in 16.G.II is prefaced by a lengthy section in verse), the style of border illustration, decorative initials and – perhaps most crucially – the illustrations, is very close to that of Margaret's book. It is likely that the two volumes were produced in the same *atélier*, probably in Rouen, and they would certainly appear to contain work by the same hands.[52] Particular comparison may be made for example, in Plates 4–7, Royal MS 15.E.VI, fol. 439v, and Royal 16.G.II, fols 8r, 33r, between the rather pudding-like representation of the faces of some of the male figures; the distinctive painting of hair, of posture and gesture (note in particular the kneeling figures in 16.G.II, fol. 8r and 15.E.VI, frontispiece [latter not illustrated]); the repetition of architectural details, such as windows; and the characteristic use of a dark blue background powdered with gold spangles for both indoor and outdoor scenes. Since Royal 16.G.II, like its larger companion-volume, came early into the royal library (it is recorded in the 1535 catalogue of the Richmond Palace library),[53] the most plausible

---

charge of the financial arrangements involved in the enterprise, John Brekenok, noted that for the sea crossing, 'one of the larger vessels, the Swallow, was reserved by the special direction of the Marquess of Suffolk' for the duchess of Bedford and her retinue; see George Smith, *The Coronation of Elizabeth Wydeville* (London, 1935), pp. 45–46.

51 See Warner and Gilson, *Catalogue of Western Manuscripts*, 2, p. 207, and Ward, *Catalogue of Romances . . . in the British Museum*, 1, 619–22, for descriptions of the volume. The style of decoration of Royal 16.G.II, 'closely resembling' that of Royal 15.E.VI was, to my knowledge, first pointed out by Warner and Gilson.

52 See J.J.G. Alexander, 'Painting and Manuscript Illumination for Royal Patrons in the Later Middle Ages', in *English Court Culture in the Later Middle Ages*, ed. by V.J. Scattergood and J.W. Sherborne (London, 1983), pp. 141–62, p. 151, for the likely location of the workshop in Rouen; at least two artists worked on the illustration of Royal 15.E.VI. It is worth noting that the English party escorting Margaret of Anjou from France spent time in this city: see Napier, quoting from a contemporary source, in *Historical Notices of the Parishes of Swyncombe and Ewelme*, p. 61.

53 Henri Omont, 'Les Manuscrits Français des Rois d'Angleterre au Château de Richmond', in *Etudes Romanes Dediées à Gaston Paris* (Paris, 1891), pp. 1–13, p. 9, no. 75.

explanation for its arrival in England is that it was brought here, along with a number of other manuscripts produced in France, as a direct result of the cultural interchange occasioned by the war with France. Sir John Fastolf, for example, is known not only to have bought books during the period of his residence abroad, but is also thought to have brought an artist back to England with him; and I have suggested elsewhere that a copy of Christine de Pizan's *Cité des Dames*, Royal 19.A.XIX, which bears the badges of the house of York on its opening pages, also entered the country at this time.[54]

Whether or not Alice obtained her copy of the *Cité* during her visit of 1444/45 we will probably never know – I have examined all the surviving manuscripts of the text now in English libraries and I can identify none as having belonged to her.[55] But it would not be surprising if she had taken advantage of the resources offered by the book-producers of northern France to acquire texts not easily available in England. She may, perhaps, have acquired her copy of 'temps pastoure' and its accompanying diverse stories at the same time. I should, though, mention one more biographical detail which could have a bearing on her knowledge of Christine's work. Her second husband, Thomas Montagu, had as his companion for two years – from the autumn of 1398 until his father's death in January 1400 – Christine's son, Jean. Thomas Montagu's father, John, himself had a reputation as a poet (Christine described him as 'Gracieus chevalier, aimant dictiez, et lui même gracieux dicteur') and Christine's early popularity amongst an English readership may well have begun with this connection.[56]

Other influences which may have helped to shape Alice's cultural milieu can also be attributed to England's relations with France during this period. The exact nature of her relationship with Margaret of Anjou, daughter of the French poet and putative artist René d'Anjou, and a known manuscript commissioner,[57] (Plate 7) may not be recoverable, but it was close enough for her to be retained by the queen for at least two years after Margaret's arrival in

---

54 On the so-called 'Fastolf Master' see Kate Harris, 'Patrons, Buyers and Owners: The Evidence for Ownership and the Role of Book Owners in Book Production and the Book Trade', in *Book Production and Publishing in Britain*, ed. by Griffiths and Pearsall, pp. 163–99, pp. 180–81; J.J.G. Alexander, 'A Lost Leaf from a Bodleian Book of Hours', *Bodleian Library Review* 8 (1967–72) 248–51. On Royal 19.A.XIX, ownership of which I tentatively associate with Cecily Neville, duchess of York, see my ' ". . . alle the bokes that I haue of latyn, englisch, and frensch": laywomen and their books in late medieval England', in *Women and Literature in Britain*, ed. by Meale, pp. 128–58, p. 135.

55 For listings of manuscripts see Kennedy, *Christine de Pizan*, and cf. P.G.C. Campbell, 'Christine de Pisan en Angleterre', *Revue de Littérature Comparée* 5 (1925) 659–70.

56 See J.C. Laidlaw, 'Christine de Pizan, the Earl of Salisbury and Henry IV' *French Studies* 36 (1982), 129–43; Charity Cannon Willard, *Christine de Pizan: Her Life and Works* (New York, 1984), pp. 42–43, 164–65, 166.

57 Margaret of Anjou's finely-illustrated prayer roll, now Oxford, Jesus College MS 124, has been attributed to the school of the metropolitan-based artist, William Abell; see J.J.G. Alexander, 'William Abell "lymnour" and 15th Century English Illumination',

England; and Alice, as the only woman named in the list of those to be banished from court during the political crisis of 1450, following her husband's summary execution, was evidently perceived as having influence in royal circles.[58] She was also one of those summoned to attend the ceremonial purification of the queen following the birth of Prince Edward, in 1453.[59] There may have been some renewal in the relationship between the two women towards the end of Alice's life, when custody of Margaret was granted to her in her capacity as Constable of Wallingford, a post which she owed to her Chaucer inheritance.[60]

Another significant relationship may have been that which she formed with Charles duc d'Orléans, who, captured at the battle of Agincourt in October 1415, and imprisoned in England until 1440, was placed in the charge of William de la Pole from 29 August 1432 until 1435/36. Charles is recorded as having been held at various of William and Alice's residences, including Wingfield, Ewelme and London, before being given into the charge of Sir Reynold Cobham (the father, incidentally, of another highly-literate Englishwoman, Eleanor Cobham, second wife of Humphrey duke of Gloucester).[61] Partly perhaps as a result of the relationship which apparently developed between Charles and the Suffolks, William himself has been credited with authorship of a number of both French and English lyrics. Whilst the theory of authorship is now largely discredited,[62] a contemporary legal testimony survives which gives an account of William's interest in music and poetry: he is said to have had various *diz amoureux* read to him, and to have initiated the performance of a love-lyric by the Burgundian-French composer, Gilles Binchois, as a diversionary activity whilst recovering from an illness in

    in *Kunsthistorische Forschungen: Otto Pächt zu seinem 70. Geburstag*, ed. by A. Rosenauer and G. Weber (Salzburg, 1972), pp. 166–72.
58 On Suffolk's downfall see Griffiths, *Reign of Henry VI*, pp. 676–84; and for Alice's dismissal from court, Griffiths, p. 691.
59 Napier, *Historical Notices of the Parishes of Swyncombe and Ewelme*, p. 93.
60 On 8 January 1472 John Paston II reported to his mother that 'As for Qween Margrett, I vndreston þat sche is remeuyd from Wyndeshore to Walyngfforthe nyghe to Ewhelme, my lady off Suffolk place in Oxenfforthe schyre.' See *Paston Letters and Papers*, 1, p. 446. Also on Alice's custody of Margaret see Napier, *Historical Notices of the Parishes of Swyncombe and Ewelme*, p. 101; J.J. Bagley, *Margaret of Anjou* (London, n.d.), p. 235.
61 For details of Charles's imprisonment see *The English Poems of Charles of Orleans*, ed. by Robert Steele and Mabel Day, EETS OS 215, 220 (1941, 1946; repr. with bibliographical supplement, 1970), p. xiii; *GEC*, 12:1, p. 445; *Fortunes Stabilnes: Charles of Orleans English Book of Love: A Critical Edition*, by Mary-Jo Am, Center for Medieval and Early Renaissance Studies, Binghamton (Binghamton, N.Y., 1994), pp. 23–25.
62 See Henry Noble MacCracken, 'An English Friend of Charles of Orleans', *Publications of the Modern Language Association*, n.s. 19 (1911) 142–80; and for modem scepticism as to the attribution, Julia Boffey, *Manuscripts of English Courtly Love Lyrics in the Later Middle Ages* (Cambridge, 1985), pp. 65–67; and *The 'Suffolk' Poems*, ed. by Jansen, pp. 14–21.

France in 1424. Binchois was apparently still part of his entourage a year later.[63] (It is worth emphasizing at this point that the English occupying forces lived abroad in some style: Suffolk's Parisian house, the Hotel d'Aligré, was on the left bank, and he only sold it, to the duke of Bedford, in 1431, when he was raising money to pay off his ransom.)[64] It may be an indication of Suffolk's liking for musical performance, and of Alice's exposure to and participation in this activity, that the chamberlain's account books for Lynn in Norfolk record payments made to the 'histrijs Comitis Suffolcie' for the years 1416/17 and, more pertinently to the present discussion, 1445/46, in which year the same 'players' also visited Great Yarmouth, whilst the Suffolks were actively engaged abroad and at court, and so would presumably not have been in need of diversionary entertainments at their normal residences.[65] Whilst there is some dispute over how the term 'histrijs' should be translated – as players, in the sense either of actors, or of musicians – the latter interpretation might seem to carry some weight, given that there are references to minstrels in Suffolk's employ having visited York on three occasions in the late 1440s.[66]

Still other records survive which show the extent to which Alice's material culture was shaped by continental influences. In her later years at Ewelme, for instance, the tapestries and hangings with which she had her house decorated were principally of Flemish manufacture some, or many, of which may have been acquired by William de la Pole through the offices of Robert Worsley, a London mercer who had extensive business interests in Bruges. In 1440, for instance, Worsley arranged for Suffolk to have imported from Flanders, through Sandwich, tapestries, carpets, beds and other forms of furnishings (including perhaps a few of the numerous cushions Alice later had listed, one of which was covered with white leather, and others of which were of 'verdure').[67] Amongst the most notable of the hangings were 'A Tapyte of

---

[63] On Suffolk and Binchois see M.A. Desplanque,'Projet d'Assassinat de Philippe le Bon par les Anglais (1424–1426)' in *Mémoires Couronnés et Mémoires des Savants Etrangers*, 33 (Brussels, 1867), p. 70; Boffey, *Manuscripts of English Courtly Love Lyrics*, pp. 99–100; and Nigel Wilkins, 'Music and Poetry at Court: England and France in the Late Middle Ages', in *English Court Culture*, ed. by Scattergood and Sherborne, pp. 183–204, p. 199; and for a more sceptical interpretation of the contemporary evidence, *The 'Suffolk' Poems*, ed. by Jansen, pp. 15–16.

[64] Stratford, *The Bedford Inventories*, p. 111.

[65] *Records of Plays and Players in Norfolk and Suffolk 1330–1642*, ed. by David Galloway and John Wasson, Malone Society Collections 11 (Oxford, 1980/81), pp. 44, 48, 11.

[66] For the debate over terminology at this period see Abigail Young, 'Plays and Players: the Latin terms for performance', *REED* Newsletter 9:2 (1984) 56–62 and 10:1 (1985) 9–16. The references to Suffolk's minstrels visiting York are to be found in Elza C. Tiner, 'Patrons and Travelling Companies in York', *REED* Newsletter 17:1 (1992) 1–36, p. 32.

[67] The artefacts are listed in Bodleian Library, Ewelme Muniments A.47 (2). For Worsley and his connection with Suffolk see Stratford, *Bedford Inventories*, pp. 429–30.

Aras of xv signes of the doom' (the subject, incidentally, of a poem by Lydgate)[68], and another 'of the story of seynt Anna of Aras', both of which, brought from the London house, hung in the chapel. (The latter bears witness to the increasing popularity of the cult of this saint during the late Middle Ages.) And, along with the expected representations in the tapestries of the courtly activities of hunting and hawking, there was in the great parlour 'a coveryng of a Bed' depicting 'men and women pleyng at cardus' – a diversion which, on the basis of the survival of high-quality packs of playing cards from around this period, would seem to have been newly-fashionable amongst the nobility.[69]

The last of the three influences which I suggested may have had significance in determining Alice's literary and cultural acquisitions was that of maternity, and this, I think, lies behind her possession of the 'boke of latin of þe morall Institucion of a prince conteynyng xxvijti chapters'. The specification of the language, together with the precise wording of the title and of the numbering of the chapters, confirms that this was indeed one of the lesser-popularized didactic works of Vincent of Beauvais.[70] Not only may the text be positively identified, but I believe that it is also possible to locate the exemplar of this book, and to recover, at least in part, the motivation behind Alice's acquisition of it. Some evidence of the restricted circulation of Vincent's treatise can be gleaned from the fact that in England copies are known to have been in the possession of various of the orders of friars: the Carmelites in Lincoln, and the Dominicans in London.[71] Of the four codices known to be still extant in British libraries, that in Cambridge, Trinity College

---

[68] *The Minor Poems of John Lydgate*, ed. by MacCracken, 1, pp. 117–20. This was also, of course, a popular subject for depiction within tapestries: see W.G. Thomson, *A History of Tapestries from the Earliest Times to the Present Day*, 3rd ed. (London, 1973), *passim*; cf. Scot McKendrick, 'Tapestries from the Low Country in England during the Fifteenth Century', in *England and the Low Countries in the Late Middle Ages*, ed. by Caroline Barron and Nigel Saul (Stroud and New York, 1995), pp. 43–60, on the subject in general.

[69] On the cult of St Anne see *Interpreting Cultural Symbols: Saint Anne in Late Medieval Society*, ed. by Kathleen Ashley and Pamela Sheingorn (Athens, Georgia, 1990); and on cards, Anne H. van Buren and Sheila Edmunds, 'Playing Cards and Manuscripts: Some Widely Disseminated Fifteenth-Century Model Sheets', *The Art Bulletin* 56 (1974) 12–30, for discussion and illustration of some of these fine surviving packs.

[70] On the dissemination (often through French translations and adaptations) of other educational and didactic works of Vincent of Beauvais (d.1264), see especially Nicholas Orme, *From Childhood to Chivalry: The Education of the English Kings and Aristocracy 1066–1530* (London and New York, 1984), esp. pp. 91–97; also Roberta Krueger, 'Constructing sexual identities in the high Middle Ages: the didactic poetry of Robert of Blois', *Paragraph* 13:2 (1990) 105–131, esp. p. 108, and ns 14–19 for additional bibliography.

[71] *The Friars' Libraries*, ed. by K.W. Humphries, Corpus of British Medieval Library Catalogues (London, 1990), pp. 178, 200.

MS B.15.11, is of especial significance.[72] Copied around 1430 by Cornelius Oesterwik in the Dominican friary at Oxford, it bears an early ownership inscription of 'John Courteys' of Exeter College, Oxford. Of the five possible candidates to be identified as the possessor of this manuscript, the only one who cannot be ruled out with a fair degree of certainty is the John Curteys who was appointed rector of Ewelme in February 1455.[73] This would appear to be the first appointment which, five years after her husband's death, was in Alice's gift, and it is quite possible that the advowson was made on the grounds of what she thought would be most fitting for the education of her only son, then aged thirteen, in preparation for the political role which he could be expected to occupy on coming of age. (There is evidence enough, of course, to suggest that family chaplains and rectors attached to particular manors performed an educative function as part of their routine duties, but additional indications of her interest in education were her joint founding with William in 1437 of the almshouse and the school at Ewelme, the latter of which was to be provided with a Grammar Master whose role was to teach the local children 'freely without exaccion of any Schole hire'; and Alice, as well as her husband, was one of those who took an active interest in Henry VI's foundation of Eton College.)[74] The terms in which John's father had talked of Alice in his last letter to his son, in which he advised him 'as ye be bounden by þe commaundement of God to do, to love, to worshepe youre Lady and Moder', and to 'obey alwey hyr commaundementes and to beleve hyr councelles and advises in alle youre werks þe which dredeth not but shall be best and trewest to you',[75] indicate that William placed every confidence in her ability to educate John for his future responsibilities. Curteys's appointment may, therefore, have been made on the basis of sound judgement, and it seems eminently reasonable to claim his possession of Vincent's text as the source for Alice's copy of it: the logical explanation would be that Curteys brought the book with him from Oxford to Ewelme, and that Alice commissioned

---

72   The manuscripts apart from Trinity at present known are: Oxford, Merton College MS 110; Cambridge, Corpus Christi College MS I.7; and a copy in the Library of the Dean and Chapter of York Minster (see Berges, *Die Fürstenspiegel des hohen und späten Mittelalters*, pp. 306–7). For a description of the Trinity codex see M.R. James, *The Western Manuscripts in the Library of Trinity College, Cambridge*, 4 vols. (Cambridge, 1900–1904), I, pp. 473–75 (no. 347).

73   A.B. Emden, *A Biographical Register of the University of Oxford to A.D. 1500* (Oxford, 1957), I, p. 529.

74   A brief history of the foundation of the Almshouse, and of the statutes relating to the school, may be found in the current *Guide to St Mary's Church Ewelme, and to the Almshouse and the School*, pp. 15–17; see also Napier, *Historical Notices of the Parishes of Swyncombe and Ewelme*, pp. 54–55. For Alice's interest in Eton, see Griffiths, *The Reign of Henry VI*, p. 268, n. 77; and for the role of household clerks and chaplains in education, Orme, *From Childhood to Chivalry, passim*.

75   This letter is often quoted. My immediate source is John Fenn, *Original Letters Written during the Reigns of Henry VI, Edward IV and Richard III*, etc. 5 vols. (London, 1787–1823), 1, pp. 33–36.

either him, or perhaps another of the clerks in her employ, to reproduce from it the appropriate text.

Alice, then, was clearly a woman of her time, and of her class. Her position was undoubtedly a privileged one, with regard both to her disposable wealth, and her exposure to a range of cultural influences through travel. And the books which we know her to have possessed, I would argue, show her participation in various aspects of contemporary culture, some of which may have been masculine in their construction – for example her ownership of a pietistic text commissioned by her second husband, and of a book of instruction designed to help her in the upbringing of her son. Of her personal piety, aside from the tantalizing reference to her command to Lydgate to write a poem on the mass for her, we know little, although it is difficult to believe that the famous cadaver tomb within which she lies buried in Ewelme church (Plate 8) was not made at her specific request, rather than at that of her son.[76] The tomb constitutes a peculiarly personal, and profound form of spirituality, and the fact that the sculptured decaying body is gazing up at painted representations of the Annunciation, and of SS. Mary Magdalene and John the Baptist, suggests particular religious allegiances on her part which would be worth investigating further.[77] She was not the only fifteenth-century English noblewoman to wish to be commemorated in this way. Isabella Despenser, countess of Warwick (and another of Lydgate's patrons), made in her will of 1439 provisions which, if only Alice's testament survived, were probably remarkably similar in the precision of their instructions.[78]

It is, perhaps, only in her ownership of of at least one text by a woman writer, Christine de Pizan, that we can begin to glimpse a culture which explicitly addressed the interests of women, a culture which, although ultimately defined by and subordinated to the assumptions and demands of a patriarchal society, and one in which contemporary social hierarchies prevailed, nevertheless offered them an opportunity to view themselves as a community, and one with its own history and sense of achievement, both practical and spiritual. And Alice was not alone amongst her sex in seeking to acquire works by this Franco-Italian author. Christine's audience abroad included queens, duchesses, and members of the bourgeoisie; and in England copies of her work are known to have been in the possession not only of

---

[76] It is assumed e.g. by J.A. Dodd, 'Ewelme', *Transactions of the St Pauls Ecclesiological Society* 8 (1920) 194–206, p. 201, that Alice's tomb was 'erected [by John] to his mother's memory'.

[77] Dodd, 'Ewelme', p. 201, notes that the painting of the Annunciation is placed over the head of the cadaver, and that of the saints above its feet. The intensely private, rather than public, nature of the act of piety underlying the construction of both the tomb and the paintings (the latter are virtually impossible to see) bespeaks personal preference on the part of the woman to be remembered.

[78] For Isabella Despencer's will see *The Fifty Earliest English Wills . . . 1387–1439*, ed. by F.J. Furnivall, EETS OS 78 (1882), pp. 116–19.

Alice, and Jacquetta of Luxembourg, but also of Anne Harling of Suffolk, widow of John, 5th lord Scrope of Bolton; Anne Neville, countess of Stafford; Lady Margaret Beaufort; and, perhaps, Cecily Neville, duchess of York.[79] Recognition of the extent to which women such as these may have been active in the promotion of writers such as Christine – in both the production and reproduction of their texts – is long overdue.

The act of recovery and reconstruction of women's culture is a painstaking one, as I have tried to demonstrate by the case of Alice Chaucer, and it is one which necessitates the piecing together of the minutiae of women's lives – of their material possessions, their networks of relationships and associations, and the day-to-day details of their existences. The voices of medieval women are mediated through sources in which they were rarely the principal concern of those whose task it was (and often, still is) to record and analyse historical experience. Yet to deny ourselves the opportunity to hear these voices, ambivalent as they may be, is to deny ourselves access to a vital part of medieval culture and, as late-twentieth century readers and academics, to acquiesce in an act of appropriation whereby the past is seen not simply as another country, but as a country which was inhabited solely by the masculine.

---

[79] On Christine's audience abroad see especially Charity Cannon Willard, *Christine de Pizan*, and 'The Manuscript Tradition of the *Livre des Trois Vertus* and Christine de Pizan's Audience', *Journal of the History of Ideas* 27 (1966) 433–44 (and cf. M. Tuetey, 'Inventaire des Biens de Charlotte de Savoie', *Bibliothèque Ecole des Chartes* 26 (1864–65) 338–442, p. 359 for a record of copies of Christine's 'Cite des Dames' and 'le livre des Troys Vertuz'; Charlotte, who died in 1483, was queen of Louis XI of France). On an English female readership of Christine's works see Meale, ' ". . . alle the bokes that I haue" ', pp. 135, 143.

Reading Women's Culture in Fifteenth-Century England: The Case of Alice Chaucer

Plate 1. Half-figure of Alice Chaucer, St Mary's Church, Ewelme

Plate 2. London, British library MS Arundle 119, fol. 4 recto

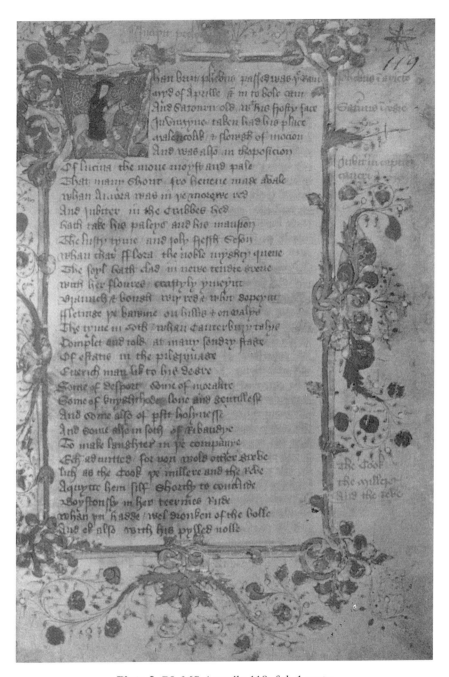

Plate 3. BL MS Arundle 119, fol. 1 recto

Plate 4. BL MS Royal 15.E.VI, fol. 439 verso

Plate 6. BL MS Royal 16.G.II, fol. 33 recto

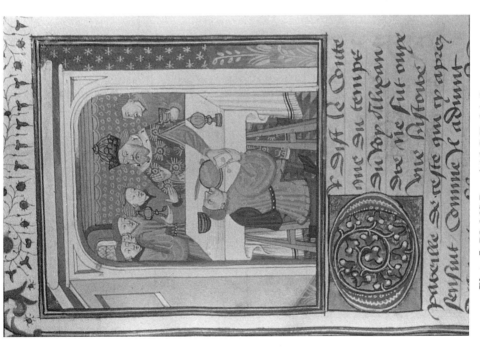

Plate 5. BL MS Royal 16.G.II, fol. 8 recto

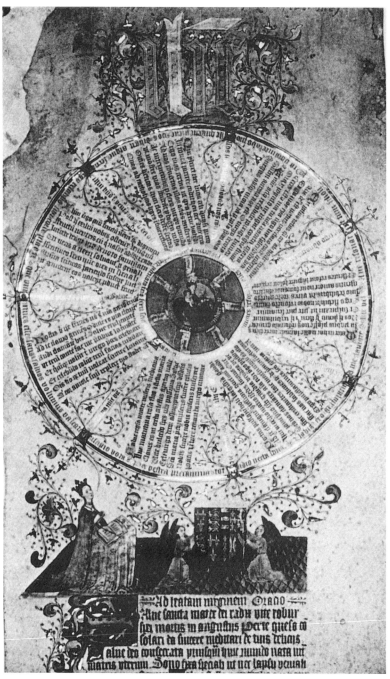

Plate 7. Oxford, Jesus College MS 124: Margaret of Anjou's prayer-roll

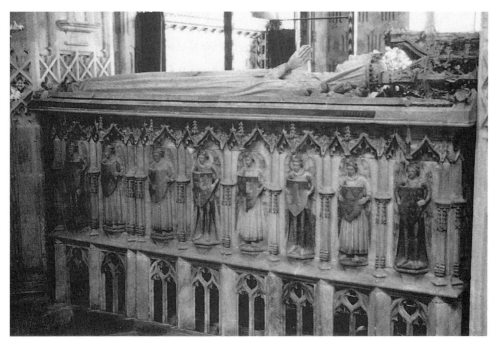

Plate 8. Tomb of Alice Chaucer, St Mary's Church, Ewelme

Blake's Chaucer: Scholasticism *post litteram*

Plate 9. William Blake, *The Canterbury Pilgrims*

Spenser's Virtue of Justice and the Four Daughters of God

Plate 10. Canterbury Psalter, fol. 150B (M.R. James)

Plate 11. Utrecht Psalter, fol. 49v (E.T. DeWald)

SPENSER'S VIRTUE OF JUSTICE AND THE FOUR DAUGHTERS OF GOD

THOMAS P. ROCHE

> It has been the fate of the *Faerie Queene* to be attacked where it is strongest. The plan, the story, the invention are triumphant. If they have faults, they are such faults as never deterred any reader except those who dislike romance and would not be allured to read it by any perfections.
>
> C.S. Lewis, *English Literature in the Sixteenth Century, excluding Drama*, p. 389

My subject today is part of a larger project on the ending of Spenser's *Faerie Queene*. I want to register my dissatisfaction with the almost universal critical agreement that the last three books of Spenser's epic are less coherent, less poetic than the first three. Most of the recent criticism, especially that about Book V, the Book of Justice, takes a politically correct stance and treats Spenser as the author of a racist pamphlet advocating the extermination, or at least, control of the Irish, and as a vicious perpetrator of colonialism. The charge is not new. It was first popularized by C.S. Lewis who claimed that 'Spenser was the instrument of a detestable policy in Ireland, and in his fifth book the wickedness he had shared begins to corrupt his imagination' (*Allegory of Love*, p. 349). Lewis's comment is the extra-literary response of an Irishman; one wonders how he would have responded to the flood of accusation at the present time.

I think that all this hullaballoo is quite wrong literarily and that we are missing the point of Spenser's poem because we miss the point of what he meant by justice. Most of the recent criticism of Spenser's virtue of justice is directed toward an act-oriented morality, that is, we read the meaning from the acts of the hero of the poem. So-and-so did such-and-such, which shows that he is behaving justly or unjustly. This will do for post-Romantic fiction, but it will not do for Spenser's allegorical poem. Spenser works from a virtue-oriented morality, as the titles of each of his books demonstrate: The Legend of the Red Cross Knight, or of Holiness; the Legend of Sir Arthegal, or of Justice. It is not so much the knight as the legend of that knight that is to be equated with the virtue, and the legends, as any reader knows, do not present the narrative as the simple story of a hero who represents a virtue. The entire narrative with all its involuted episodes presents the virtue that Spenser is rehearsing for our edification and delight. Of all the critics of Spenser, and of late there have been too many, only Rosemond Tuve was aware of the

> Yet would not let iust vengeance on her light;
> But rather let in stead thereof to fall
> Few perling drops from her faire lampes of light;
> The which she couering with her purple pall
> Would haue the passion hid, and vp arose withall.

The misreading occurs in the central lines of the stanza with their repeated use of the word *let*: 'Yet would not let iust vengeance on her light; /But rather let in stead thereof to fall / Few perling drops. . .' Mercilla gives the sentence of doom for Duessa in one of the most glorious puns in Renaissance literature. The misreaders assume that Spenser meant to have us read both *let*s with the more common meaning of *allow*, but Spenser knew that the word *let* had two contradictory meanings, both *to allow* and also *to prevent*, and he uses the second meaning in the first line to test our reading skill: that is, she would not prevent just vengeance from falling on her, but allowed instead some perling drops to fall. The pun on the two meanings encapsulates the problem of justice for this episode, and as I shall argue for the entire book.

This is not history as history; it is not the trial of Mary Stuart as recorded in numerous documents; it is Spenser's attempt to deal with the significance of that event in his virtue-oriented world. Elizabeth never met her cousin Mary Stuart, and so it is useless to think that Spenser is depicting Elizabeth's dramatic confrontation with her cousin, as in the Donizetti opera out of Schiller. Hence those 'few perling drops' are a portrayal of Mercy not reconciled with Justice, as embodied in the trial of Mary. Mercy weeps because she cannot become part of the justice meted out to Duessa, who is not repentent, and only to this extent is the scene an exculpation of Elizabeth's hard-won agreement to the execution of her cousin.[9]

IV

Critics of Book V continually complain about the repetitiousness of the adventures divided between Arthur and Arthegall in the last four cantos of the book, as if the rescue of besieged monarchs were all one story, and if you have read one you have read them all. This is to miss the point of Spenser's rewriting of history. The sameness of all these incidents points not to a lack of narrative ability on Spenser's part but to a deliberate neutering of individual characteristics in order to emphasize the encompassing evil of the underlying threat in all these 'historical' episodes, and that is the judicial power of the Roman church, which is the unifying element of all four cantos. Duessa as Mary Stuart is Mary Stuart as a Roman Catholic, who seeks to undermine the justice of Elizabeth's kingdom; Burbon as Henri IV is Henri as lapsed protestant, for whom 'Paris vaut bien une messe'; Gerioneo is Spanish

---

[9] See Dunseath and Tuve comment from preceding note.

political power in the Low Countries using the judicial power of the Roman Church and its instrument of torture, the Inquisition; Grantorto is that same power as the subverter of peace in Ireland. Spenser sees Roman Catholic power as the global threat.

I agree with all the critics of Book V that Grantorto is one of the greatest lack-luster presentations in the poem. We find none of the elaborate preparation for the Dragon fight in Book I, so brilliantly analysed by Carol Kaske,[10] nothing of the *paysage moralise* of the Bowre of Bliss, nothing like the eeriness of the Masque of Cupid in Book III; Grantorto is all swash and buckle (5.12.14ff.), armed as a great tyrant should be, but Arthegall's reaction is to the point:

> But th'Elfin swayne, that often had seene *like sight*,
> Was with his ghastly count'nance nothing queld...
> (5.12.16; italics mine)

This is a cigar-store tyrant, Spenser is telling us, frightening only if you do not know his lack of power. This may be a failure or imaginative fatigue on Spenser's part, but I would rather like to suggest that it is a purposeful dimming of the evil opponents of these last two books because Spenser did not want to aggrandize the reality of the evils he was decribing. He seems to be insisting on what Hannah Arendt has called the 'banality of evil'. He is downplaying, stereotyping the evil in order to establish the rationale of goodness that runs through the book and contravenes the evil that we all must acknowledge in this world. It is to this rationale of good that I will devote the remainder of this paper.

V

Let us get back to my idea that the Four Daughters of God may have something to do with Spenser's depiction of justice in Book V. In canto 9 in the presence of both Arthur and Arthegall the queen Mercilla metes out justice to a deposed queen, Duessa, and in canto 12 Arthegall the knight of justice rescues Irena, another besieged queen. Thus the knight of justice has important connections with two queens representing Mercy and Peace at the beginning and end of the most historically oriented set of cantos in the entire poem, but as I previously mentioned none of the history happens as Spenser depicts it – with the exception of the execution of Duessa and the ambiguous support of Burbon. None of it is true, and it is that very absence of truth both in Spenser's depiction of recent history and the absence of that fourth daughter of God, Truth, that makes me think that Spenser was playing with that ancient foursome. Let me try to convince you that I may be right.

---

[10] Carol Kaske, 'The Dragon's Spark and Sting and the Structure of Red Cross's Dragon-fight: the *Faerie Queene* I. xi–xii', *Studies in Philology* 66 (1969) 609–638.

Habitually Spenser ends each book of his poem almost immediately after the defeat of the major vice, but in Book V, which could have ended with the freeing of Irena in the 26th stanza of canto 12, he continues the adventures of Arthegall after his recall to the Faery Court for 17 stanzas, of which 9 stanzas are devoted to elaborate descriptions of Envy, Detraction, and the first appearance of the Blattant Beast, the major vice of Book VI. This episode has usually been interpreted as Spenser's defense of Arthur Grey, 14th Lord Grey de Wilton, for whom Spenser was secretary when Grey was Lord Deputy of Ireland, and I see no reason to dispute this historical identification. On the other hand, I do not see that we have to be confined to this historical identification, since Arthegall in the poem is many things beside his identification with Lord Grey, the most important of which is Justice.

I would rather consider the allegorical problems that Spenser was facing in his poem at this point, and I will begin by reminding you that in the medieval reconciliations of the Four Daughters of God, Truth is always besieged by Envy and Detraction.[11] Truth, who does not appear in any recognizable guise in this book, is there by implication through the active presence of her traditional enemies. Truth cannot be presented in this part of the poem because Spenser has deliberately not told the truth about the historical situations he has depicted.[12] For him the Truth is the un-truth of his prophetic history, and it is this untruth that is being undermined by Arthegall's recall to the Faery Court through the actions of Envy, Detraction, and the Blattant Beast. Truth, that fourth Daughter of God, is being invoked by her very absence from the poem.

The truth that is lacking from Spenser's poem is not a failure of imagination on his part but a clear look at the failure of the Christian community that cannot avail itself of the reconciliation prophesied by Psalm 85, that total reconciliation of Justice and Mercy, Truth and Peace through the Incarnation, as shown in the illuminations from the Utrecht and Canterbury Psalters, uniting the prophecy of the Psalmist to the greater glory of the Incarnation and its consequences for labouring fallen man. Milton has his God the Father echo the sentiment in Book III of *Paradise Lost*:

> man therefore shall find grace,
> The other [Satan] none: in mercy and justice both,
> Through heaven and earth, so shall my glory excel,
> But mercy first and last shall brightest shine.   (131–34)

God's mercy is predominant, both in the eye of Milton's God and in Spenser's depiction of Mercilla. But the execution of Mary Stuart as an act of supreme mercy is the stumbling block for modern readers. Needless to say, Mary was

---

[11] Chew, pp. 88–89.

[12] This strategy may have been derived from Virgil's story about the gates of horn and ivory in Book VI of the *Aeneid*, in which Aeneas escapes from the underworld through the gate of horn, the gate of false dreams.

put to death unlike Adam and Eve, but no matter how much we see *realpolitik* in that execution today Spenser is presenting Elizabeth-Mercilla as the exemplar of mercy, joined both by Arthur finally and Arthegall steadfastly. Spenser is telling us that the claims both of justice and mercy have been met in this execution of Duessa because of the participation of Arthegall with Mercilla. We get nowhere in resolving the moral conundrum if we think of – or read only – Mary Stuart because such historical reading simply leads us back to the historical problem of Mary Stuart. We as readers of Spenser's poem must keep our mind on Duessa, the Scarlet Whore of Babylon from Book I, the mistress of Orgoglio, the *doppelganger* of Una – evil, not a person, a name for duplicity. And that is how Spenser thought of Mary Stuart and the reason why he presents her case in the figure of Duessa.

I think that the critical reaction to Mercilla would have been quite different if Spenser had presented Elizabeth's case against Mary in the figure of Justitia or had put Arthegall in charge of the trial. It would have been shorter, and Talus who only deals with mob scenes would have accompanied some noble justiciar to behead Duessa. But that is not the narrative that Spenser presents. Mercilla accedes to the demands of justice and weeps, not out of sympathy but at the just loss of a monarch, an irony surely not lost on Charles I. Mercilla's exacting justice leads to her wanting her 'passion' to be hid because emotions should have nothing to do with justice. Spenser in this stanza is getting as close to justifying Elizabeth for her execution of Mary as he could without engaging in discursive polemics. In his poem Elizabeth cannot lose, not only because Spenser believed that she was right and just in her decision, but also because he shows it through the virtues with which he associates her decision. Mercilla fulfils the claims of justice. The mercy she shows is not in those 'few perling drops', but in the mercy shown to all those others whom she is saving from Duessa's deceits, symbolized earlier by that unused sword at her feet, 'Whose long rest rusted the bright steely blade, (5.9.30.7).

As you can see from my preceding presentation, I am not in sympathy with the current wave of criticism that denies Spenser anything he says about Ireland because of the scoundrel he must have been for not attending to post-colonial political correctness. That he was a platonist, no one has ever denied, but that his platonism, by which I mean his total adherence to a virtue-oriented morality, requires an attempt to judge his created figures by reference to the centuries-old tradition of the virtues and their inter-relationships has not been granted to him, although the evidence is patently obvious if one attends to the way he turned the epic tradition inside-out. Spenser's *Faerie Queene* abandons the single narrative line of Homer, Virgil, Ariosto, and Tasso by making each new book the adventure of a different knight and by identifying each book with the name of a virtue so that the meaning of each book becomes a label to guide our reading. We read about Red Cross under the label of Holiness and about Arthegall under the label of Justice, so that we cannot avoid Spenser's effort to force us to see virtues rather than merely figures. I suppose that we will never be able to read Spenser fully unless we accept a platonic realm of ideas as the ultimately real, of which we are merely the third-hand particulars, and I do not see this happening in the near future. Perhaps Spenser saw this even as he wrote his poem and knew that the truth he wanted so much to depict would never be actualized. At least this is what I want to suggest about those last cantos of Book V, in which I see Spenser playing his narrative of recent history against a paradigm of those Four Daughters of God – Justice and Mercy and Peace – and that most elusive of them all – Truth. I think also that this may be the reason that he places at the midpoint of the Mercilla canto the picture of the poet Malfont, with his tongue nailed to a post at the entry to the domain of Mercilla, at that very point in his poem where he is about to tell that which is not true about the kingdom he was celebrating.

Spenser saw to it that he failed the primary task of the historian – truth. He did so, it seems to me, in order to insist that he was playing for stakes higher than historical veracity, in which the virtues of Justice and Mercy achieve a Peace refuted by the Truth of our earthly achievements. He is asserting what he saw as the limits of the Four Daughters of God in the world in which he lived. At least that is what his poem seems to be telling me.

BLAKE'S CHAUCER: SCHOLASTICISM *POST LITTERAM*

STEFANIA D'AGATA D'OTTAVI

In 1809 William Blake decided to hold a public exhibition of some of his pictures and wrote a *Descriptive Catalogue* to accompany it and explain for the first time to the public his ideas about art, which had hitherto remained unknown. The Exhibition, which was a complete failure, like everything Blake did during his lifetime, included nine paintings and seven drawings, all accurately and polemically described in the *Catalogue*. The pictures are watercolours, or in Blake's words 'portable frescos', and the artist's violent rejection of the fashionable oil painting, extravagant as it is, has some extremely important theoretical implications. Blake writes:

> All Frescos are as high finished as miniatures or enamels, and they are known to be unchangeable; but oil being a body itself, will drink or absorb very little colour, and changing yellow, and at length brown, destroys every colour it is mixed with, especially every delicate colour...[1]

This is contrary to the artist's aim, which is explained at the very beginning of the *Descriptive Catalogue*:

> Clearness and precision have been the chief objects in painting these Pictures. Clear colours unmudded by oil, and firm and determinate lineaments unbroken by shadows, which ought to display and not to hide form...[2]

Permanence is what interests Blake as it interests Wordsworth, but while Wordsworth's archetypes belong to the natural world, Blake's belong to the spiritual existence, which to him is the only reality.[3]

The third picture in the Exhibition is labelled 'Sir Jeffrey Chaucer and the nine and twenty Pilgrims on their journey to Canterbury'. It is dated 1808 and was painted with the intention of providing a counterpart to the picture

---

[1] William Blake, 'A Descriptive Catalogue', in *Blake. Complete Works*, ed. G. Keynes (London, 1972), p. 566. All quotations from Blake's works, unless otherwise stated, are from this edition. Blake expresses the same ideas in his *Prospectus of the Engraving of Chaucer's Canterbury Pilgrims* (Keynes, pp. 586–590) and in his *Public Address* (Keynes, pp. 591–604).
[2] *A Descriptive Catalogue*, p. 564.
[3] William Blake, *A Descriptive Catalogue* (Oxford and New York, 1990).

representing the same subject by Thomas Stothard, a painter working under the protection of the publisher Robert Hartley Cromek, who had, in Blake's opinion, 'stolen' his idea and painted the picture before him. The picture, which Blake later engraved, is tempera on canvas and measures 18½ inches by 53¾ inches (i.e. 46.4 cm by 136.5 cm); it is in fairly good condition although faded in colour, and is part of the Stirling-Maxwell Collection at Pollok House, Glasgow (Plate 9).[4]

Blake claims fidelity to Chaucer's description of the Pilgrims, and often quotes from the *Prologue* of the *Canterbury Tales* to justify the way he represents them.[5] For example, the Knight and the Squire lead the procession, while the Reeve ends it, as Chaucer says. However, after this outward compliance with his source, the order and the way the Pilgrims are represented and described suit the painter's own purposes which, I shall argue, are not only quite different from those of the medieval poet, as could well be expected, but unconscious of, or uninterested in, the new attitude Chaucer and his age show toward nature and knowledge. The fact is that when Blake wrote his *Descriptive Catalogue* almost all his major poetry had been composed and his system had reached completeness and maturity. He therefore looked at literary and pictorial traditions from the point of view of the symbolic system he had developed. This seems to revive, in a strangely interesting way, some of the ideas Chaucer's age and Chaucer himself were abandoning, slowly and unobtrusively, as the way is with the Middle Ages, but still definitely, while pretending to give credit to tradition and authority.

After giving the order in which the pilgrims are presented, Blake adds:

> The characters of Chaucer's Pilgrims are the characters which compose all ages and nations: as one age falls, another rises, different to mortal sight, but to immortals only the same; for we see the same characters repeated again and again, in animals, vegetables, minerals, and in men; nothing new occurs in identical existence; Accident ever varies, Substance can never suffer change nor decay. Of Chaucer's characters, as described in his Canterbury Tales, some of the names or titles are altered by time, but the characters themselves for ever remain unaltered, and consequently they are the physiognomies of universal human life, beyond which Nature never steps. Names alter, things never alter. I have known multitudes of those who would have been monks in the age of monkery, who in the deistical age are deists. As Newton numbered the stars, and as Linneus numbered the plants,

---

[4] I am greatly indebted to Mrs Winnie Tyrrell, of Pollok House Photolibrary, for her kindness in having Blake's painting photographed and for sending me photographs and slides in a very short time.

[5] The edition of Chaucer actually used by Blake is still the subject of debate. Blake often quoted from memory and it is always difficult to find the exact source of his quotations. However, Alexander Gourlay has convincingly argued that Blake used the 1687 Speght edition of Chaucer's works. See A. Gourlay, 'What was Blake's Chaucer?', *Studies in Bibliography* 42 (1989) 272–283.

so Chaucer numbered the classes of men. The Painter has consequently varied the heads and forms of his personages into all Nature's varieties; the Horses he has also varied according to their Riders, the Costume is correct according to authentic monuments.[6]

The characters, therefore, represent the whole of human life, not at a certain period, but in eternity, and this is emphasized by the comparison with scientific discoveries and classifications. The representation of the pilgrims must therefore be absolutely consistent with their transcendent and eternal significance.

A first glance at the picture will show that the procession coming out of the Gothic archway of the Tabard Inn is composed, with few exceptions, of stiff, hieratic and dignified figures which surely remind us that Blake had started his career with his apprenticeship to the engraver James Basire, who had made him study and reproduce the Gothic monuments in Westminster Abbey, but also that his Pilgrims are not meant to represent temporal characters, but the eternal nature of man.

Before coming to what is really Blakean about this representation, we should notice that in his interpretation the painter was less far from tradition than might be thought at first. The idea that the Canterbury Pilgrims represent the immutable nature of mankind is well established in eighteenth-century criticism. In the *Preface* to his *Fables Ancient and Modern* (1700), Dryden, although he accepts the idea that Chaucer's barbaric strength has to be 'methodized', writes of the Pilgrims:

> . . . Their general characters are still remaining in mankind, and even in England, though they are called by other names than those of monks, and friars, and canons, and lady abbesses, and nuns; for mankind is ever the same, and nothing lost out of nature, though everything is altered.[7]

And, at the end of the century, in 1776 Sir John Hawkins expresses the same idea:

> Chaucer . . . has feigned an assemblage of persons of different ranks, the most various and artful that can be imagined, and with an amazing propriety has made each of them the type of a peculiar character.[8]

If examined further these writings would show a tendency to sort out pairs of Pilgrims according to their characters and an attention to physiognomy which gives their descriptions almost a pictorial quality (*Ut pictura poesis*) that Blake must surely have found interesting. But here the similarities end. Blake

---

6   *A Descriptive Catalogue*, p. 567.
7   John Dryden, *Fables Ancient and Modern*, ed. Keith Walker (Oxford, 1987), p. 563.
8   Quoted in Betsy Bowden, 'The Artistic and Interpretive Context of Blake's "Canterbury Pilgrims" ', *Blake: An Illustrated Quarterly* 13 (1980) 164–180.

adds to these views his own peculiar 'visionary' outlook and his theory of contraries, on the existence of which all knowledge is based. Chaucer's list of Pilgrims is therefore transformed by Blake into a complex allegory of life, where the classicist belief in the imitation of nature is thoroughly discarded (as his *Annotations to Sir Joshua Reynolds's 'Discourses'* show): his Muses, he says, are not the Daughters of Mnemosyne, or Memory, but of Beulah, or Imagination.

He takes advantage of the Prologue's ambiguity: the narrator describes the Pilgrims *before* they start for Canterbury, and the order in which they are mentioned is not necessarily the one in which they ride, so the painter is relatively free to invent his own, and this Blake does by following his archetypal mythology. Mankind is here 'divided' – so to speak – into nine and twenty characters, the division being the consequence of the loss of eternal life after the original sin and the Fall. Each character is therefore eternal in two ways: it represents a single aspect of human nature, which – Blake says – never changes, and it is part of the 'Eternal Man' together with his fellow pilgrims. The pilgrimage itself symbolizes life: man comes from eternity and must return to it. The Gothic archway of the Tabard Inn, reminiscent of the tombs in Westminster Abbey Blake used to copy when apprenticed to Basire, is the place the Pilgrims will have to go back to, literally and symbolically. The whole pilgrimage thus becomes the journey of mankind. [9]

I anticipate here (but I will come to it later in greater detail) what seems to me to be a point of great interest in Blake's interpretation of Chaucer. This complex allegorical picture seems in some ways to go back to a 'scholastic' method of interpretation of both life and art. The transcendent and symbolic significance attributed to every detail, the idea that all the parts must fit in to form an organic whole is typical of the aspiration of the Schoolmen to bring all knowledge under the control of theology and to assign to art the aim of making the eternal truth known. The unity of sciences, the conception of theology as 'the science of sciences' (*scientia scientiarum*) is the subject of heated debates at the end of the thirteenth century and throughout the following age at the most important universites, and it is by no means taken as a matter of course by the intellectuals of the fourteenth century. The new logic and theory of language which had slowly developed during the thirteenth century had begun to argue against the existence of a single science and had begun to give value to 'secular' disciplines, which need not have the same aim as theology. An important consequence of this outlook is the interest in the observation of the world for its own sake, even when the study of nature does not seem to agree with the teachings of theology. Loss of universal knowledge, doubts as to the possibility of getting to know the world completely are the price that has to be paid for the independence of science. And if an overall

---

[9] Karl Kiralis, 'William Blake as an Intellectual and Spiritual Guide of Chaucer's "Canterbury Pilgrims" ', *Blake Studies* 1 (1969) 139–190.

picture of the world is called into question, the use of allegory becomes doubtful. This of course does not mean that allegorical poetry comes abruptly to an end, but simply that non-allegorical interpretations of poetry become possible.

Whether Blake was not aware of the new secular interest of Chaucer's age or he was not interested in it, the fact is that he seems to look exactly for those eternal meanings Chaucer's age was slowly setting aside (this is why I have called, somewhat paradoxically, his attitude 'Scholasticism *post litteram*')

It is a crucial point in Blake's system that knowledge can only exist in the fallen world if 'contraries' co-exist, eternally, always fighting against each other, never reduced to unity:

> Without Contraries is no progression. Attraction and Repulsion, Reason and Energy, Love and Hate, are necessary to human existence.

This is *The Marriage of Heaven and Hell*.[10] The Pilgrims are therefore usually represented in pairs, each having his or her counterpart in some place in the picture, sometimes more than one counterpart, according to the point of view from which they are observed. A look at the picture will show some of these symmetries. There is first a broad division into two halves provided by the figure of the Host, which separates people of higher rank from those belonging to a lower class.[11] The central position of Harry Bailey is the visual counterpart of the importance Chaucer gives him and of the role he plays in *The Canterbury Tales*. His gesture, which points to both parts of the procession, his left hand indicating the knight, the first to tell a tale, and his right the parson who is the last to tell his own, his imposing dimensions justify Blake's description of him:

> For the Host who follows this group, and holds the centre of the cavalcade, is a first rate character, and his jokes are no trifles; they are always, though uttered with audacity, and equally free with the Lord and the Peasant, they are always substantially and weightily expressive of knowledge and experience; Henry Baillie, the keeper of the greatest Inn, of the Greatest City; for such was the Tabard Inn in Southwark, near London: our Host was also a leader of the age.[12]

The attitude we have just seen explains also Blake's indulgence with 'negative' characters: their 'eternal' significance implies that both positive and negative are necessary to the progress toward eternity.

Blake achieves the symmetry he is after in various ways: physical propinquity (i.e. two or more Pilgrims actually riding together), position of

---

[10] William Blake, *The Marriage of Heaven and Hell* (Keynes, p. 149).
[11] Clare Pace, 'Blake and Chaucer. "Infinite Variety of Character" ', *Art History* 3 (1980) 388–409.
[12] *A Descriptive Catalogue*, p. 569.

the body, details of dress, and, as far as can be gathered from the rather faded condition of the picture, colour contrast or concordance.

The Parson and the Pardoner form a pair, though they are at some distance from each other: they are both represented in profile, right profile the Parson, left profile the Pardoner who seems to look at him defiantly: the one is pure goodness ('an Apostle, a real Messenger of Heaven, sent in every Age for its light and its warmth'), the other pure evil ('The Age's Knave, who always commands and domineers over the high and low vulgar'), but still they have something in common ('But alas! you will not distinguish him – i.e. the Parson from the Friar or the Pardoner, they are also "full solemn men", and their counsel, you will continue to follow').[13] The Prioress and the Wife of Bath also form a pair, riding midway in the front half and in the back half of the procession. The Knight and the Squire, who lead it, have their counterparts in the Poet and the Philosopher, who are at the end.

Symmetries are, however, not merely binary, nor are they merely visual: affinities and contrasts intersect throughout the picture in a very complex way, and verbal symmetries in the *Descriptive Catalogue* provide additional links among the Pilgrims: The Wife of Bath is defined 'a scourge and a blight' and is explicitly opposed to the Prioress:

> The characters of Women Chaucer has divided into two classes, the Lady Prioress and the Wife of Bath. Are not these leaders of the ages of men? The lady prioress in some ages predominates; and in some the wife of Bath, in whose character Chaucer has been equally minute and exact; because she is also a scourge and a blight...[14]

But this expression is also used for the Pardoner:

> This man is sent in every age for a rod and a scourge, and for a blight, for a trial of man, to divide the classes of men...[15]

so as to relate the two characters by similarity, whereas the Prioress and the Wife of Bath are related by contrast. The Prioress/Second Nun pair is contrasted by the Pardoner/Summoner pair, who are instead related by verbal likeness. The Physician and the Man of Law form a pair balanced by the Monk and the Friar: the word *master* is used by Blake for these four characters.[16] Blake sometimes gives full account of the reasons which have induced him to place his Pilgrims at a certain position of the procession: for example, the Sergeant at Law rides between the Plowman and his brother the Parson:

---

[13] *A Descriptive Catalogue*, p. 570.
[14] Ibid., p. 572.
[15] Ibid., p. 570.
[16] Bowden, p. 185.

> . . . as I wish men of Law would always ride with them, and take their counsel, especially in all difficult points.[17]

And Blake goes on:

> The Doctor of Physic is in this groupe, and the Franklin, the voluptous country gentleman, contrasted with the Physician . . .[18]

After which we come to important generalizations:

> Chaucer's characters live age after age. Every age is a Canterbury Pilgrimage; we all pass on, each sustaining one or other of these characters; nor can a child be born, who is not one of these characters of Chaucer . . . Thus the reader will observe that Chaucer makes everyone of his characters, perfect in his kind, every one in an Antique Statue . . . the Franklin the Bacchus; as the Doctor of Physic is the Esculapius, the Host is the Silenus, the Squire is the Apollo, the Miller is the Hercules, etc. Chaucer's characters are a description of the eternal principles that exist in all ages . . . Chaucer has divided the ancient character of Hercules between his Miller and his Plowman . . . The Plowman of Chaucer is Hercules in his supreme eternal state, divested of his spectrous shadow, which is the Miller, a terrible fellow, such as exists in all times and places, for the trial of men, to astonish every neighbourhood, with brutal strength and courage, to get rich and powerful to curb the pride of Man . . . Visions of these eternal principles or characters of human life appear to poets, in all ages . . .[19]

The comparison of the characters of the Pilgrims to the Greek Gods makes Blake's meaning clearer: we now see that to him *The Canterbury Tales* are not merely an allegory of Chaucer's age, but a picture of the 'eternal principles' always acting in nature. In his own mythology the loss of Eden has resulted in what the poet calls 'fall into division', some sort of splitting of the original unity of man (Albion) into four parts (the 'zoas'), four mythological characters always fighting to achieve control over Albion. Every aspect of human life is thus composed of contrasting principles, unity being impossible in the fallen world. This is specially evident in the last pair of characters he describes, i.e. the Clerk of Oxford and 'Chaucer'. He has described Chaucer before as 'the great poetical observer of men, who in every age is born to record and eternize its acts . . .', but now he sets him against the 'philosopher':

> This character (i.e. the Clerk) varies from that of Chaucer, as the contemplative philosopher varies from the poetical genius. There are always these two classes of learned sages, the poetical and the philosophical. The painter has put them side by side, as if the youthful clerk had put himself

---

[17] *A Descriptive Catalogue*, p. 570.
[18] Ibid., p. 570.
[19] Ibid., p. 571.

under the tuition of the mature poet. Let the Philosopher always be the servant and scholar of inspiration and all will be happy.[20]

The last part of the *Descriptive Catalogue* contains an attack on Stothard, the rival painter. I will not analyse this in detail, but a few remarks will show clearly why Stothard's painting could not be acceptable to Blake, apart from the personal polemical note. Stothard's is an oil painting, and this would in itself be enough to meet with Blake's disapproval: the blurring of the outline caused by the use of oil colours leaves everything indistinct; now in Blake's theory, true knowledge, which is attained by means of imagination, consists of separation: the indifferentiated cannot be known, the human mind proceeds by division:

> Nature has no Outline, but Imagination has. Nature has no Tune, but Imagination has. Nature has no Supernatural and dissolves: Imagination is Eternity.[21]

Besides, Stothard's pilgrims are human beings, not eternal principles. His picture has a theatrical and dramatic organization which is 'human' and not 'eternal'. He therefore accuses Stothard of 'betraying' Chaucer's intentions and this he does in his usual plain language:

> When men cannot read, they should not pretend to paint . . . all is misconceived and its mis-execution is equal to its misconception.[22]

A correspondence between Blake's interpretation of Chaucer's Pilgrims and his own mythological characters could easily be established. If we did so, we would find that the Wife of Bath is represented as The Whore of Babylon or that the Prioress is similar to Tirzah or that 'Chaucer' has something in common with Los, and that the adjective 'mild' for the young Squire recalls one of Blake's most important symbols of innocence.[23] But what seems to me more important is the fact that the system he had been building induces Blake to interpret Chaucer's Pilgrims in terms of abstracted one-sided characters. If they must each have their 'contrary' or 'spectrum', as sometimes Blake calls it, each must represent *one* aspect of life and the more restricted, the better. As a consequence of this, he ignores the ambiguity of Chaucer's characters and divides 'positive' and 'negative' traits by creating characters either wholly 'good' or wholly 'bad', while in Chaucer the *same* character possesses contrasting connotations to the point of making it purposely unpracticable to decide whether he is 'good' or 'bad', thus rendering moral judgement impossible.[24] Blake's plurality of symbols always refers to the 'eternal' type,

---

[20] *A Descriptive Catalogue*, p. 572.
[21] William Blake, *The Ghost of Abel* (Keynes, p. 779).
[22] *A Descriptive Catalogue*, p. 575.
[23] Bowden, p. 187.
[24] Jill Mann, *Chaucer and Medieval Estates Satire* (Cambridge, 1973).

or the archetype, while in Chaucer the referent is human, mutable and ambiguous and all the way through the medieval poet seems to be wondering what nature is like and whether knowledge of nature and mankind is possible to man.

I will try to analyse two aspects of the deep changes in the theory of knowledge I have mentioned before. The first is more general and concerns sign theory and language, the second is more closely related to art.

It is well known that Scholasticism had attempted to reconcile Aristotle's thought with Christian doctrine and had set up a complex system which has been compared to a Gothic Cathedral (Panofski).[25] At the end of the thirteenth century some outstanding philosophical personalities, the most famous of whom, but by no means the only one, is William of Ockham, had begun to question the validity of the assumptions which formed the basis of the doctrine, and new theories had been developed which questioned the unity of sciences and the privileged place of theology. The relatively recent discovery of new theological and philosophical texts together with a closer study of the older ones has clearly shown that these masters do not deny that there is *one* truth and that this is contained in the Holy Text. They simply state that the search for eternal truths is not the object of philosophical research and must be left to theologians; but the study of secular sciences has a dignity and an independence of its own and must be pursued without trying to reconcile it with the teaching of theology. It is not even certain that the human mind can arrive at Truth: research 'ut naturalis' – says Nicholas of Autrecourt concerns not the realm of Truth, but that of the probable.[26] In the words of Etienne Gilson, the last years of the thirteenth century witness the end of the honeymoon between philosophy and theology.[27] One very important consequence of this transformation is the distinction between 'logica fidei' and 'logica naturalis', a distinction which did not escape the Church's attention in the person of the Archbishop of Paris, Etienne Tempier, who labelled it 'the theory of double truth' and in 1277 condemned its articles and the *artistae* who had promoted them.[28]

All this is relevant to literature in a number of ways. First of all, artist means 'magister artium', i.e. 'philosopher' and the relationship between literature and philosophy (from Gower's 'philosophical Chaucer' to the mention of philosophers – Strode and Bradwardine, for instance – in Chaucer's works) is well known to medievalists. Second, and more important, there is a gradual change in the subjects of literary works, and their aim is no

---

[25] Erwin Panofski, *Gothic Architecture and Scholasticism* (2nd edn, Princeton, 1957).
[26] E.A. Moody, 'Ockham, Buridan and Nicholas of Autrecourt', *Franciscan Studies* 7 (1947) 113–146.
[27] Etienne Gilson, *History of Christian Philosophy in the Middle Ages* (London, 1955), p. 165.
[28] Roland Hissette, *Enquete sur les 219 articles condamnés à Paris le 7 Mars 1277* (Louvain-Paris, 1949), p. 238.

longer exclusively the revelation of truth, which we have seen to be probably unattainable by the human mind.

The relative freedom acquired by secular art – in spite of the always formally declared edifying aim – gives intellectual experience a value of its own, while on the other hand, it sets its limitations much more clearly. Doubt takes the place of certainty: freedom has a price. The notion of *sign* and of linguistic sign in particular changes significantly. Augustine had given it a symbolic value ('Signum est enim res, prater speciem quam ingerit sensibus, aliud aliquid ex se faciens in cognitionem venire'),[29] thus establishing a one-to-one relationship between the word (if we limit ourselves to verbal signs) and what it represents. The way this definition suits medieval philosophy up to Scholasticism is evident: everything in the world (and in texts) recalls something which is beyond nature; poetry, in particular, reveals what lies beyond the *integumentum*, i.e. supernatural realities. Examples are Guillaume de Conches' *Commentary* on Macrobius,[30] the first part of the *Roman de la Rose*, where the characters of Guillaume de Lorris are symbols of abstract qualities. In the second part Jean de Meun's refusal of all allegorical interpretations (of dreams, for instance) and the insistence on the literal interpretation of natural phenomena are certainly not a rejection of the supernatural, but the statement that it is not the object of the intellectual activity of philosophers. Their task, in the words of Boethius of Dacia, is the study of the soul within the body, while the theologian's field of analysis is the soul separated from the body.

These ideas have an interesting – but not unexpected – counterpart in the divorce between grammar and logic which occurs in language theory. The study of the word, not as a grammatical category (i.e. noun, adjective, etc.), but within the context of the proposition (terminist logic), which had begun as early as the twelfth century, was revived and greatly modified during the thirteenth and fourteenth centuries. Grammar shows the way individual languages work, logic is concerned with the way *language* works – Robert Holkot says, and according to him the object of philosophical enquiry is not reality, but language.[31] The sign is defined in terms of *suppositio*, that is what takes the place of objects within the proposition. The expression *supponit pro*, i.e. 'stands for', becomes one of the most frequently encountered in the writings of the philosophers. The relationship between the forest of signs and reality (*res extra*, in Ockham's words) is by no means certain: the ambiguity of language cannot guarantee a consistent and unambiguous knowledge of reality, and the question arises whether it can be known at all (we have seen Holkot's extreme position). In the fourteenth century literary works show very clearly that the intellectuals are thoroughly aware of the problem.

---

[29] Augustine, *De Doctrina Christiana*, ed. G. Combès and J. Farges (Paris, 1949), p. 238.
[30] Peter Dronke, *Fabula* (Leiden und Koln, 1985).
[31] William Courtenay, *Schools and Scholars in Fourteenth-Century England* (Princeton, 1987).

I shall briefly concentrate again on the *Prologue* of *The Canterbury Tales*, as this is the main object of Blake's analysis, and shall try to show in what way the Pilgrims are – so to speak – the product of the separation between philosophy and theology.

The new logic, we have seen, has its foundations in sign theory and is a development of 'terminist logic', i.e. of a kind of logic which analyses the word within the context of the proposition, where it stands for the object (*supponit pro*). But if the meaning of the word depends on the kind of proposition it belongs to, it can no longer be absolute, eternal and immutable; meanings become, to say the least, questionable. Moreover, what object does the word stand for? The relationship between word and object is no longer universal. The problem arises: how far can words describe reality? Is there an element of ambiguity in every statement?

In showing people who represent the class they belong to, but also who do not completely fulfil the conventions of the classification, Chaucer seems to question the clichés according to which the social classes are normally labelled and to wonder whether things are more complicated than they look. When he describes comic aspects of his pilgrims he does not seem to be making fun of individuals, but of a too simplistic and stereotyped view of a class. His characters are not entirely 'good' or 'bad', but a mixture of positive and negative qualities, thus making an absolute point of view impossible.

Chaucer invents some peculiar technical devices to show the ambiguity of his characters. I will mention only some of them. First of all, he applies the same word to different people. *Courteisie*, for example, does not indicate the same quality when applied to the Knight and to the Squire: in the father it corresponds to an ideal of heroic life, in the son it refers to love. The same word is also used for the Prioress and there it refers to her good manners; the Friar, a different character indeed, is 'curteys'.[32] So, what is *courteisie* after all? It does not stand for a single quality, but its meaning depends on the context in which it is used and on the character to whom it is attributed. This confers ambiguity on *both* the quality *and* the character.

The Prioress has many of the qualities which can traditionally be attributed to a nun, but she is also shown to be a woman of high rank, and of a kind of beauty which is not only spiritual: 'Hir mouth ful smal and therto softe and reed'(153). So the crowned A on her gold brooch and the sentence *Amor vincit omnia* leave reasonable doubt that *love* does not stand for the love of God only. This is not merely a separation of the religious and the secular, but a mixture of both values in a character which should be the symbol of spiritual love. In a similar way, the love-knot of the Monk is mentioned immediately after the character's inclination toward worldly pleasures, and immediately before his eyes that *stemed as a forneys* are described (202). The Friar is *worthy* and so are the young women of his town whose marriages he made *at*

---

[32] *The Riverside Chaucer*, gen. ed. Larry D. Benson (Oxford, 1988), pp. 23–36.

his owne cost. But *worthy* is also used for the Merchant, meaning that he has, to the highest degree, the qualities of the class he belongs to. But what are these qualities? The solemnity with which he speaks his mind may either come from his dignified personality or from his intention to conceal his true nature under a pompous way of speaking.

Another way of showing the ambiguity of the Pilgrims is to present them as they *appear*: the Sergeant at Law is entirely described from this point of view. Nothing is explicitly told about his activities. The description is centred on his professional skill, but nothing is said of the way he puts this to use. The reputation he enjoys is emphasized, but this is because he *semed* competent. He is said to be often in court, to have many cases to deal with, *And yet he semed bisier than he was* (322), which seems to contradict the preceding lines. But, what does 'bisier' mean? Jill Mann has shown that the word had a wider semantic field than it has now. Is it possible that it had a derogatory connotation, like the modern word 'busybody'? A similar ambiguity can be detected in the word *purchasour*. Did he buy land on behalf of other people who trusted his knowledge of the law, or did he buy it for himself both because he had become rich in a more or less honest way and because he could use his legal expertise to make good bargains, possibly at the expense of less skilled people? The exploration of the implications of these words only shows how difficult it is to throw light on the activity of this shifty character.[33]

Traditional symbols of innocence are often applied to activities the innocence of which is – to say the least – doubtful. The beard of the Franklyn is *Whit . . . as is the dayesye* (332), and provides a contrast with his sanguine complexion. The abundance of food in his house, a sign of his gluttony, is emphasized by the word *snewed*. The dagger and the purse are part of his array, but they are also symbols of violence and bribery. The contrasting qualities of this pilgrim are repeated in the mention of Epicurus and Saint Julian, with both of whom he is compared. But the mention of Epicurus, although relatively traditional, is important within the context of the *Prologue*. The expression *felicitee parfit* (338) is the English translation of *Summum bonum*: every pilgrim has his own idea of what perfect happiness consists of, and as they are outstanding specimens of the class they belong to, this means that the idea of *summum bonum* varies according to social class, and is related to interests and professions; therefore it can be neither an absolute value nor a transcendent one. The Shipman is called *a good felawe*, which must refer to his ability in his calling, not to his moral character about which we are left with no illusions. He may be 'good', but he is certainly not *nyce*, being a thief and a murderer. His ability in sailing his ship, thus saving himself from drowning, is equal to his ability to 'send by water' his enemies, i.e. drown others. Let us for a moment go back to Blake's description of this character and the difference will be evident:

---

[33] Mann, p. 91.

The Shipman or sailor is a genius of Ulyssean art; but with the highest courage suparadded.[34]

The Parson and the Plowman are brothers in more than one meaning: the family connection and the fulfilment of the Christian ideal. They both help the poor, the Parson spiritually, the Plowman materially. The Parson is described as a character of such perfection as to seem 'too good to be true'. Litotes is the prevailing figure of speech in the description of this character: we are told what he was not, as if to imply that he is an exception among the representatives of his class. There is at first sight little ambiguity in the Miller: his connotations are entirely on the negative side. But just because it is impossible to find even one positive quality in him, the difficulty does not lie in distinguishing between his good and bad qualities, but in deciding whether he is a human being at all. Ram, sowe, foxe, bristles are explicitly mentioned in his portrait, while his human aspects show a degraded sort of humanity: he steals, uses foul language, and yet knows how to make profit for his master and for himself.

In trying to show that the words Chaucer uses to introduce the Pilgrims can be interpreted in different ways according to the contexts they belong to, the figure of the Clerk must receive special attention, because it appears to be particularly interesting for what I am trying to demonstrate. First of all, he is a philosopher, he certainly studies logic and probably prepares to study theology. In her analysis of this character Jill Mann has observed that for him study seems an end in itself as nothing is said about the aim of studying and teaching which in the conventional presentation of philosophers is that of achieving the *summum bonum*.[35] But this is exactly the point: the *summum bonum* is not necessarily a transcendent one after the 'honeymoon' between philosophy and theology has come to an end. Happiness can be achieved in this world, independently of man's immortal destiny. Research *ut naturalis* is just as possible and rewarding as theological research: methods and aims can be different, but they are equally justified. This is the doctrine Siger of Brabant, Boethius of Dacia and other 'Averroists' had been teaching at Paris and Oxford Universities, and which had been condemned by Tempier. Among these intellectuals, it is Boethius of Dacia who deals with the problem in greater detail. In his short treatise *De Summo Bono* he argues that knowledge can give perfect happiness and can be obtained in this world. Philosophical research has its own field of analysis and its results need not necessarily be consistent with those obtained by theology. The nature of the *summum bonum* can be understood by reason alone.[36]

No wonder the Church found it dangerous and condemned it, but it resisted

---

34 *A Descriptive Catalogue*, p. 571.
35 Mann, p. 76.
36 Boethius of Dacia, 'De Summo Bono', *Corpus philosophorum Danicorum Medii Aevi*, VI (Copenhagen, 1976), pp. 369–377.

persecution and influenced the writings of authors such as Cavalcanti, Dante, Jean de Meun and Chaucer. The fourteenth century was acutely aware that the harmony between man and the world could no longer be taken for granted. The analogy between what is finite and what is infinite is impossible: the *logica fidei* and the *logica naturalis* develop along different lines. Nature is no longer the mirror of the creator. Jean de Meun's Nature is not Alain de Lille's.

As a consequence of this new world picture, it is now possible to understand why allegory tends to lose some of its importance. Allegory is based on a close correspondence between objects and between the objects and the words which represent them: every word must be the sign of something definite and immutable. No allegory is possible if the sign is ambiguous. We have seen how this works in the *Prologue* of the *Canterbury Tales*. What Blake does is to build an allegory out of Chaucer's Prologue, an allegory based on his own mythology and on his own conviction of the eternity of human nature. He makes Chaucer's Pilgrims the abstract representatives of Mankind at all times and in all places, the eternal contraries which exist in the fallen world and which make knowledge possible. In ignoring the ambiguity of Chaucer's characters, Blake has revived, though in a different context, the ideal the Schoolmen had pursued for such a long time.

BROWNING'S MEDIEVALISM

ANGELO RIGHETTI

An exhaustive reading of Browning's medievalism is beyond the scope of this paper: what is proposed here is a fresh investigation through significant specimens into its relevance and uses within an oeuvre covering fifty-seven years of poetic activity and foreshadowing the Victorian revival – often a revision – of medieval themes, figures, settings, in painting (the Preraphaelites), in poetry (Rossetti, Morris, Tennyson, Swinburne), in prose (Carlyle, Ruskin),[1] a revival that had been partly carried out, as regards the approach and working methods, in some very popular historical romances by Scott (*Ivanhoe*, 1819, *Quentin Durward*, 1823, *The Betrothed* and *The Talisman*, 1825). *Sordello* (published in 1840, but composed between 1833 and 1839) – in spite of the poet's later statement to the contrary that the eponymous hero's historical background is mere 'decoration'[2] – can be associated to them for its combination of fictional organization and perusal of 'documentary' sources. As it stands the poem is a major experiment and the noblest failure in Browning's 'medieval' poetics, as it gives indirect evidence of the poet's awareness of his 'belated' romanticism (I'm using the qualifier in Harold Bloom's sense), besides betraying the consciousness that in the poem 'there is too much inexperience of life' (Keats's words expressing his dissatisfaction with his medievalist rewrite of Boccaccio's tale, *Isabella, or, the Pot of Basil*, 1820).

At this stage of Browning's life and writing experience amounts to the vicarious one derived from most disparate, encyclopaedic reading, extending from the volumes of *Biographie universelle* (1811–1822) to the *Wonders of the Little World* by Wanley (1678), from the romantic poets (Shelley, Byron, Keats, Coleridge, Wordsworth, in order of preference) to Shakespeare, Spenser and Chaucer (that he boasted he could quote from memory), from the Bible to *The Pilgrim's Progress* to books of sermons and devotions, from

---

[1] Cf. A. Chandler, *A Dream of Order* (London, 1970). *Browning Institute Studies*, 1980 (a special issue on 'Victorian Medievalism'). M. Girouard, *The Return to Camelot* (New Haven and London, 1981). A.H. Harrison, *Swinburne's Medievalism* (Baton Rouge, 1988).

[2] Cf. Browning's dedication of *Sordello* to his French friend J. Milsand in the 1863 edition of *The Poetical Works*: 'The historical decoration was purposely of no more importance than a background requires; and my stress lay on the incidents in the development of a soul: litle else is worth study', in I. Jack, ed., *Browning. Poetical Works 1833–1864* (Oxford, 1975), p. 157.

Homer's epic to treatises like *The Art of Painting* by the Dutch artist Gerard de Lairesse, to the lives of artists narrated by Vasari or Baldinucci or Bellori: in short, a range of reading that saturates the poet's mental space in his formative years.[3]

An integral and influential part of Browning's reading curriculum is constituted by Dante[4] who provides him with the title character and the story (the stories) of *Sordello*, but also with a model for many of his love poems written between 1840 and 1855 (*Dramatic Lyrics*, 1842; *Dramatic Romances and Lyrics*, 1845; *Men and Women*, 1855). From the Florentine, his circle and earlier troubadour poets Browning derives, reshapes and reelaborates a set of topoi expressive of emotional, intellectual and 'philosophical' attitudes to be adapted to his own existential journey, preoccupations, and/or double binds, and carries out intertextual operations that benefit from the 'rereadings' and 'misreadings' of Dante passed on by an ideal chain of readers including Chaucer, Renaissance and metaphysical poets, romantic poets, Byron and Shelley especially.

Lyrical motifs from the occitanian tradition are developed in various *loci* of Browning's poetry as is evident in 'Eyes, calm beside thee . . .',[5] an early sonnet reminiscent of Dante's '*Tanto gentile e tanto onesta pare . . .*' and '*Dei tuoi begli occhi il molto acuto strale . . .*',[6] but with the interpolation of a contrast between the Lady's admirers voicing their admiration, and the poetic I's *amor de lonh* characterized by silence and tears. In other poems the theme of passion is revisited as both an idealization of the loved one and a source of suffering in a style modelled on Jaufré Rudel's famous lines: 'I am stricken by joy that slays me, / and by a pang of love which ravishes my flesh,/ whence will my body waste away' (cf. Browning's 'Rudel to the Lady of Tripoli' or 'Time's Revenges').[7] Or the poet's emotional tension is attuned to Cavalcanti's love poems (for instance, '*Tu m'hai sì piena di dolor la mente . . .*': 'You filled my mind with grief') in which the '*donna umile*', i.e. willing to reciprocate her lover, turns into a '*fiera donna, che niente / par che pietate di te voglia udire . . . Io vo' come colui ch'è fuor di vita*' ('a ruthless woman deaf to your sighs / and who won't pity you . . . I go like one who's lifeless'),

---

3 Cf. W.C. DeVane, *A Browning Handbook* (New York, 1955). J. Maynard, *Browning's Youth* (Cambridge, Mass., 1977).
4 Cf. S. Ellis, *Dante and English Poetry. Shelley to T.S. Eliot* (Cambridge, 1983), pp. 66–101.
5 See it in R. Browning, *The Poems*, ed. by J. Pettigrew, supplemented and completed by T.J. Collins (New Haven and London, 1981), vol. 2, p. 940. See also my comments on the sonnet in R. Browning, *Poems / Poesie* (Milan, 1990), pp. 336–37.
6 Cf. Dante Alighieri, *Vita Nuova. Rime*, ed. by F. Chiappelli (Milano, 1965); all quotations hereafter are taken from this edition.
7 Translation by Harrison, *Swinburne's Medievalism*, pp. 30–31. See also, J. Rudel, *Les chansons*, ed. by A. Jeanroy (Paris, 1965).

so that the power of love brings about a life bordering on death, in Rossetti's words, 'a continual death in love' (cf. *'Donna me prega . . .'*).[8] Echoes of such strained emotional attitudes are to be heard in Browning's 'Time's Revenges', 'A Woman's Last Word', 'Serenade at the Villa', and 'Women and Roses', whereas in 'By the Fire-Side' (cf. st. XLIV–XLVI)[9] the poet makes a restatement of Dante's 'ontological promotion of the lover'(s)[10] as the love of woman is the supreme goal, love fulfilled the 'moment one and infinite'(l. 181).

This 'philosophy' is renewed in 'The Last Ride together' (st. II, III, IX),[11] with its metaphysics of love that 'deifies' the lover (l. 21) in an exaltation of the concept and poetic practice of love vassalage.[12] Moreover, an original contribution to the time-honoured love poetry of the Provençal tradition revitalized by the poets of the Dolce Stil Nuovo, Dante and Petrarca (and later in England, by metaphysical poetry) is given by Browning in a few poems singing love as separation and absence from the loved woman, in an attempt to suggest an intermittent dialogue with a lover who is present and yet absent, far and near, abstract and concrete, living and dead, as is the case with 'Two in the Campagna', or 'One Way of Love', and, after Elizabeth Barrett's death, with 'Prospice', 'Amphibian', and 'St Martin's Summer'.[13] In the latter lyrics Browning tends to gradually reduce the impact of Dante's metaphysics of love (cf. *Vita nuova*) considered as a *figura* of divine love, by privileging the paradox of a living, physical presence of the absent, dead lover that is its own metaphor and justification.

In the context of Browning's medieval poetics 'Childe Roland to the Dark Tower Came' deserves a special mention, albeit a cursory one here, as it has

---

[8] For the text of Cavalcanti's poems quoted here, cf. G. Contini, ed., *Letteratura italiana delle origini* (Firenze, 1970), pp. 164–65 and 171–75. Rossetti's words are the title of his translation of Cavalcanti's *'Se m'hai del tutto obliato mercede . . .'* ('Though thou, indeed, hast quite forgotten ruth . . . '), in *The Early Italian Poets* (1861) (London, 1905), p. 282.

[9] Cf. R. Browning, *The Poems*, vol. 1, pp. 453, 539, 578, 702, and 552 respectively.

[10] Cf. Contini, *Letteratura italiana*, p. 300: *'l'amore promuove ontologicamente l'uomo e per analogia lo rende partecipe delle verità supreme'* ('love gives man an ontological promotion and by analogy lets him share supreme truths').

[11] Cf. Browning, *The Poems*, vol. 1, pp. 608–810.

[12] For a very perceptive discussion of the *durée* and metamorphoses of the concept of courtly love and its religious implications in Victorian literature, cf. J. Maynard, *Victorian Discourses on Sexuality and Religion* (Cambridge, 1993). For seminal studies on the subject, see C.S. Lewis, *The Allegory of Love* (Oxford, 1936) and D. de Rougemont, *Love in the Western World* (1940, originally in French: *L'amour et l'Occident*), Revised and Augmented Edition, tr. M. Belgion (Greenwich, Conn., 1956). For recent critical discussions on the topic, cf. E.T. Donaldson, 'The Myth of Courtly Love', in *Speaking of Chaucer* (New York, 1979), pp. 154–63. B. O'Donoghue, ed., *The Courtly Love Tradition* (Totowa, 1982). L. Benson, 'Courtly Love and Chivalry in the Later Middle Ages', in R. Yeager, ed., *Fifteenth Century Studies* (Hamden, 1984), pp. 237–57.

[13] Cf. Browning, *The Poems*, vol. 1, pp. 728, 734, 815; vol. 2, pp. 5 and 454.

been the object of much critical speculation.[14] The poem is connected with Arthurian romance, but the knight's quest has been metamorphosed and textualized into an existential one, as the form of the journey that still structures the narrative-descriptive monologue emphasizes the minority Victorian 'philosophy' of tension and effort instead of result and success.

While Arthurian matter is taken from Malory and *Sir Gawain and the Green Knight* (in the reminiscence of the quest for the Holy Grail and the Green Chapel respectively,[15] 'Childe Roland' 's inspiration and approach to the narrative is drawn from largely allegorical works such as the *Inferno* or *The Pilgrim's Progress*. But if Browning shrewdly recycles this reading he also makes use – as a 'reagent' for his modern version of romance – of an antiromance like *Don Quixote*, and, for the grotesque (ludicrous) overtones of certain passages (especially st. XXX e XXXI) even of Wordsworth's *Idiot Boy*. Besides, the poet's historical awareness of the decline and irretrievable loss of the age-long tradition of Arthurian romance, and his use of fictional material deliberately torn from its integrated, totalizing medieval *Weltanschauung* turn this material into the scattered tesserae of a mosaic whose grand design has ben dissolved. And the narrator/quester is only allowed to partially reorganize through his memory and confused mind a matter that is given by Roland an appearance of finality, although the story remains extremely fragmentary and contradictory and often resembles the transcription of oneiric processes.

Indeed, the knight's quest takes place in a 'waste land' (Barbara Melchiori's felicitous definition) conjured up by Browning with the analytical eye of a botanist, but the frequent use of the pathetic fallacy gives natural objects a ghostly aspect, so that details that appear hardly significant receive an almost metaphysical charge, sparked off by an absolute lack of time coordinates, as even the seasonal cycle of *Sir Gawain* is discarded. Rather, the cyclical movement is represented here by obsessive allusions to Dante's

---

[14] For a brief survey of the critical debate on 'Childe Roland' cf. Browning, vol. 1, pp. 117–18. Cf. H. Bloom's three major contributions to the debate: 'Browning's "Childe Roland"': All Things Deformed or Broken', in *The Ringers in the Tower* (Chicago, 1971), pp. 157–67; 'Testing the Map: Browning's "Childe Roland" in *A Map of Misreading*', (Oxford, 1975), pp. 106–22; 'Browning: Good Moments and Ruined Quests', in *Poetry and Repression. Revisionism from Blake to Stevens* (New Haven and London, 1976), pp. 175–204. See also, B. Melchiori, *Browning's Poetry of Reticence* (Edinburgh, 1968), esp. pp. 127–39, on the 'waste land' in 'Childe Harold'. A. Righetti, ed., R. Browning, *Poems / Poesie*, for a reappraisal of the poem and detailed annotations, pp. 371–76. F. Marucci, 'Nel labirinto delle isotopie: "Childe Roland to the Dark Tower Came" di Browning', in L. Innocenti, F. Marucci, P. Pugliatti, eds., *Semeia. Itinerari per Marcello Pagnini* (Bologna, 1994), pp. 331–43 (no acknowledgement of Bloom's work).

[15] Cf. ll. 2069–2210: the allusions are discussed for the first time in my annotations in Browning, *Poems / Poesie*, p. 375 (no acknowledgement of them in Marucci, 'Nel labirinto delle isotopie').

infernal circles and *bolge*.[16] Ultimately, the 'dark tower', a faint memory of long-lost myth and impossible quests (the Holy Grail, the Green Chapel) cannot become a symbol, and at the most it indicates the poet's anxiety at the Sisyphean task of restoring romance and its religious foundation to a bourgeois, skeptical age.

In *Sordello* Browning takes up the challenge of producing a fictional re-creation of the character Dante has fixed in the reader's memory for ever through a few touches in canto VI of the *Purgatorio* (ll. 58–72, *passim*) emphasizing his magnanimity, moral nobility and superiority: '*anima . . . sola soletta . . . anima lombarda . . . altera e disdegnosa, / E nel mover delli occhi onesta e tarda . . . ombra tutta in sè romita*' ('a spirit . . . Stands solitary . . . thou Lombard spirit . . . in high abstracted mood, / Scarce moving with slow dignity thine eyes': tr. H.F. Cary, 1812), and with some brief mentions in the following cantos (VII–IX). A poet, courtier, faithful advisor of princes and noble Ladies, a valiant soldier and leader, Sordello has all the features of a romance hero harmonizing many lives into one, and in this plenitude lies the troubadour's greatest attraction for Browning. But if it is true that Browning picks up this extraordinary suggestion from Dante – and scanty though strategic hints are given on Ezzelino the Tyrant in the *Inferno* (XII) and Cunizza in the *Paradiso* (IX) in the historical context of the struggle between Guelphs and Ghibellines in thirteenth century Italy – the Victorian poet must still come to terms with his 'betters', that is with the romantic heritage of subjectivity, both as self-consciousness and self-expressiveness – on the one hand, and with his own gradually vanishing faith in romantic self-portrayal and self-projection, even when they hide behind Byron's ironic mask, Don Juan – on the other.

Dante affords Browning the essential elements of a story, both historical and transfigured by a halo of romance, into whose details he enquires by wading through page after page of documentary-anecdotal accounts of political events in northern Italy during the thirteeenth century: the entry under Sordello in vol. 43 of *Biographie universelle* (1811–1822); G.B. Verci's *Storia degli Ecelini* (1779); L. Muratori's *Rerum Italicarum Scriptores* (1723–1751, vol. 8); S. Sismondi's *Républiques italiennes* (1809–1818); (incidentally, Byron considered Muratori and Sismondi required reading for his works on Italian matters of the past).[17] Through this reading the poet soon

---

[16] Cf. R.E. Sullivan, 'Browning's "Childe Roland" and Dante's "Inferno" ', *Victorian Poetry* V (1967) 296–302; for Browning's refunctionalization of some Dantean images and *loci* (not pointed out by Sullivan) from both the *Inferno* and *Purgatorio*, see my comments in Browning, *Poems / Poesie*, pp. 373–76, notes 8, 14, 15, 16, 18, 19, 20, 23, 31, 34.

[17] For a concise and satisfactory introduction to the sources, bibliographical and critical problems of *Sordello*, cf. Browning, *The Poems*, vol. 1, pp. 1039–41); see also the entries under Sordello, Ezzelino and Cunizza in *Enciclopedia dantesca* (Roma, 1970–1976), and Sordello, *Le poesie*, ed. by M. Boni (Bologna, 1954).

comes to realize that he risks getting lost in a maze, in a 'dark wood' of stories/histories conflicting with one another, in a number of versions of a multi-faceted personage, a recognized poet, courtier, knight errant, political leader. Actually, a superfetation of mostly fictional biographies relying on *very few* facts, namely, that Sordello was born at Goito near Mantua, that he was a troubadour (testified by a small collection of poems handed down the centuries), and who according to his near contemporary Rolandino da Padova's (Rolandini patavini) *Cronica in factis et circa facta Marchie Trivixane* had abducted Cunizza, wife of Guelph Count Rizzardo di San Bonifacio: 'mandato Eccelini sui patris, Sordellus de ipsius familia dompnam suam latenter a marito subtraxit'.[18]

On the slight evidence of this far from transparent incident the anonymous author of one *vida* (biographical outline) of Sordello constructs a romance akin to Paolo and Francesca's, telling us that when the poet was at Rizzardo di San Bonifacio's court '*el s'enamoret de la moiller del comte, et ella de lui*'.[19] Although he is reticent concerning the outcome of the affair, the 'biographer' actually develops a suggestion made by Rolandino who ends the story of the abduction with the suspicion that 'cum qua (i.e. Cunizza) in patris curia permanente dictum fuit ipsum Sordellum concubuisse', thus crediting the poet with a liaison Dante does not (*cannot*) mention, because Sordello is placed in the *Purgatorio* among late penitents who met with violent death (nor for that matter can he involve Cunizza as she is to appear among the elect in the IX canto of the *Paradiso* because her worldly passions have been redeemed by grace and have changed into divine love).

In various earlier accounts the singer of courtly love becomes the protagonist of a love affair and a romantic elopement against the will of Cunizza's family, and ends up being stabbed to death by Ezzelino's hired ruffians. In another variant to this romance Sordello is the son of a poor knight of Mantua, falls in love with Cunizza, elopes with her, then prefers war to love, proves valiant in Provence, and eventually makes an honourable marriage. Here the romance of sinful and adulterous love has been toned down to the traditional happy ending of comedy – lawful marriage – in what I

---

18   Quoted from E. Raimondi, *Metafora e storia. Studi su Dante e Petrarca* (Torino, 1970), p.136. Apart from the direct sources mentioned above Browning could get the information about Cunizza's elopement with Sordello from Cary's annotated edition of *The Divine Comedy*, entitled *The Vision: or Hell, Purgatory and Paradise of Dante Alighieri* (1819. In the Notes to the *Paradise* (IX) one can read: '(Cunizza) eloped from her first husband, Richard of St Boniface, in the company of Sordello . . . with whom she is supposed to have cohabited before marriage', a sentence that sounds like an exact translation of Rolandino's account cited above; quoted from Ellis, *Dante and English Poetry*, p. 91. Cary's blank verse translation was done in three stages: the *Inferno,* 1805; the *Purgatorio* and *Paradiso* were published in 1812, and the whole *Vision* was out in 1814. Lord Byron's wry comment on it was that Dante was 'slain' by his translator: cf. *Byron's Letters and Journals*, ed. by L.A. Marchand (London, 1973–1994), VII, p. 58.

19   Cf. M. Boni, *Sordello*, in *Enciclopedia Dantesca*, p. 1026.

would call, after Borges's fondness for paradoxical anachronisms, a Victorian version of romance. There is another version of the romance Browning had to deal with in his investigations into 'historico'-fictional sources, one that blends the intrigue of romance with the virtues of a 'Victorian' solution: Sordello, after resisting the advances and prayers of Beatrice, Ezzelino's sister, finally flees to Mantua, followed by her, disguised as a man (yet another staple device of comedy). He eventually marries her: it is worth noticing that here Cunizza is no longer involved as Sordello's lover, which allows Browning to fictionalize the heroine of his poem as Palma.

The core of romance meant as a scene of extreme, uncontrolled and transgressive experiences that cannot be reconciled[20] – the love affair of both historical and mythic Sordello and Cunizza – is not exploited in the way one would expect of Browning, i.e. to confront the reader with the oppositon between sympathy and judgement (compare the Paolo-Francesca episode and its source of inspiration, the romance of Lancelot and Guinevere), as is the case with 'My Last Duchess', or with *The Ring and the Book*, some twenty-five years later, where yet another abduction is the gist of the story (a priest, Caponsacchi, kidnaps an unhappily married woman, Pompilia!), in order to 'force' the reader to choose between a verdict of moral condemnation and one of acquittal based on emotional complicity.[21] Nor does Browning explore the motif of social inequality between Cunizza and the troubadour as a source of conflict and a real obstacle to the love relationship of Sordello and Palma, who, it should be noted, is *about* to be betrothed, *not* married to Rizzardo di San Bonifacio.

And yet, the melodramatic organization of a very fragmentary plot makes it compulsory for Browning's *inventio* to produce the denouement through which Sordello is recognized as the long-lost son of Taurello Salinguerra, and as such is invested with the leadership of the Ghibelline faction, only to meet with an unlikely tragic ending: Sordello is found dead by lover and father just on the eve of his achievement as a lover, as the leader of the Emperor's party, as a warrior, and after his triumph as a poet. Which goes to suggest that in post-Enlightenment times the re-creation of a hero out of its tessellated identities is no longer possible as it used to be for the Sordello of medieval history and legend, and Browning for his part obliquely admits his incapacity to deal with the 'hero' and the 'heroic' even in the terms and with the compromise worked out by Lord Byron or Shelley (the latter is conjured up at the beginning of the poem, only to disappear like the ghost of Hamlet's father).

The stories/history about Sordello have all the ingredients of romance, but Browning at this early stage of his poetic career is less interested in the hectic

---

[20] Cf. R. Chase, *The American Novel and Its tradition* (Garden City, N. Y.), 1957, p. 25 (quoting from H. James's 'Preface' to *The American*).

[21] Cf. R. Langbaum, *The Poetry of Experience* (1957) (Chicago, 1985), pp. 75–108 and 109–36.

sequence of events (adventure) and the conflict of situations (in his words, mere 'decoration') than in the 'development of a soul'. This means for him fathoming Sordello's soul, or mental states, in an attempt to trace out the stages of a *Bildung* through the contemplation rather than the achievement of growth and metamorphosis, through the contemplation of poses and role-playing in the troubadour's mind.

Despite a similarity in working methods, i.e. the exploration of half-historical, half-legendary sources, that associates him to Scott, Browning lacks Scott's zest for adventure, for coups de théâtre, for peripeteia, nor does he succeed in resuscitating remote public events (the struggle between Pope and Emperor, or the Guelph and Ghibelline factions) by writing the spiritual biography of the main character. Sordello, on account of his status, both historical and legendary, can theoretically serve as a *persona* to express Browning's spiritual autobiography, but the Victorian poet fails to propose and support it as an emblematic one in the way Lord Byron had done with Childe Harold, and above all with Don Juan, where the fictional hero's story, the Lord's personal history, and crucial phases of European History between 1789 and 1822 are magically reconciled and made significant to one another and to the reader.[22]

Even though the subject and the hero are well chosen the development of both story and protagonist is entangled in the erratic goings-on *of* and *in* Sordello's mind, in his ruminations and abstract aporias: man vs. poet; action vs. contemplation; fulfilled love vs. sublimation of desire. And the charge of having been 'willfully obscure, unconscientiously careless or perversely harsh' (B. owning up, many years later, in 1872) was not so much aimed by his critics at his nondevelopmental fictional approach, nor at a presentational mode anticipating the dramatic monologue and privileging the self-perpetuating digressive, dilatory approach of the oral tale, but rather at a working method that by obstinately unearthing obscure (and often pseudo) historical details (no matter how much the poet may deny it), loses sight of the essentials and fundamentals of romance.

Now, by way of closing remarks, and yet sticking to the subject of Browning's medieval poetics, I would like to take a look at the way the same story (at least part of it) is dealt with by Verdi in his earliest opera. In 1839, when Browning was still wrestling with the problems of writing and rewriting *Sordello*, Giuseppe Verdi and his librettist, Temistocle Solera took up the 'romantic' nucleus of Sordello's life but made Cunizza the protagonist, even though the title of the opera is *Oberto, conte di San Bonifacio*.[23] She is the only

---

22 Cf. J. McGann, *The Beauty of Inflections. Literary Investigations in Historical Method and Theory* (Oxford, 1985), esp. the chapter on 'The Book of Byron and the Book of a World', pp. 255–93.
23 See the libretto in L. Baldacci, ed., *Tutti i libretti di Verdi* (Milano, 1975), pp. 1–13.

'historical' character of the opera whereas all the other ones that have some connection with historical events are given new names and families. So Guelph Rizzardo da San Bonifacio is fictionalized into Oberto, Leonora's old father, and Ghibelline Taurello Salinguerra is rechristened Riccardo Salinguerra. Once all historical, scholarly, chronicle-based references have been removed the composer can concentrate on the four characters whose savage feelings of love and/or hate, jealousy and/or thirst for revenge provide the machinery and the arena of the melodramatic action and bring about the final catastrophe.

Riccardo is made the catalyst of all the fatal attractions and rejections of the opera: he loved and seduced innocent Leonora, but is now in love, betrothed to and about to marry Cunizza. Apparently, if we keep an eye on history, his is a 'political' engagement, but Verdi is not in the least interested in that; what matters for him is that Riccardo stands for love and lust, and as is well known, variety is the soul of desire. So, according to this logic Leonora's 'right' to marry her seducer by way of compensation must be trampled on by Riccardo, who unashamedly accuses her with perjury: '*ebben . . . l'amai / spergiura la trovai*' ('I loved her, and found her unfaithful'), but she unexpectedly finds on her side Cunizza who generously sacrifices her own love to return the seducer to his former abandoned lover.

This however turns out to be no solution as the motif of revenge is grafted onto the romance because the father *must* avenge the wronged honour of his daughter. Which entails that the action is supported and made coherent by unreconciled experiences typical of romance, a prey to the 'rich passion for extremes' (James) of which tragedy is the necessary outcome. And with the finality and inevitability of impending fate old Oberto challenges Riccardo to a duel and is struck dead; Leonora enters a convent out of despair as she feels guilty for the death of her father ('*ad ucciderlo qui venni / con la man del seduttor*': 'I came here to kill him through my seducer's hand'), since he has been forced by his sense of honour to an unequal fight; Riccardo, the villain of the piece, asks forgiveness and goes into exile; Cunizza is left alone on the stage, a desolate witness to hate, death, and futurelessness. Here, then, is an alternative and rather essential use of almost identical characters and historical-legendary action-events: Verdi and Solera go directly to the heart of the matter, exploiting the timelessness and *durée* of Romance and in so doing, achieving its 'eternal return'.

LOVE AND TRANSGRESSION IN SOSEKI'S STORY OF THE MAID OF ASCOLAT

TOSHIYUKI TAKAMIYA

The episode of the Maid of Ascolat is no doubt one of the most touching scenes in the whole corpus of Arthurian literature.[1] Her innocent and unrequited love for Lancelot, which results in her tragic death, has been dealt with and enjoyed generation after generation. As you will see from my table,[2] it was first introduced in the Old French *Mort Artu*, and later immortalized by Malory in the *Morte Darthur* during the revival of medieval chivalry in the late fifteenth century. Furthermore, thanks to Tennyson's *Lancelot and Elaine*, the Maid's fame grew to the extent of inspiring a large number of paintings and book illustrations by the Pre-Raphaelites and their followers.[3]

In 1905, Natsume Soseki (1867–1917) composed an Arthurian novella

---

[1] I am very grateful indeed to Professor Piero Boitani, Professor Anna Torti, and all those concerned with the J.A.W. Bennett Lectures for inviting me to Perugia. While I was a research student in Cambridge 1975–78, I benefited from Professor Bennett's lectures, particularly those on medieval English devotional writings which he conducted in Easter term 1978. In his final lecture, he suggested that he would give an additional lecture in the following week, but when I turned up I could not find any other student in the lecture room. He then kindly invited me to tea in his office on the Sidgwick Site. This turned out to be a memorable occasion: he told me that he had intended to talk about Walter Hilton by referring to my critical edition of *Of Angels' Song*. Thus, alas, a rare chance was lost for my text to be mentioned in a Cambridge lecture room! I am also indebted to Professor Andrew Armour for offering his expertise and correcting my English.

[2] This table is a slightly revised and abbreviated version of what was published in Toshiyuki Takamiya and Andrew Armour, 'Kairo-ko: A Dirge', *Arthurian Literature* II (Cambridge, 1982), pp. 92–126; see especially pp. 99–101. The problem of spelling variants in Ascolat/Astolat is discussed in Toshiyuki Takamiya, ' "Ascolat" in the Winchester Malory', in *Aspects of Malory*, eds. Toshiyuki Takamiya and Derek Brewer (Cambridge, 1981), pp. 125–26.

[3] For a list of Victorian treatments of the Maid of Ascolat and the Lady of Shalott in art, see William E. Fredeman, 'Appendix: The Laureate and the King: An Iconographic Survey of Arthurian Subjects in Victorian Art', in *The Passing of Arthur: New Essays in Arthurian Tradition*, eds. Christopher Baswell and William Sharpe (New York, 1988), pp. 277–305, especially pp. 283–89. In 1985 George P. Landow organized an admirable exhibition at Brown University called 'Ladies of Shalott: A Victorian Masterpiece and Its Contexts', issuing an extremely useful catalogue with the same title.

Table: the Transmission of the Story of Ascolat

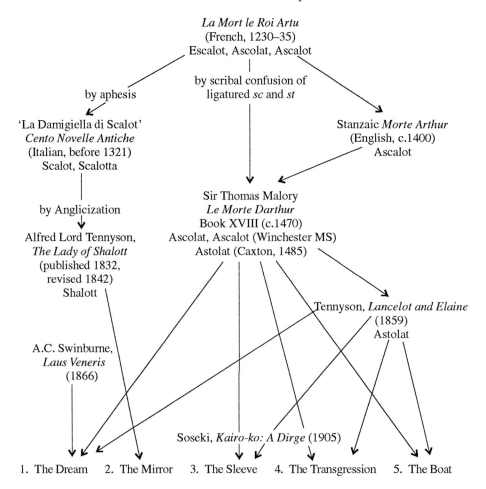

called *Kairo-ko: A Dirge*.[4] He was then on his way to literary fame as the most celebrated novelist in Japan and arguably the first to incorporate the Western concept of ego into the modern Japanese novel. His masterpieces have survived to this day, despite the many changes that have taken place in literary tastes and trends this century. *Kairo-ko* is based on Malory's work, Tennyson's *Lancelot and Elaine* and *The Lady of Shalott*, and some minor sources. One can trace the ultimate source of Tennyson's *Lady of Shalott* as far back as the *Mort Artu*. Thus Soseki's piece is unique in its use of multiple sources dealing with the same episode. *Kairo-ko* is best, however, in its treatment of love, in the Arthur-Guinevere-Lancelot and Lancelot-Guinevere-Elaine triangles, depicting Lancelot's acute sense of having wronged Guinevere. Full of torment and agony, *Kairo-ko* was in fact the first of many of Soseki's novels dealing with illicit love. The present paper will focus on this Japanese Arthurian story, comparing it with its sources.[5]

Soseki's awareness of Western medieval literature – namely, Chaucer, Malory and Boccaccio – can be traced back to his two years of study in London, from October 1900 to December 1902. This was a traumatic period in his life, full of anguish and the torments of a growing inferiority complex. As the first recipient of a scholarship granted by the Ministry of Education, it was his professional duty in London to improve his understanding of English literature; however, his efforts at improvement made him increasingly aware of the difficulty he faced and of the insecurity of his own cultural identity. Moreover, he was disturbed by the stipulation that he concentrate more on the language than on the literature.[6]

---

[4] An English translation of Soseki's *Kairo-ko: A Dirge*, with an introduction, is available in *Arthurian Literature* II; see note 2 above. All the citations from *Kairo-ko* refer to this edition. Cf. Norris J. Lacy, ed., *The New Arthurian Encyclopedia* (New York, 1991), pp. 130, 424.

[5] Soseki's major sources for *Kairo-ko* are as follows: part one, 'The Dream' (Malory, *The Morte Darthur*, Book XVIII, Chapters 8–9; Tennyson, *Lancelot and Elaine*, ll. 73–159; A. C. Swinburne, *Laus Veneris*, stanzas 29, 32, 50, 55–57, 78, 80–81, 101–02); part two, 'The Mirror' (Tennyson, *The Lady of Shalott*, Parts 1–3); part three, 'The Sleeve' (Malory, Book XVIII, Chapter 9; *Lancelot and Elaine*, ll. 241–396); part four 'The Transgression' (Malory, Book XVIII, Chapter 15; Book XX, Chapter 3; *Lancelot and Elaine*, ll. 568–610); and part five, 'The Boat' (Malory, Book XVIII, Chapters 19–20; *Lancelot and Elaine*, ll. 1–33, 899–1154 and 1233–74; *The Lady of Shalott*, Part 4). The Soseki Library, now intact in Tohoku University Library, contains three editions of Malory and a large number of Tennyson's texts, of which the following carry notes and underlinings by Soseki: Sir Thomas Malory, *Le Morte Darthur*, ed. A.W. Pollard, 2 vols. (London, Macmillan, 1900); Tennyson, *Lancelot and Elaine*, with introductions and notes by F.J. Rowe (London, Macmillan, 1895). A list of his library, in his own handwriting, makes a reference to Swinburne's *Poems and Ballads*, vol. 1, which contains *Laus Veneris*: see note 9 below.

[6] See Hisaaki Yamanouchi, 'The Agonies of Individualism: Natsume Soseki', in *The Search for Authenticity in Modern Japanese Literature* (Cambridge, 1978), pp. 44–81, with a useful list of Soseki's works in English translation. Soseki's treatment of

After arriving in London, Soseki was permitted to attend Professor W.P. Ker's lectures at University College, but he stopped after just two months. The longer he stayed in London, the more neurotic he became. And he barely ever left London during the two years of his stay, making just two short trips – one to Cambridge, the other to Pitlochry in the Highlands. Some time later his landlady related that he would often confine himself to his bed-sitter for days on end. Because of his characteristic habit of marking the books he was reading – a habit for which we are now very grateful – he did not work in libraries, not even at the British Museum. Instead he lived on bread and water alone, spending his grant on large numbers of books: his diary indicates that he once made a purchase of more than one hundred in Charing Cross Road.[7]

These periods were evidently not wasted, however, for it seems that he devoted himself to reading extensively in English literature, in spite of the mental anguish that he was suffering. This laborious study was to bear fruit after his return to Japan, in his lectures entitled *A Theory of Literature* and *Form and Style in English Literature*, which were both published at a later date.[8] I think it is a great pity that Soseki did not publish his *Theory of Literature* in English, since it would certainly have been comparable in structure and content to I.A. Richards's *Principles of Literary Criticism*, first published in 1924. At any rate, while preparing these series of lectures to be given at the Tokyo Imperial University, Soseki accumulated quite a large quantity of notes and memoranda, and one of his notebooks carries the following remark on female literary characters:

> The female characters suitable for Japanese environments are the patient Griselda in Boccaccio, Godiva in Tennyson and Landor, and Elaine in Tennyson's Arthurian legend.

This praise for submissive women strongly suggests that Soseki's values matched those of Victorian society in general.

On his return to Japan in 1902 Soseki took up a lectureship in English at the Tokyo Imperial University. It was there, in the autumn of 1905, that he composed *Kairo-ko*, one of his earliest literary undertakings. Soseki was simultaneously engaged in writing a serial novel, *Wagahai wa Neko de aru* (*I am a Cat*, 1905–6), a satirical masterpiece depicting a university professor's life as seen through the eyes of his cat. This work, which achieved immense popularity, is written in a plain, colloquial style that has little in common with the deliberately archaistic language adopted in *Kairo-ko*.

---

medieval English literature is discussed in Toshiyuki Takamiya, 'Medieval English Literature and Soseki', *Soseki Museum in London Occasional Papers* 1 (1986) 15–25.

7   Perhaps the best account of Soseki's London life is found in Jun Eto, *Soseki and his Times* (in Japanese), vol. 2 (Tokyo, 1970).

8   Soseki's lectures and writings on English literature, annotated by Hisaaki Yamanouchi, are edited in *The Complete Works of Soseki* (in Japanese), new edition, vol. 13 (Tokyo, 1995).

Any reader of *Kairo-ko* will no doubt find himself somewhat bewildered from the outset by the multi-layered enigma that he encounters. First, there is the problem of the title, which was no less puzzling ninety years ago than it is now. In fact, I have met very few Japanese intellectuals who can read this title written in Chinese characters and guess its proper meaning. 'Kairo' literally means 'dew drops on a shallot leaf', and is derived from a line in an ancient Chinese dirge, originally composed for a nobleman who had committed suicide. Thus it implies 'Human life is as evanescent as the dew drops on a shallot leaf'. Still extant are two letters in which Soseki explains the meaning of his title and its origin; unexplained is the pun on Shallot, which can have hardly been accidental, though there is no concrete evidence to support such an assertion. As for the 'ko', this refers to a song or poem characterized by a slow but steady rhythm. Thus, pedantic though it sounds, the title of *Kairo-ko* is meant to refer to a lament or dirge – in this case for the death of a young maiden called Elaine, whose name originated in Malory.

Soseki's Arthurian story is divided into five parts, following a preface which, though untitled, should be regarded as the author's apologia. The story begins with 'The Dream' which relates a meeting between Lancelot and Guinevere, her recounting of a dream in which the two are bound together by a coiled snake, and Lancelot's departure for a tourney. In 'The Mirror' the Lady of Shalott may look at the world only through a mirror set in front of her, or else she will die. When Lancelot passes, however, she turns and gazes directly at him; but before dying, she puts a death curse on him – Soseki's original idea. In 'The Sleeve' Elaine of Astolat prevails on Lancelot to wear her red sleeve on his shield at the tourney. Then, in 'The Transgression', Guinevere learns of Lancelot's apparent love for, or dalliance with, Elaine, while Mordred and others denounce the Queen for her sinful adultery with Lancelot. The final part, called 'The Boat', tells how Elaine, grieving for the wounded and absent Lancelot, dies; her body is placed in a boat and borne to Camelot, along with a letter proclaiming her love.

Though spiced with images of violence and pain, with which love is associated, this elegant and lyrical work is a striking blend of Western material, both medieval and Victorian, with Japanese and Chinese textures. Recently Mrs Mihoko Higaya convincingly argued that Soseki's treatment of Guinevere's dream drew in part on *Laus Veneris*, the famous poem treating Venus and Tannhauser, which was composed by the Pre-Raphaelite poet A.C. Swinburne.[9] Colour images abound in the following account of Guinevere's dream, given by her towards the end of part one:

'It was on a day when all the roses were in bloom. There were just the two of us, lying together among the roses – white, red and yellow. We watched the sun set on that happy day; the endless twilight was filled with joy. I was

---

[9] Mihoko Higaya, 'Soseki and Swinburne: A Source Study of the Pre-Raphaelite Features in Kairo-ko', *Comparative Literature Studies* 30 (1993) 377–87.

wearing the crown', she explained, raising a finger to her forehead. *Twice coiled around its base was a golden serpent, with finely etched scales and two sapphire eyes set in its upraised head.*

'*This crown began to burn into my flesh and around my head I heard a strange sound, like that of cloth being rubbed. This golden snake wound in my hair had begun to uncoil itself. Its head slithered towards you, leaving its tail on my breast. I watched it stretch like a curling wave, and then we were entrapped in its slimy coils,* bound so tight that there was no hope of release. You lay at arm's length, but I had no strength to draw nearer, no means to draw away. Yet loathsome though it was, that bond became a solace for my anguished heart, for to sever it would have been to separate us. *But how cruel that we had to endure its bites and stings till the day the flesh rotted from its bones. Assailed thus by pleasure and pain, I looked on as the red roses burst into flame and engulfed the snake that bound us. Soon, the golden scales about its middle began to change colour, giving out a bluish smoke and an evil odour. It suddenly snapped in two. "With this, may both body and soul vanish for eternity," I prayed, when I heard someone beside me laugh mockingly,* and I awoke. But waking too, the voice continued to echo in my ears. The memory of it filled me with cold dread when I heard the echo of your laughter in this room.' (p. 106: emphases added by Higaya)

For these italicized passages, Higaya suggests the following parallels from Swinburne's poem:

> . . . sleeping with her lips upon their eyes,
> Heard sudden serpents hiss across her hair. (st. 29)
>
> Her gateways smoke with fume of flowers and fires,
> With loves burnt out and unassuaged desires. (st. 32)
>
> The queen whose face was worth the world to kiss,
> Wearing at breast a suckling snake of gold: (st. 50)
>
> . . . the edged light slips,
> Most like a snake that takes short breath and dips
> Sharp from the beautifully bending head,
> With all its gracious body lithe as lips
> That curl in touching you; right in this wise
> My sword doth, seeming fire in mine eyes,
> Leaving all colours in them brown and red
> And flecked with death; then the keen breath like sighs,
> The caught-up choked dry laughter following them. (sts. 55–57)
>
> She walked between the blossoms and the grass;
> I knew the beauty of her, what she was,
> . . . The beauty of her body and her sin.
> And in my flesh the sin of hers, alas! (st. 78)

Ah, with blind lips I felt for you, and found
About my neck your hands and hair enwound,
The hands that stifle and the hair that stings,
I felt them fasten sharply without sound.

Yea, for my sin I had great store of bliss:
Rise up, make answer for me, let thy kiss
Seal my lips hard from speaking of my sin,
Lest one go mad to hear how sweet it is. (sts. 80–81)

And I forgot fear and all weary things,
All ended prayers and perished thanksgivings,
Feeling her face with all her eager hair
Cleave to me, clinging as a fire that clings

To the body and to the raiment, burning them;
As after death I know that such-like flame
Shall cling to me for ever; yea, what I care,
Albeit I burn then, having felt the same? (sts. 101–02)[10]

Despite the general opinion that Soseki did not care for Pre-Raphaelite poems, Mrs Higaya has detected that virtually every single stanza of *Laus Veneris* resembles 'The Dream' in one way or another, and, moreover, that there lies a close parallel between the central arguments of *Kairo-ko* and *Laus Veneris* – the sinfulness of Lancelot and Guinevere, on the one hand, and the English poem's portrayal of amorous rapture heightened by the awareness of sin and the presentiment of ruin, on the other. 'Soseki assimilated' she concludes, 'the basic themes, as well as the picturesque images and phrases, of *Laus Veneris* into his own writing'.[11]

Now we should turn to Soseki's preface which reads as follows:

From the point of view of its simple, unsophisticated charm, Malory's famous Arthurian romance is without doubt a work of great value. However, because it is a product of the Middle Ages, when viewed as a novel it is open to the criticism of being desultory. For this reason, if one is interested in extracting and condensing part of the whole, it becomes virtually impossible to remain faithful to the original. Accordingly, in writing this piece I have taken the liberty of sometimes inverting the sequence of events, inventing new situations and remoulding the personalities of certain characters. The result is something which comes close to being a novel. However, I must say that I have done this merely because it seemed interesting, and not because I wanted to provide the reader with an introduction to Malory. I hope that he will bear this in mind.

To tell the truth, I have often thought the Lancelot depicted by Malory resembled a rickshaw man, Guinevere being his light-o'-love. Were it for this alone, I think there would be sufficient reason to warrant a revision.

---

[10] Higaya, p. 383.
[11] Higaya, p. 382.

> Also, I need hardly say that, in composing this short story, I made frequent reference to Tennyson's 'Idylls of the King'. This epic is invaluable not only as a classic masterpiece of grace and beauty, but also because the character portrayal succeeds in making nineteenth-century men and women act out their parts on the medieval stage. I had originally intended to read it through again in order to refresh my memory, but I realized that in doing so I would be unconsciously tempted to imitate it, and so gave up the idea. (p. 103)

Soseki thus reveals that his intention is to produce a modern rendering of an Arthurian romance; however, here too the reader may find it difficult to grasp exactly what the author is trying to say. It should be noted that, in disparaging Malory's treatment of Lancelot and Guinevere because the former resembles a rickshaw man and the latter his girlfriend, Soseki is suggesting that they have something in common with such simple-minded, uncouth characters. There is a possibility that he was thinking of the argument put forward by Swinburne, who denounced Tennyson's characterizations in *Idylls of the King*. Tennyson, by the way, was defended by such English critics as Robert William Buchanan and James Thomas Knowles.[12] In an 1872 article entitled 'Under the Microscope', Swinburne makes the following observation:

> Mr Tennyson has lowered the note and deformed the outline of the Arthurian story, by reducing Arthur to the level of a wittol, Guinevere to the level of a woman of intrigue, and Launcelot to the level of a 'correspondent' . . . the debased preference of Mr Tennyson's heroine [i.e., Guinevere] for a lover so much beneath her noble and faithful husband is as mean an instance as any day can show in its newspaper reports of a common woman's common sin.[13]

It seems that Soseki reversed Swinburne's position, denouncing Malory and praising Tennyson's characterizations. The reason why Soseki stands with Buchanan and Knowles is clear from his remark in the preface that Tennyson's 'character portrayal succeeds in making nineteenth-century men and women act out their parts on the medieval stage'; such a portrayal suited Soseki, who wanted to describe the sense of transgression, the distress and the struggle of the fatal lovers. Quite possibly Soseki had read the following passage by Knowles:

> Lancelot in the splendour of his double nature (a double star with just such complicated orbit) moves, and must always move, upon a level with the

---

[12] This view in terms of the celebrated controversy over the 'Fleshly School of Poetry' was put forward in Masaie Matsumura, 'The English Literary Background of "Kairo-ko": Mainly Tennyson' (in Japanese), in *Meiji Literature and Victorian Age* (Tokyo, 1981), pp. 105–48, especially pp. 109–13.

[13] A.C. Swinburne, *Under the Microscope* (London, 1872), pp. 37–38. Soseki probably had access to it in Swinburne's *Studies in Prose and Poetry* (London, 1894), a marked copy of which is contained in the Soseki Library.

King himself, in interest, and even closer to ordinary sympathy. The ceaseless inner war which tears him before our eyes, breeds in a sense of nearer kinship than we dare to claim the Royal calm. But through it all how lofty and how great he is: no wonder that he 'knew not he should die a holy man', and no wonder also that he did so die.[14]

Judging from what Soseki read, wrote and lectured on, his interest in Malory remained mainly linguistic and stylistic. When he says in his preface to *Kairo-ko*, 'From the point of view of its simple, unsophisticated charm, Malory's famous Arthurian romance is without doubt a work of great value', he must have been thinking especially of Malory's style. Soseki's observation is reminiscent of several contemporary views on Malory's style, which Soseki encountered.[15] But if he valued such simplicity, one may wonder why Soseki employed such a complicated and antiquated style in *Kairo-ko*. Two decades ago, in answering this question, Professor Jun Eto brought forth an ingenious theory of literary-visual interaction, which states that the intricately entwined, interlaced, and claustrophilic atmosphere that he claims is predominant in many Pre-Raphaelite paintings, influenced Soseki's choice of style in writing *Kairo-ko*.[16] Eto was thinking of the illustrations of the *Lady of the Shalott* which William Holman Hunt and Dante Gabriel Rossetti contributed to Moxon's Tennyson poems (1857). It is perhaps interesting to note that Soseki liked not only to paint but also to view Victorian paintings in London. Our English translation of *Kairo-ko* in *Arthurian Literature* (1982) indirectly lent support to this theory, since reactions in the West were very much in this vein. For instance, a certain Englishman wrote to me saying that *Kairo-ko* reminded him 'so very much and so appropriately of just a story as Dante Gabriel Rossetti might have written in his youth for the *Oxford and Cambridge Magazine*, which Rossetti and Morris edited'.[17] Another suggested some affinity in atmosphere and tone with Swinburne's *Tristram of Lyones* (1882).

---

14 James Thomas Knowles, 'The Meaning of Mr Tennyson's "King Arthur"', *Contemporary Review*, May 1873, p. 947.
15 In his detailed *Studies in Soseki Natsume* (in Japanese), vol. 1 (Tokyo, 1981), pp. 347–447, Saburo Oka mentions that Bayard Tuckerman's *A History of English Prose Fiction* (New York and London, 1899) and John Earle's *English Prose: Its Elements, History and Usage* (London, 1890) were particularly influential in forming Soseki's view of Malory's style: a copy of the former, bearing Soseki's annotations, was found by Oka in the University of Tokyo Library at Komaba, and a copy of the latter is in the Soseki Library.
16 Jun Eto, *Soseki and the Arthurian Legend: A Comparative Study of Kairo-ko* (in Japanese) (Tokyo, 1975), pp. 145–274. Although rather controversial, this monograph, now reprinted in a paperback edition, was instrumental in encouraging popular interest in *Kairo-ko*. For the Pre-Raphaelite influence on Japanese art at the turn of the century, see *The Journal of Pre-Raphaelite Studies*, new series, III (1994), Special Issue: 'Japan and the Pre-Raphaelites' (Guest Editor: Hiroyuki Tanita).
17 Quoted from a letter written by Colin Franklin, FSA, the author of various books on private presses, including the Kelmscott Press.

There certainly lies in *Kairo-ko* the poetic environment of the Pre-Raphaelites, who were influenced by medievalism in the nineteenth century. It is understandable that, like most of his fellow Victorians, Soseki preferred Tennyson's characterization of Lancelot and Guinevere. Nevertheless, there is evidence indicating that, in writing *Kairo-ko*, he actually turned to Malory in some instances: he follows, for example, Malory's spelling for Lavaine's brother: Tirre, rather than Tennyson's Torre. Merlin's prophecy concerning Guinevere's adulterous love, mentioned in part three, is also taken from the *Morte Darthur*. Perhaps what is most puzzling about Soseki's preface is the total absence of any mention of Tennyson's *The Lady of Shalott*, despite its prominent position in the construction of part two, entitled 'The Mirror', and in the denouement of the story. It is certainly to Soseki's credit that he incorporated, instinctively perhaps, the supernatural elements of the *Lady of Shalott* into the story of the Lily Maid of Astolat: only a novelist's sixth sense can have hinted to him that Astolat and Shalott shared a common origin. On the other hand, the inclusion of the *Lady of Shalott* undoubtedly makes the structure of Kairo-ko all the more intricate and enigmatic.

As well as playing an important part in the plot and imagery of *Kairo-ko*, mirrors had a special significance for Soseki, who was a victim of smallpox at an early age. Professor Sneeze, a self-caricature of Soseki, suffers from the same problem in *I am a Cat*, Chapter 9. The frequent use of mirror imagery in his novels certainly indicates his inferiority complex and obsession with his own reflection. It seems that his stay in London only exacerbated this condition, as can be seen by the following account of his experiences there:

> Everyone I see in the street is tall and good-looking. That, first of all, intimidates me, embarrasses me. Sometimes I see an unusually short man, but he is still two inches taller than I am, as I compare his height with mine when we pass each other. Then I see a dwarf coming, a man with an unpleasant complexion – and he happens to be my own reflection in the shop window. I don't know how many times I have laughed at my ugly appearance right in front of myself. Sometimes, I even watched my reflection that laughed as I laughed.[18]

Prior to the composition of *Kairo-ko*, he wrote in the same year *Maboroshi no Tate* or *The Phantom Shield*, dimly set in an Arthurian background, which features a man gazing at his shield.[19] This motif was evidently derived from the beginning of *Lancelot and Elaine*, in which Elaine gazes at Lancelot's shield. Soseki's shield serves as a mirror, since its inner side 'gleams brightly like a mirror and reflects anything that comes by'. Thus the man gazing at his

---

[18] Translated by Yamanouchi (see note 6 above, pp. 48–49) from 'A Letter from London', published in April-May, 1901.

[19] Oka discovered that Soseki used as a source for his *The Phantom Shield* John Rutherford, *The Troubadours: their Loves and their Lyrics* (London, 1873), an unannotated copy of which is contained in the Soseki Library: see note 15 above, pp. 487–519.

shield is at the same time gazing at a mirror, and Soseki drew on *The Lady of Shalott* for this image.

The mirror in *Kairo-ko* which 'was said to be the work of Merlin, the famous sorcerer', is taken from neither Tennyson nor Malory. What seems possible is that both Tennyson and Soseki independently found the description in *Faerie Queene* of Merlin's mirror, connected with a folk-tale motif called 'death from unrequited love', though there is no curse attached to the mirror in Spenser's poem.[20]

The inclusion of *The Lady of Shalott* could also be explained from the viewpoint of *Kairo-ko*'s structure. At the outset of this paper, I touched upon the two eternal triangles, but it is possible to see the main characters of *Kairo-ko* as forming a structure in which Lancelot is surrounded by the three women – namely Guinevere, Elaine and the Lady of Shalott. King Arthur may or may not be a wittol – that is, a cuckolded husband who keeps silent about his wife's liaison – but he does not play an important role in this episode whether handled by Malory, Tennyson or Soseki. The structure resembles to a certain extent that of *The Tale of Genji*, one of the Japanese courtly romances, written in the first quarter of the eleventh century.

Well known is the fact that the element of courtly love plays an indispensable part in chivalric romances in Europe, but it can hardly be seen in Japanese equivalents such as *The Tale of the Heike*. Perhaps one should call them war epics rather than chivalric literature, since the Japanese authors or minstrels deliberately ignored female characters and questions of love. However, complicated love relations are abundant in the earlier, courtly literature. Soseki's library, now preserved intact at Tohoku University, contains many books from this period including *The Tale of Genji*, whose first four volumes are mainly concerned with the rivalry between Prince Genji's various ladies. It is therefore possible to assume that, while writing *Kairo-ko*, Soseki had in mind such intricate relationships as described in *The Tale of Genji*.[21] Adulterous love inevitably involves transgression. We found it extremely difficult to translate Soseki's 'tsumi' into an appropriate English term. It should not always mean 'sin', since he sometimes uses its Buddhist connotations: in the end we chose 'transgression' for the title of the fourth part of *Kairo-ko*, in which the term is particularly abundant, although it appears in the other parts as well. Depending on the situation, Soseki's 'tsumi' bears almost all of the connotations normally attached to it in Japanese, except that concerning violations of national law. It sometimes means even 'actions disturbing the communal order'.

---

20 *Faerie Queene*, Book III, Canto II, xvii–xviii. The Soseki Library holds no less than five editions of the poem.
21 Murasaki Shikibu, *The Tale of Genji*, tr. with an introduction by Edward G. Seidensticker (New York, 1977); *The Tale of the Heike*, tr. with an introduction by

In part four, Guinevere's sense of transgression is intensified, as we see in the following passage:

> The remorse that stems from having harmed another who knows that he has been harmed, is not so painful to bear as the remorse which comes from harming a victim who is unaware of it. Even if there be no retribution, the man who scourges the saint will be sure to feel the horror of his deed if he repents. In the same way, the shame that Guinevere felt in front of a husband who displayed his suspicions openly, was less painful to bear than if Arthur were still unaware of the sin secreted in her breast. The shock of this realization pierced her to the quick with a dagger of ice-cold fear. (p. 119)

As far as Lancelot is concerned, passages suggesting his transgression are to be found throughout *Kairo-ko*, but I shall quote from the dialogue between the hermit and Elaine in the fifth part called 'The Boat':

> 'The hermit did restore him, but he may as well have been in the other world. For it was not Lancelot that lay there, ranting like a man possessed. In his delirium he would sometimes rave about sin, or the Queen – Guinevere – or Shalott. His brow burned with a powerful fever that even the potions of the kindly hermit could not allay.'
> 'If I had only been at his side', Elaine thought to herself.
> 'After passing the night, the fever gradually abated and Lancelot returned to his old self. Yet no sooner had he gathered his wits than he told me to leave him. Of course, the old hermit was worried for him and forbad me. Two days passed, and on the morning of the third, we awoke and looked over to the sickbed to see how our patient fared . . . but he was gone! With the point of his sword he had scratched on the wall the words "Sin pursues me – I pursue Sin" '. (p. 123)

Thus Soseki's story differs from those in Malory and in Tennyson in putting far greater stress on the sinfulness of adulterous love between Lancelot and Guinevere. Professor Eto suggests that this is because *Kairo-ko* was a preliminary attempt to express his guilty obsession with the illicit relationship that he had formed with his sister-in-law, Tose, a theme which was developed in later novels.[22] This theory, though interesting and certainly possible, is based on circumstantial evidence alone; it has caused fierce controversy among critics, and Soseki's intent remains a mystery.

Debra N. Mancoff, in discussing mid-Victorian attitudes to Arthurian art, rightly distinguished between public voices and private visions: although

---

Helen Craig McCullough (Stanford, Ca., 1988). I owe this suggestion to Professor Andrew Armour, Japanologist at Keio University.

[22] Jun Eto, note 16 above, 311–22. His interpretations recently led Yoshiyuki Fukuda to write a play entitled *Romance: Soseki's Love*, which was performed in Tokyo in 1995. Shohei Ooka published several articles contradicting Eto's view: see Ooka, *Soseki Natsume the Novelist* (in Japanese) (Tokyo, 1988), pp. 132–99.

many artists drew heavily on Malory's *Morte* for materials and inspiration, their motives were diverse. For example, William Dyce, who painted the murals in the Queen's Robing Room at Westminster, and Tennyson the Poet Laureate, used Arthurian materials as a means of imposing Victorian morals and virtues on the public, whereas Pre-Raphaelite painters and poets such as Rossetti and Swinburne, as well as such followers as William Morris and Edward Burne-Jones, turned their attention to immoral aspects of the legend – infidelity, desire, and too passionate spirituality – in which they found some impetus with which to describe their private visions: the inner struggles with love and with an overly mechanistic society.[23] It is worthy of note that these Victorian *enfants terribles*, who were once so enthusiastic about *The Lady of Shalott* and *Sir Galahad*, which Tennyson wrote in his youth, later turned their back on his *Idylls of the King*. Despite Soseki's apparent attachment to Tennyson's characterization of Lancelot and Guinevere, his inclinations were in fact more in the Pre-Raphaelite vein in that, regardless of his motivation, he wished to express his sense of transgression in *Kairo-ko* as a private vision.

---

[23] Debra N. Mancoff, *The Arthurian Revival in Victorian Art* (New York, 1990), pp. 136–67.

THE END OF UTOPIA – THE TREATMENT OF ARTHUR AND HIS COURT IN CONTEMPORARY GERMAN DRAMA

JOERG O. FICHTE

The topic of our conference, *mediaevalitas*, the precise meaning of which, I must confess, still escapes me, made me ponder on what things medieval mean to us nowadays. In the fifty years since World War II we obviously have witnessed a great revival of interest in the Middle Ages, something that has not only changed the premises of our own discipline, the scholarly approach to the study of medieval life and literature, but has also created a general awareness of what was once considered a distant past. The Middle Ages have become alive, flourish again and are presented to us in a great variety of media: poetry (although there is a definite shift from the written word to song), imaginative re-workings of medieval masterpieces (T.H. White, *The Once and Future King*, an adaptation of Malory's *Morte Darthur*, or Adolf Muschg, *Der Rote Ritter*, a modern version of Wolfram's *Parzival*), countless sword and sorcery novels (Mary Stewart's books), detective or mystery stories, especially those by Umberto Eco and Ellis Peters, fanciful biographies of medieval authors (Dieter Kühn, *Ich Wolkenstein, Herr Neidhart*), comic strips (from 'Prince Valiant' to 'The Wizard of Id'), movies dealing with Robin Hood and the Knights of the Round Table, musicals (*Camelot*) and finally drama, the genre to be discussed here. The reasons for this revival are manifold and often contradictory. The Middle Ages are seen as an image of a better past, a world less complicated and more harmonious because of the supposed absence of conflicting ideas. Especially in fantasy literature we are transported into an imaginary romantic world without technology and natural sciences, in which an elementary order reigns supreme and the good always defeats the bad. This apparent simplicity appeals to those who are either unwilling or incapable of facing and dealing with the complexities of modern life. The Middle Ages thus become an alternative to modern times, a place of escape from reality, a radically reduced utopian vision of what is considered to be a social, ethical and religious ideal.

Alternatively, the Middle Ages can be used as *chiffre* for political and ideological purposes, as mirror of the present which is reflected and refracted in the past. Rather than offering an escapist vision, this projection of the Middle Ages serves as a corrective to modern times. Medieval themes and topics are presented in parabolic form as comments on what is perceived to be a deficient present. Christoph Hein's *Die Ritter der Tafelrunde*, one of the two plays to be discussed, belongs to this category.

Finally, the Middle Ages have been revived because of their mythic potential. Authors have tried to isolate and recast those myths in modern form, whose power and relevance have survived, that is, especially the stories outlining the rise and fall of civilizations. King Arthur's ascent to power, his founding of the Round Table as implementation of the concept of a perfect society, and his subsequent decline are paradigmatic of this mythic story pattern, which has inspired many treatments during the subsequent centuries and in modern times. Tankred Dorst's *Merlin oder Das wüste Land* is one more testimony to the fact that the story has lost nothing of its fascination.

When Dorst published a rough draft of his play in *Theater heute* in 1979, it was instantly suggested that he was riding the wave of the Middle Ages boom, an insinuation he rightly rejected. In an interview with Peter von Becker he maintained that the play was written at Peter Zadek's request for a particular place, a fish market (which reminded Dorst of a cathedral) in the vicinity of the Hamburg harbour.[1] The play was supposed to take on shape in the process of its production, i.e., Dorst at that point did not regard it as a finished product, but as a living organism that was subject to change. Although the project was not realized, the play itself retained this incomplete shape because with 97 scenes distributed over more than 370 pages it defies production in its entirety. It would take fifteen hours to stage it. The original production in Düsseldorf in 1981 and the more famous second production in Munich in 1982 took place on two consecutive evenings reducing Dorst's text to twice 4½ hours of playing time. In short, the enormous size of the text not only encourages but also forces every director to construct his own dramatic version from Dorst's epic collection of dramatic and non-dramatic scenes – roughly one third of the printed text is non-dramatic scenes (including an exchange of letters between Ginevra and Isolde). There are also songs and poems interspersed and a singer and a chronicler who occupy the position of epic commentators. In view of the play's length and the diversity of the material available, the individual director has an even greater influence on the interpretation and subsequent staging of the play. Thus, the director of the Zurich production renamed the drama *Merlin oder Der Traum von König Artus' Tafelrunde* (*Merlin or the Dream of Arthur's Round Table*), leaving out the important reference to T.S. Eliot's 'Waste Land' and reducing the play to a chivalric fairy tale and a knights-in-shining-armour spectacle that promoted escapism rather than conveying Dorst's message.[2] When speaking about the

---

[1] Peter von Becker, 'Merlin: Magier und Entertainer. Theater als Phantasiestätte', *Theater heute* 20/4 (1979), p. 34.

[2] Rüdiger Krohn, 'Mehrfach gebrochenes Mittelalter. Tankred Dorst *Merlin* auf der Bühne und in der Kritik', in *Mittelalter-Rezeption. Ein Symposium*, ed. Peter Wapnewski (Stuttgart, 1986), p. 303.

play, we should, therefore, heed Dorst's advice who maintained: 'The book is my production'.[3]

In order to get a feeling for the main characters, Dorst, according to his own account, started to write the play from the end, that is, he began with the scene in which the sons rebel against their fathers' utopian ideas gone stale.[4] Writing the play from the end is important not only as a device but also as a concept. For Dorst this end, an end when all dreams of a perfect body politic have failed, is both the point of departure and conclusion. After the final battle the pagan gods driven out by Christ at the very beginning of the play return to their haunts. Although set in the past, *Merlin*, as Dorst maintains, is a modern story; it is an illustration of the failure of utopias.[5] The story narrates the beginning and the end of our civilization. In this sense it is a paradigmatic story without, however, being a parable. We are not supposed to read it allegorically, that is, construct a second contemporary level to which the historical action set forth corresponds. Rather, Dorst's epic manner of presentation, which includes not only dramatic and narrative passages but also mixes historical and modern characters (Mark Twain, Dagobert the garbage man, and assorted weirdos in Mordred's company), creates an anachronistic present. In the person of Merlin, moreover, past, present and future coalesce, obscuring any distinction between these three modes of time. Thus, in the very beginning Merlin sees the whole of human history without being able to tell what is past and what is still to come. Only his father, the Devil, knows this distinction. For Merlin, on the other hand, this seeming contemporaneousness is nothing more than a welcome means of escaping responsibility. He can always point to the future and invoke different moral standards to justify his actions or to explain deviant human behaviour. Ironically, there is only the Devil to correct him. Merlin's prophetic gift and his concomitant incapacity to alter the course of history give Dorst's play a sense of fatedness. And having the final battle between Arthur and Mordred followed by a necrologue on the whole planet spoken by a divine intelligence from an eternal perspective intensifies this feeling. It is a bleak vision of a planet that has been destroyed by either its intellectually inferior inhabitants or by some kind of natural catastrophe. Thus, Dorst's play dramatizes the feeling of impotence in the face of possible nuclear disaster and impending doom and of deep-rooted pessimism in regard to social and human progress. He never allows the spectator to escape into a fantasy world, but constantly confronts him with the problems of his own world. The illusion of a play action created on stage is repeatedly disrupted, in order to break down the separation of stage and audience. A gentleman from the audience, for instance, who doubts the magic

---

3   Heinz Klunker, 'Untergang des Abendlandes mit Goldrand', *Theater heute* 23/3 (1982), p. 31: 'Meine Inszenierung ist das Buch.'
4   Peter von Becker, 'Merlin: Magier und Entertainer. Theater als Phantasiestätte', p. 34.
5   Günther Erken, ed., *Tankred Dorst* (Frankfurt, 1989), p. 175.

of the perilous seat and tries to sit on it, is consumed by flames. The audience is forced to participate in the decline of the Round Table, the image of civilization, and is thus made to realize that all utopian ideas of a better world are bound to fail because they become obsolete once they have been accomplished. Man like Merlin may have a vision of 'Eine schöne geordnete Welt' (A beautiful ordered world),[6] but once this dream is accomplished, it vanishes, since there is no way of stopping the process of time. History refutes utopia, as Merlin tells Arthur on the eve of the decisive battle.[7] In this respect Dorst's play is a 'Lehrstück' (didactic play), but a negative one, since there is no hope of changing the process of history and the condition of man. In addition to being foiled by history, Merlin's efforts at achieving a better world are constantly frustrated by human nature itself. Unintentionally but not unwittingly he does his father's bidding: to liberate man to do evil. In a sense he is an inverted Mephistopheles, someone who tries to do good but does evil.[8] This dilemma becomes immediately apparent. The Round Table, i.e., the symbol of the utopian ideal of a perfect society, can only be gained by means of a beautiful woman, who will obviously be one of the causes of the failure and eventual disintegration of the new society. The Devil, of course, is aware of this. When Arthur upon seeing a picture of Ginevra and her dowry, the Round Table, decrees: 'Den Tisch muß ich haben!' (I must have this table!) and as an afterthought adds 'Ginevra', the Devil chuckles: 'Bravo, bravo! Eine schöne Frau! Ich bin entzückt!' (Bravo, bravo! A beautiful woman! I am delighted!)[9] Merlin's joy vanishes instantly. He takes the picture from the scaffold and tramples on it. To make things worse, he is immediately shown a vision of Ginevra lying in a meadow with a strange knight, who is not Arthur. Before the Round Table is founded, its destruction is already a foregone conclusion.

In this prelude, moreover, Dorst develops the three themes of his play that are inextricably intertwined: the utopian vision of a new civilization, bracketed by love, which threatens its harmony, and death, which terminates all human endeavours. The action surrounding the establishment of the Round Table vacillates between these two poles, i.e., the ideal is constantly threatened by the forces of destruction (time, age and death) and by love as an irrational, antisocial force. Once the knights have assembled and taken their seats, Death in the guise of a Chinese acrobat appears in their midst, kills the King of Cornwall and lures an armed knight away. This scene foreshadows the reappearance of Death just before Arthur's battle against Mordred: ' – Da ist doch

---

[6] Tankred Dorst, *Merlin oder das Wüste Land* (Frankfurt, 1981), p. 41.
[7] Ibid., p. 360.
[8] Dieter Hensing, 'Die Marionetten und Spieler bei Tankred Dorst – Tradition und Verarbeitung', in *Literarische Tradition heute. Deutschsprachige Gegenwartsliteratur in ihrem Verhältnis zur Tradition*, ed. Gerd Labroisse and Gerhard P. Knapp (Amsterdam, 1988), p. 282.
[9] Tankred Dorst, *Merlin*, p. 80.

jemand über mich hinweggesprungen, sagte König Artus und sah sich verwirrt um' (Somebody just jumped over me, said King Arthur, and looked around confusedly).[10] He does not see the Chinese acrobat. The scene in which Death appears at the Round Table is juxtaposed to a scene called 'Die Grünen Augen' (Green Eyes), when Lancelot falls in love with Ginevra, the final cause of the dissolution of the utopian social idea embodied in the Round Table. This ideal is presented in a scene, ironically called 'Democracy'. We are shown a vision of a peaceful world conjured up by Merlin. Before our eyes the Round Table turns into a paradise. The lion eats grass. Sir Orilus takes off his armour, reclines peacefully upon the flowery meadow and sings a song in praise of God's creation. The reaction to this presentation is mixed. Arthur welcomes the idea of a world without strife – his knights are not convinced. They fear for their *raison d'être*. Mark Twain, though, the Connecticut Yankee at King Arthur's court, is enthusiastic. Being an utter rationalist, he mistakes the vision for an adumbration of American democracy. In order to demonstrate his point, he produces a little steam engine: 'Der technische Fortschritt hat auch den gesellschaftlichen Fortschritt zur Folge! Die Maschine arbeitet, der Mensch wird frei!' (Technological progress will insure social progress! The machine does the work, man becomes free!).[11] For Mark Twain, the pragmatist, progress, especially technological progress, is the road to paradise, whereas, in reality, it leads to destruction, as Dorst illustrates by painting a macabre picture of an apocalyptic battle to end all hopes of spiritual regeneration. There is a strong criticism of the uncritical acceptance of technological development that in Dorst's eyes must lead to ecological destruction and the death of civilization. Parzival's brutal slaying of Ither in the next scene counteracts the vision of a peaceful society. The grass eating lion is juxtaposed to the ravenous Parzival who cuts Ither peacemeal out of his armour like a lobster out of his shell.

Parzival is one representative of the young generation. He personifies horrible, pitiless innocence and naive, but monstrous violence.[12] Whatever he touches withers and dies. Because of his incapacity for human interaction he turns the world into a waste land. Needless to say, he does not achieve the mystery of the grail, even though in the end he is made to realize his personal shortcomings by Merlin, who confronts him in the guise of Trevrizent. There is no indication, however, that Parzival will ever change his life. He remains the outsider, who eventually fades out of the picture. Parzival, of course, is only one member of a lost generation. There are more, all of them ludicrously immature like Sir Beauface and Sir Persant or in some way psychologically crippled like Agrawain and Mordred. They are divided into two groups: those

---

10 Tankred Dorst, *Merlin*, p. 355.
11 Ibid., p. 111.
12 Peter von Becker, 'Merlin: Magier und Entertainer. Theater als Phantasiestätte', p. 35; Reinhard Baumgart, '*PARSIFAL 1982* in Bayreuth, bei Syberberg und in Dorsts 'Merlin'', *Theater heute* 23/10 (1982), p. 23.

who ridicule the old values and have no sense of the passing of time (their life will be nothing more than a dream) and those who feel victimized by the generation of fathers and forefathers. Agrawain uses the image of the tower of fathers he carries on his shoulders, in order to impress upon us that a start from scratch is impossible. We cannot act as if there were no past, that is, every attempt at creating a better future is impeded by the liabilities of the past. 'Wie werde ich fertig mit den Heldentaten meines Vaters?' (How do I manage to deal with my father's heroic deeds?) asks Mordred, an obvious reference to the conflict of generations in the late sixties and early seventies.[13] Mordred, of course, uses this reference to his undesirable heritage as a mere excuse for his own moral failure. His facile self-analysis as a victim of an unloving hostile father, whom he blames for his own deficiencies, is constantly held up to ridicule by Dorst, who rejects the idea that psychoanalysis is a social panacea. In spite of all of his posturing – he even masquerades as a Christ figure – Mordred is evil by design, as his engineering of the murder of his mother Morgause and her lover Lamorak proves.

The murder shows that even the most sacred family ties are no longer binding, i.e., human depravity has reached its apex and society heads for destruction. Ironically, the murder is followed by Galahad's claim of the perilous seat. Although a light radiates from him as a vague promise of salvation, Galahad is isolated. Dorst describes him as an albino, a bloodless figure without substance, who will redeem neither himself nor the world. Shortly before the final battle, he dances back and forth between the two opposing armies like a self-styled Christ in a mad attempt at reconciliation, before he is crushed and night falls. Thus, the search for the grail, to which Merlin urges the Arthurian knights as an attempt to forestall destruction, is bound to fail. The grail as an idea is nothing but a phantom. As an object it is a stone from Lucifer's crown, i.e., it is tainted by the original fall. Therefore, it can be no cure for men living in a postlapsarian world.[14] It is no viable alternative to the 'pragmatic', albeit insufficient visions of the generation of fathers. As a matter of fact, the questers of the grail, the idealists, the founders of ideal societies, and the initiators of new orders promising happiness to all are the true agents of the devil.[15] The search for this phantom called grail must end in frustration and defeat because change has to come from within. Although Merlin tries to convince the various searchers to change their life, as

---

[13] Tankred Dorst, *Merlin*, p. 171; Rüdiger Krohn, 'Tankred Dorst: *Merlin* oder *Das wüste Land*', *Deutsche Gegenwartsdramatik*, ed. Lothar Pikulik (Göttingen, 1987), p. 22.

[14] The concept of the grail as a stone from Lucifer's crown has been taken from Wolfram. The meaning, however, is changed. There is no connection between the Devil, who lost the gem because of his pride and Mary, who won it because of her humility. Thus, the promise of salvation associated with the stone is lost in Dorst. Cf. Roswitha Wisniewski, 'Wolframs Gralstein und eine Legende von Lucifer und den Edelsteinen', *BGDSL* 79 (1957) 43–66.

[15] Tankred Dorst, *Merlin*, p. 268.

always he is unsuccessful. In answer to his harrowed question ' – Was ist mit der Vollkommenheit?' (What about perfection?) he is transported into a waste land, causing him to say: 'Ich will nicht mehr! Ich will mit der verdammten Weltgeschichte nichts mehr zu tun haben!' (I am done. I will not be bothered any more with this damn history of the world!).[16] Shortly thereafter he withdraws into the enchanted forest of Broceliande, while the message appears written in the sky: 'Du mußt dein Leben ändern!' (You must change your life!). One hundred million people look at this message, but no one seems to take notice of it.[17]

The final act 'Untergang' (Extinction) chronicles the events of the *Morte Darthur* from Ginevra's trial to the destruction of Arthurian society. Dorst follows his sources, T.H. White and Malory, fairly closely. Without much delay the action is hurried to an end. After the apocalyptic battle only a mountain of corpses is left. With broken legs Arthur drags himself towards Mordred and kills him. Chaos reigns; the idea of a better society is dead; utopia has been devoured by time. In other words, the process of history destroys all utopian ideas. In this respect, Dorst's concept of utopia differs from that current in both the Middle Ages and the Renaissance.[18] The utopian vision of a society ruled by reason and justice, in which truth, love and peace reign supreme, as developed by Conscience in Passus III of *Piers Plowman* (Kane and Donaldson, B-Text, ll. 284–330), can be realized, as can the society founded on the precepts of reason alone, described by Thomas More in his *Utopia or The Best State of a Commonwealth*. For Dorst, however, no goal exists that could be reached as final telos like earthly Paradise or an ideal human community. Once a utopian idea has been attained it has to be replaced by another, since finality equals death. Life proceeds in an ever repetitive cycle of chaos, creation, completion, decline and return to chaos. The return of the pagan gods chased out in the beginning of the play illustrates this movement. The grail, once the hope of a meaningful renewal of a society become habituated to the values represented by the pristine utopian ideal of the Round Table, disappears as does Arthur, who is transported to Avalon. In contrast to medieval concepts, no return and salvation is possible. Even Galahad, the self-styled Christ, is removed from this world not by way of a mystical ascent as in the *Queste del Saint Graal* of the Vulgate Cycle, but when he is crushed in the onslaught of the two opposing armies. He symbolizes the inability of even the chosen ones to realize a higher goal or state of being. Although he appears to be an avatar of Christ, his so-called love will not bring salvation to anyone because it is essentially narcissistic and self-centred.[19]

---

16 Tankred Dorst, *Merlin*, pp. 194–95.
17 Ibid., p. 278.
18 Cf. Walter Haug, 'Die Sache mit dem Teufel oder Das Mittelalterlich-Utopische und das Modern-Utopische', *Arbitrium* 1 (1983) 100–108.
19 Gerhard P. Knapp, 'Grenzgang zwischen Mythos, Utopie und Geschichte: Tankred Dorsts *Merlin* und sein Verhältnis zur literarischen Tradition', in *Literarische*

In the final scene Merlin, a prisoner of his own making, caught in the briar hedge, sings a song from Purcell's *Indian Queen* (1695) on the captivating power of love. In a more profound sense, Merlin's song suggests that love too like time and death has been a destructive force. In the form of irrepressible passion (Lancelot and Ginevra), hedonistic lasciviousness (Morgause), self-gratifying abandon (Gawan), and denial leading either to pathological self-destruction (the Maid of Astolat) or hateful destruction of others (Mordred), irrational love has defeated all attempts at rationality. Merlin's song, couched in the aesthetically pleasing form of an aria, is a statement of resignation. The artist speaks, whereas the visionary has failed to realize his dream.

Merlin's self-induced imprisonment raises the question of the role of the artistic imagination in the construction of ideal worlds. To what extent is the artist responsible for his creations? Merlin denies any responsibility: ' – Ich bin ein Künstler, was geht es mich an!' (I am an artist, what have I got to do with it!) is his response to a vision of the horrors of failed utopias.[20] Being an artist, so Merlin claims, puts him above any moral norms. The end, however, proves him wrong. The artist like any other man is responsible for his visions. As a matter of fact, Dorst seems to suggest, he is even more responsible because men live by his visions. Once the Merlins of this world, that is, the artists, the magicians, the *magistri ludi*, leave the stage, fantasy dies. There will be no more utopian visions, concepts, however, that are in constant need of revision and renewal.

In contrast to the atemporality of Dorst's mythic play *Merlin*, Hein's drama, *Die Ritter der Tafelrunde*, is extremely timebound. After being cleared for production by GDR cultural officials – not a smooth process from what we know now – it was first staged in Dresden in April of 1989. Then it disappeared from the programme to be quickly revived in the autumn of the same year, when the Wall fell.[21] The play was subsequently staged in Halle, Schwerin, Leipzig, Kassel, Franfurt/Oder, Bielefeld and Mainz. Although its author, Christoph Hein, objected to the concept of literature as a comment on day-to-day politics,[22] the play was seen in both East and West Germany as a

---

Tradition heute. Deutschsprachige Gegenwartsliteratur in ihrem Verhältnis zur Tradition, ed. Gerd Labroisse and Gerhard P. Knapp (Amsterdam, 1988), p. 250.

20 Tankred Dorst, *Merlin*, p. 195.

21 Hartmut Krug, 'Rezension: *Ritter von der Traurigen Gestalt*', *Theater heute* 30/7 (1989), p. 24.

22 Christoph Hein, *Die fünfte Grundrechnungsart. Aufsätze und Reden* (Frankfurt, 1990), p. 193: Interviewed by the *Berliner Zeitung* (4/5 November 1989) about the political situation, he said: 'Das alles ist sicher ein Stoff für Literatur, aber drei Generationen nach mir. Kunst strickt ungern mit heißer Nadel.' (All of this is certainly material for literature, but three generations after me. Art does not like to knit with a hot needle.) On the other hand, Hein in his address at the tenth meeting of the society of GDR authors on 25 November 1987 had insisted: 'Theater ist ohne Engagement nicht denkbar, ein öffentliches Engagement, ein politisches Engagement, ein Engagement

parable on the state of the GDR. Hein, who always calls himself a chronicler not a preacher,[23] produced a play that in this concrete situation became a statement, a political argument, and perhaps even agitation: 'The GDR as Arthur's realm, the Party executive office as Round Table. Hein's "comedy", dealing with the myth of the aged King Arthur and his quarrelling knights around the table in doomsday mood, is in reality a fable of the political leadership of the GDR' – so stated Max Thomas Mehr, a spokesman for the majority opinion, in *TAZ*, 26 October 1989.[24]

Unlike Dorst's magical play featuring many settings and more than sixty dramatis personae, Hein's drama is very conventional, suited to his pose as chronicler. It consists of four acts, written in prose. The unities of time, manner and place are observed. The entire action takes place in one setting, a hall in Arthur's castle. The Round Table is the major stage prop. There are some assorted chairs, many of them empty, among them the perilous seat that is no longer dangerous. Anyone can sit on it, even Jeschute, a woman, and Mordret's class mates. The cast of characters is limited to nine. There is little to no action on stage, in order to convey the impression of paralysis. The characters seem to be frozen into this setting, unable to move or do anything. All that is left to do in this play is talk, talk that runs the whole gamut from meaningless chitchat, idle reminiscences, petty bickering, empty threats to the uttering of vain, unsubstantiated hopes. The see-sawing dialogue is punctuated by occasional insights, when the characters try to assess their situation and grope for meaning in their meaningless lives. The society, represented only by the political elite (the people are conspicuously absent from Hein's play), is characterized by drunkenness, boredom and a profound sense of failure. The Round Table has deteriorated to a coffee table, where even women have a place now that most of Arthur's knights are gone. A leg has broken off, but the carpenter has never bothered to fix it. Later on the table becomes Parzival's editorial desk. 'Irgendwelche mystisch-metaphysischen Bestandteile sind nicht nachzuweisen' (Any mystical-metaphysical properties cannot be proven), as Mordret remarks, the radical, nihilistic representative of a frustrated young generation.[25]

---

für die eigene Zeit.' (Theater without commitment is unthinkable, that is, commitment to public affairs, commitment to politics, and commitment to one's own time.) Christoph Hein, *Die fünfte Grundrechnungsart*, p. 121.

23 ' "Die alten Themen habe ich noch, jetzt kommen neue dazu". Gespräch mit Sigrid Löffler (März 1990)', in *Christoph Hein. Text, Daten Bilder*, ed. Lothar Baier (Frankfurt, 1990), p. 38.

24 Klaus Hammer, ed., *Chronist ohne Botschaft. Christoph Hein. Ein Arbeitsbuch* (Berlin/Weimar, 1992), p. 258: 'Die DDR als Artusreich, das Politbüro als Tafelrunde. Heins "Komödie" um den Mythos vom altgewordenen König Artus und seinen zerstrittenen, in Endzeitstimmung verfallenen Rittem am runden Tisch ist in Wirklichkeit eine Fabel über die politische Führung der DDR.'

25 Christoph Hein, *Die Ritter der Tafelrunde. Eine Komödie* (Frankfurt, 1989), p. 27.

The play is dedicated to an assessment of the achievements of Arthurian society and its future goals. Central subject of this discussion is the grail. The nature of the grail is defined by the various members of the Round Table in a variety of different ways. Ultimately, it turns out to be a utopian concept intimately related to the vision of a perfect socialist society. In consequence, Arthur and his knights represent the aged leaders of a spiritually bankrupt communist state. Orilus personifies the old fighter, who still clings to the now outmoded ideals, which, he feels, can be revived by martial activities or at least a great tournament that will inspire admiration for the old guard in the young people. He reminisces about the good old days of law and order and a common enemy, Klingsor, representing some leading politician of West Germany or some figure like Goldstein in *1984*, who becomes the object of consolidated hatred. Keie functions as chief ideologist who resists any change. There is something tough and Stalinistic about him. He is adamantly opposed to new ideas, even though he realizes that Arthur's knights have sacrificed their lives for a future nobody wants. He despises the younger generation and advises their liquidation. Parzival is the disillusioned intellectual and editor of a critical newspaper that contains nothing worth reading and, if read at all, is read only by a small coterie. All of his ideals have vanished. Although totally disillusioned, he still defends the system and the measures that were taken in its name like the elimination of political enemies and deviators from the party line. In contrast to the hardliners, he is aware that the great vision has faltered: 'Einen Frieden der Krämerseelen, eine Ordnung der Polizeikasernen' (A peace for the petty and narrowminded, an order of police barracks), he retorts, when Orilus praises the civilizing effect of the *pax Arthuriana*.[26] Lancelot, who returns at the end of the second act from his unsuccessful search for the grail, is at first speechless and then voices his utter disappointment. He has actually seen and experienced the people's discontent, because he is the only one of Arthur's knights who has had contact with the real world. Now he has grown old physically and spiritually – Mordret calls him a dinosaur – and has lost his former identity as courtly lover. He is hardly recognized by even Ginevra. Gawain has made a separate peace. He has gone to the Castle of the Hundred Maidens, a metaphor for private enjoyment – this, at least, is Parzival's interpretation, whereas the more optimistic Arthur interprets Gawain's decision to leave the court as the beginning of a new simple bucolic life, a possible alternative to the failed official vision represented by the Round Table.

The women in this play have all been badly abused by the men and are thus doubly disappointed. Jeschute, the wife of the bully and bore Orilus, only believes in the pleasures of the flesh. Out of sheer boredom she has an affair with Mordret. Kunniware, a young and idealistic girl, is in love with the older married Parzival, who once had a brief affair with her, but now has lost all

---

[26] Christoph Hein, *Die Ritter der Tafelrunde*, p. 28.

interest in her. She is hopelessly out of place in this superannuated society of old men. Ginevra, dissatisfied with the state of affairs and frustrated by the absence of her former lover, has taken to reading literature as means of escape from reality. It is her protest against the social malaise, a retreat from society into a private sphere.

Arthur is well aware of the failure of his court. He tries to reform the society of the Round Table, an attempt, however, that is bound to fail. In contrast to Keie and Orilus Arthur knows that the old times are past and gone forever: 'Aber alles verändert sich, und das ist gut so.' (Everything changes, and that is good).[27] He regards the present development as a process of change not of dissolution. And he welcomes this change as something positive: 'Es muß etwas Neues entstehen.' (Something new must come into existence).[28] If the Round Table should be in the way of obtaining the grail, i.e., the realization of the socialist utopia, it should be removed. Undoubtedly there is still some hope, even though the implementation of Arthur's vague ideas is questionable because of Mordret, who represents an utterly cynical young generation. The grail means nothing to him; it is a mere phantom, as are all traditional social and moral values cherished by the older generation. Although he has no vision of his own (and in this respect he is a typical representative of the no-future-generation), he will destroy the now useless society. The final scene shows him to clean up the royal hall. All chairs are put on top of the Round Table with the exception of the perilous seat awaiting the redeemer. Thus, there is still a slight hope that something new may replace the outmoded regime, even though it is more than doubtful that a new beginning is possible in view of the general breakdown of the old order and its ideals. Mordret, supposedly, has to create a new order and find a new way, after the Round Table has been consigned to a museum.

In a statement in the *TAZ* (14 June 1990) Christa Wolf gave a precise definition of one of the dilemmas of GDR politics in its final stages, the conflict of generations: 'My generation', she maintained, 'exchanged one ideology for another at a very early stage; this generation only grew up late and slowly, that is, became mature and autonomous (some did not grow up at all). This is the reason for its (our) difficulties with the younger generation. There is a great insecurity because our own departure from ideological precepts and from the strong ties to rigid structures was not very successful, because the young people can perceive so little independence of thought and action, and are, therefore, unable to find reliable public figures who could provide guidance. Thus, in relation to the young generation, our childhood catches up with us which has not been sufficiently dealt with.'[29] Christa

---

27 Christoph Hein, *Die Ritter der Tafelrunde*, p. 58.
28 Ibid., p. 68.
29 Wolfgang Emmerich, *Die andere deutsche Literatur. Aufsätze zur Literatur aus der DDR* (Opladen, 1994), p. 178: 'Meine Generation hat früh eine Ideologie gegen eine andere ausgetauscht, sie ist erst spät, zögernd, teilweise gar nicht erwachsen gewor-

Wolf's assessment of the difficulties caused by the older generation's insufficient understanding of its own past seems to be a perfect description of the situation in Hein's play. She speaks about a generation of political leaders, intellectuals and authors that is represented by writers like Fühmann, Strittmatter, De Bruyn, Loest, Kant, Müller, Neutsch, Noll and herself, who had experienced the Third Reich either as children, soldiers, BdM girls or naive enthusiasts. They were reformed in the new faith, that is, one ideology was substituted for another. The closed world view of Fascism was replaced by the equally closed world view of Marxism.[30] Some members of this generation, so Wolf suggests, never came to grips with their past. They correspond to the ideological hardliners like Keie and Orilus in Hein's play, who have no understanding of or sympathy for the legitimate complaints of the younger generation, a generation aware that the old ideas have lost their meaning and must be replaced by something new, if Arthur's realm, the GDR, is going to survive. Mordret, the representative of this young, bored and extremely frustrated generation, does not know what this saving new idea will be. He only knows that the old concepts represented by the Round Table have to disappear. Consigning this antiquated piece of furniture, i.e., this symbol of real existing socialism, to the museum, at least creates room for breathing. The hall, metonymy of the GDR, has to be cleared first so that something new can replace the bankrupt ideology of the fathers.

Implicit in Hein's play is the belief voiced by Arthur himself that something new to save society is still possible. Even though we are left in doubt what this new concept will be, it is definitely not the sort of capitalist democracy practised in West Germany. Although a vociferous critic of the political regime of the GDR and the actual state of socialism, Hein like Christa Wolf and many other intellectuals believed that socialism could be changed and democratized. Thus, he supported the appeal 'Für unser Land' (For our country), which Christa Wolf read on 4 November 1989 in the name of many intellectuals who did not want their country to be annexed by West Germany. There was still hope for a radically reformed new democratic socialist society, a society that was to embark upon the so-called third path, that would insure the existence of an East German state in its present territory minus its failed political-economic system, or at least would provide the socio-political and ideological foundation for a reunified Germany.[31] In a

---

den, will sagen, reif, autonom. Daher kommen ihre - unsere Schwierigkeiten mit den Jüngeren. Da ist eine große Unsicherheit, weil die eigene Ablösung von ideologischen Setzungen, intensiven Bindungen an festgelegte Strukturen so wenig gelungen ist, die Jungen so wenig selbständiges Denken und Handeln sehen und daher kein Leitfiguren finden, auf die sie sich verlassen können. So holt uns, im Verhältnis zu den Jungen, unsere nicht genügend verarbeitete Kindheit wieder ein.'

30 Ibid., p. 212.
31 Bernhard Spies, 'Der Anteil der sozialistischen Utopie an der Beendigung der DDR-Literatur. Am Beispiel Christoph Heins', *The Germanic Review* 67 (1992), p. 117.

letter of 20 November 1989 to the Rowohlt-Verlag Hein insisted: 'We are undertaking a very daring experiment in our country: For a few weeks now we have been trying to build here a socialist society. . . . There is a chance for our hope; it is, however, the first and at the same time the last one. If we should fail, McDonald will eat us.'[32]

In view of these hopes, the play's assessment by the offical SED newspaper *Das Neue Deutschland* 'Hein did not write an absurd endgame. He offers a realistic startgame' is not so far off the mark as it may at first seem.[33] The play, after all, is called a comedy, which means, according to classical concepts, a drama that starts in turbulence and ends in harmony. There appears to be a reconciliation between Arthur and Mordret with the under-standing that the young generation will have to take over and bring about change. The search for the grail, the utopian concept of true socialism, has failed, but the idea lives on.[34] There is still hope, even though Hein refuses to subscribe to hope as principle in Bloch's sense. 'I know hope as principle does not work any more. I cannot piece together hope, just in order to maintain the principle. . . . Therefore, I shall not be able to work with the principle, but in order to live as a man, I must work with hope.'[35] In his insistence on hope for some better future Hein is a typical representative of the third generation of GDR authors (before 1976/1979) for whom literature becomes both a medium of criticism and the search for a utopian socialism. The theme is treated by Hein in the form of a dramatic trilogy. *Lasalle fragt Herrn Herbert nach Sonja* (Lasalle Asks Mr. Herbert About Sonja) sketches the beginning of the social utopia; *Schlötel oder Was Solls* (Schlötel or So What) is a presentation of the real existing socialism in the GDR; and *Die Ritter der Tafelrunde* (The Knights of the Round Table) is a chronicle of the decline of practised socialism in the final phase of East Germany.[36] Although Hein offers no positive

---

32 Christoph Hein, *Die fünfte Grundrechnungsart. Aufsätze und Reden 1987-1990*, p. 210: 'Wir haben ein sehr gewagtes Experiment in unserem Land vor: Wir versuchen seit ein paar Wochen, hier eine sozialistische Gesellschaft aufzubauen. . . . Es gibt eine Chance für unsere Hoffnung, allerdings ist es die erste und gleichzeitig die letzte. Wenn wir scheitern, frißt uns McDonald.'
33 Gerhard Ebert, 'Parabel auf das Streben nach menschlicher Vervollkommnung', *Das Neue Deutschland*, 3 May 1989: 'Doch Hein schrieb kein absurdes Endspiel. Er bietet ein realistisches Beginnspiel.'
34 Karla Kochota, 'Austreibung des Grals?', in *Chronist ohne Botschaft. Christoph Hein. Ein Arbeitsbuch*, ed. Klaus Hammer (Berlin/Weimar, 1992), p. 225.
35 Christoph Hein, 'Mut ist keine literarische Kategorie. Gespräch mit Alois Bischof', in *Christoph Hein. Texte, Daten, Bilder*, ed. Lothar Baier (Frankfurt, 1990), p. 95: 'Ich weiß, das Prinzip Hoffnung funktioniert nicht. Ich kann mir die Hoffnung nicht zusammenbasteln, um das Prinzip aufrechtzuerhalten. . . . Also werde ich mit dem Prinzip nicht arbeiten können, aber ich muß, um überhaupt als Mensch leben zu können, mit Hoffnung arbeiten.'
36 Antje Janssen-Zimmermann, 'Schlötel, Lassalle und König Artus. Aktuelle Anmerkungen zu Dramen von Christoph Hein', in *Christoph Hein. Texte, Daten, Bilder*, ed. Lothar Baier (Frankfurt, 1990), p. 172.

vision of what the future should bring, there is still hope of something better to come, although Hein like Heiner Müller knows that any practice eventually destroys utopias, whose earlier play *Praxis als Esserin der Utopien* (Practice as Eater of Utopias) had made just this point. In spite of ever-threatening, and in the final analysis certain failure, Hein clings to the hopeful idea, that something good may yet happen, even though in his writings we only get negative versions. All of his attempts at creating humane utopias fail, yet by this failure he asserts his belief in man's capacity for good.[37] His conviction, shared by many of his colleagues, that after the failure of the gerontocratic regime in East Germany something new and better could develop in the future, is a testimony to this hopeful disposition.

History, of course, soon ended these utopian hopes of Hein and other reformist intellectuals. The people who on November 4th in Berlin had been encouraged to dictate the course of change were no longer interested in yet another experiment in socialism. Hein seems to be aware of this mood, when he deplores the state of affairs in an interview conducted with Sigrid Löffler in March 1990: 'The independence of the GDR has been wasted and lost over here, not through the fault of West Germany. This decrepit system has no chance of bringing about the reunification upright and with dignity. There will be no agreement, therefore, just a takeover by the FRG.'[38] Political developments after the peaceful revolution in 1989 once more proved the radical divorce between poetic vision and practical politics. And Hein's play, that was meant to be a play promising a new beginning, became an endgame. The productions in Halle and Schwerin in the months after Honecker's ouster and enforced retirement, show no more rapprochement between Arthur and Mordret. The young man is on his own. There is no knowing of what the future holds in store, and what is worse, there is no hope.[39] *Die Ritter der Tafelrunde*, originally a play not totally devoid of optimism about man's ability to create utopian visions of a better future, is now made to carry the same message as Dorst's *Merlin*: History destroys utopias. And what is worse, the vision vanishes at the very moment when a new start appears to be within reach because the practice, perhaps in the guise of McDonald, has once more eaten utopias.

---

[37] Bernhard Spies, 'Der Anteil der sozialistischen Utopie an der Beendigung der DDR-Literatur. Am Beispiel Christoph Heins', p. 115.

[38] Christoph Hein, ' "Die alten Themen habe ich noch, jetzt kommen neue dazu." Gespräch mit Sigrid Löffler (März 1990)', p. 44: 'Die Selbständigkeit der DDR ist hier verludert und vertan worden – und nicht durch die Schuld Westdeutschlands. Dieses marode System hier hat keine Chance, aufrecht und mit Würde eine Vereinigung herbeizuführen. Es wird deshalb auch kein Agreement geben, sondern eine Übernahme durch die BRD.'

[39] Ingeborg Pietzsch, 'Rezension über Passé? "Die Ritter der Tafelrunde" von Christoph Hein in Halle und Schwerin', *Theater der Zeit* 45/2 (1990), p. 17.

Epilogue

Christoph Hein's last statement regarding the future of the GDR was made in March 1990, that is, five years ago. Time has proved him right. The so-called third way propagated by East German intellectuals has not been realized. As a matter of fact, quite the opposite has taken place. Instead of a search for the values of a humane socialism, there has been a return to the vices of Fascism. A small but very visible group of young people in both the old and the new states has drawn attention to themselves because of their criminal activities directed primarily against foreigners, those seeking asylum in Germany and against Jewish institutions. Needless to say, the outrages committed by the neo-Nazi skin-heads have provoked a public debate that has also been carried into the theatre. In particular Frank Castorf, the 42-year-old director of the Berliner Volksbühne, has come under attack because, without engaging in any moral diatribe, he shows skin-heads on a rampage on stage, thus representing everyday German reality, as he proclaims, and for admitting in an interview with the *Junge Welt*:[40] 'I still remember six or seven years ago, I sat in the cafeteria in Chemnitz, in Karl-Marx-Stadt, and thought, to counter the decadence of the GDR, the lack of movement: We need a new "Stahlgewitter", that is, Fascist-like or maybe just vital thoughts, or . . . something that means movement.'[41] There is the use of the ominous word 'Fascist-like' and the obvious reference to Ernst Jünger, one of the spiritual fathers of the new nationalism, who coined the phrase 'Stahlgewitter' and was an apostle of vitality. The choreographer Johann Kresnik, incidentally, was just in the process of producing the dance theatre piece 'Ernst Jünger' in Castorf's Volksbühne – it turned out to be an anti-Jünger performance –, in order to celebrate the theatre's seventieth anniversary. In the same interview Castorf once more emphasized this need for vitality by again linking it with right wing ideology: 'Expressionism, Dadaism, that is, those artistic movements that one hundred years ago presented new thought as a form, . . .

---

40 Peter Iden, 'Ein Irrer. Frank Castorf bekennt sich', *Frankfurter Rundschau* (10 January 1995), p. 8, who calls Castorf a madman and is grateful for the fact that Castorf is just a 'Theatermann und ohne politische Entscheidungsfunktion' (man of the theatre without the power of making political decisions). For a collection of statements see Stefan Ripplinger, 'Ladenhüter. Alle Welt denkt über Castorfs Interview mit der jungen Welt nach. Herausgekommen ist dabei nicht allzu viel. Eine Presseschau', *Junge Welt* (24 January 1995), p. 17.

41 'Ungekappte Sätze', *Junge Welt* (13 January 1995), p. 11, a corrected version of Castorf's statements made during an interview with Dirk Nümann, 'Stahlgewitter in der Volksbühne', *Junge Welt* (30 December 1994): 'Ich weiß noch, vor sechs, sieben Jahren saß ich in Chemnitz, in Karl-Marx-Stadt, in der Kantine und dachte gegen die Dekadenz der DDR, die Nichtbewegung: Wir brauchen wieder ein neues Stahlgewitter, also faschistoide oder vielleicht nur vitale Gedankengänge; oder . . . etwas, das Bewegung heißt.'

is longing for vitality that once existed, for courage, for power, for all those things which are most likely to be found in the rightist radical store, not in the enlightened, liberal realm of the Tuscany faction.'[42] Castorf also attacks the complacent sixty-eighters and the 'Toskana-Fraktion' (Tuscany-faction) of the Social Democrats, whose 'heuchlerischer Antifaschismus' (hypocritical anti-Fascism) reminds him of the officially proclaimed anti-Fascism of the GDR. He regards the pogroms and violence of the young as a reaction against this pretence.[43]

How does this affect the meaning of our two plays? It is obviously of some relevance in reference to Hein's figure of Mordret. Although Mordret, the representative of the frustrated young generation in Hein's *Ritter der Tafelrunde*, does not voice any Fascist sentiments, he is the perfect example of a potential Fascist, as defined by Castorf, that is, somebody whose longing for action could take on Fascist-like forms. In other words, the seeds are there in Hein's play, from which some of the deplorable actions have issued in the years after the reunification. Mordret has not just consigned the Round Table to the museum, he has become active in a way not envisioned by Hein.

I have been careful to state that the rise of neo-Fascism is not restricted to the new states. Tankred Dorst's latest play *Die Schattenlinie* (The Shadow Line), which just premiered on 28 January 1995 in Vienna, also shows the intellectual demise of the generation of sixty-eight and the rise of a new generation dedicated to self-gratification and violence. As in the case of *Merlin* Dorst draws on the storehouse of ancient myth; this time he makes use of the Lear story, which he presents as a farce, since the protagonist, Mr Malthus, lacks any tragic potential. An effete liberal and father of three children, a cripple, a skin-head and a daughter torn between the loyalty towards her father and the financial attractions of her yuppy banker friend, he is mercilessly revealed as an impotent chatterbox indulging in occasional outbursts of violence directed against the members of his own family but incapable of any redeeming social actions. His inarticulate but extremely violent neo-Nazi skin-head son, acting upon what he calls his creed 'der Mensch ist 'ne Fehlentwicklung! Der muß wieder aus dem Programm!'[44] (man is an evolutionary mistake! He has to be taken out of the programme!), makes short shrift of his father's proclaimed ideals of tolerance, liberalism and social commitment by cruelly and gruesomely murdering a negro who appears in Mr Malthus's house, in order to demonstrate to his father the limits of tolerance. Driven almost to insanity by his adamant but futile adherence to

---

42 *Junge Welt*, p. 11: 'Der Expressionismus, der Dadaismus, also die Kunstströmungen, die ja vor hundert Jahren einfach ein neues Denken als eine Form vorgestellt haben ... ist ja auch eine Sehnsucht nach Vitalität, die einfach mal vorhanden war, nach Mut, nach Kraft, nach all den Sachen, die wahrscheinlich heute im rechtsradikalen Fundus zu finden sind, und nicht im aufgeklärt-liberalen Bereich der Toskana-Fraktion.'
43 Robin Detje, 'Landschaft mit steinernen Gästen', *Die Zeit* 5 (27 January 1995), p. 52.
44 Tankred Dorst, *Die Schattenlinie* (Frankfurt, 1994), p. 68.

the belief that all social and personal problems can be resolved in a rational and humane fashion, Malthus withdraws to a garbage dump, where, babbling madly in a rhetoric befitting his son, he waits for the reappearance of the slain negro: 'Komm endlich Nigger! – Hey! Hörst du, ich sage Nigger zu dir! Hätte ich früher nicht über die Lippen gebracht, oder?'[45] (Come on, nigger! – Hey! You hear, I call you nigger! Wouldn't have crossed my lips before, would it?). The garbage dump is an extremely potent symbol. All the humanitarian ideals proclaimed by the social reformers have become refuse. Thus, Dorst's latest play too is a dismissal of utopian ideals, this time of those cherished by the generation of sixty-eight, now destroyed by its own children.

---

[45] Tankred Dorst, *Die Schattenlinie*, p. 83.

Index

Abell, W. 95 n
Achilles 73
Adam 113
Adicia 108
Aeneas 68, 112 n
Agatha, St 65
Agnes, St 65, 68
Agrawain 157, 158
Alan of Lille (Alain de Lille) 1–14, 128
  De planctu Naturae 3–14, 47 and n
Albion 121
Alceste 49 and n, 64, 68
Aldhelm *De virginitate* 64
Aldwell, S.W.H. 84 n
Alexander, J.J.G. 94 n, 95 n
Alison 65
Allen, J.B. 76, 77
Andreas Capellanus *De amore* 35 n
Anne, St 68, 98 and n
Anne of Bohemia 13 n
Anslay, B. 90
Apollo (*see also* Phoebus) 72, 73, 121
Aptekar, J. 104 n, 109 n
Aquinas, St Thomas *In decem libros Ethicorum Aristotelis ad Nicomachum Expositio* 25 n, 26
Arachne 71
Archer, R. 82 n, 83 n
Arendt, H. 111
Ariadne 69
Ariosto, L. 113
Aristotle 29, 33, 73, 123
  Nicomachean Ethics 25 and n, 26 and n, 27 n, 34
  Physics 72 n
Armour, A. 139 n, 150 n
Arn, M.-J. 44 n, 96 n
Artegall 103, 104, 107, 108 and n, 109 and n, 110, 111, 112, 113
Arthur 107, 108 and n, 109 and n, 110, 111, 113, 139 n, 141, 146, 149, 150, 153–69
Ashley, K. 98 n
Assembly of Ladies 50 n
Athena (*see also* Minerva *and* Pallas) 69, 71
Atropos 73
Auden, W.H. 'Dame Kind' 1, 14 and n
Augustine, St *De civitate Dei* 68; *De doctrina christiana* 66, 70, 72, 74, 124 and n
Avalle, d'A.S. 35 n
Avril, F. 62 n

Bacchus 121
Backhouse, J. 43 n, 62 n
Bagley, J.J. 96 n
Baier, L. 161 n, 165 n
Bailly, H. 119
Baker, D.N. 7 n, 9 n
Bakhtin, M. 32 n
Baldacci, L. 136 n
Baldinucci, F. 130
Baldwin, A.P. 19 n
Barden, G. 17 n
Baret, J. 65 n
Baron, H. 77 n, 78 n
Barron, C. 98 n
Bartholomaeus Anglicus *De proprietatibus rerum* 12 n
Barton Palmer, R. 46 n
Basire, J. 117, 118
Baswell, C. 139 n
Baumgart, R. 157 n
Beadle, R. 59 n, 60 n, 93 n
Beatrice 135
Beauchamp, R. Earl of Warwick 91
Beaufort, E. Earl of 60
Beaufort, M. Lady 101
Becker, P. von 154 and n, 155 n, 157 n
Belge 107

Belgion, M. 131 n
Bellori, G.P. 130
Bennett, H.S. 17 and n
Bennett, J.A.W. 1 and n, 12 n, 13 and n, 43 n, 51 and n, 55 n, 57 and n
Benoît de Sainte-Maure 52 n
Benskin, M. 92 n
Benson, C.D. 20 n
Benson, L.D. 11 n, 15 n, 45 n, 50 n, 131 n
Bergen, H. 52 n
Berges, W. 87 n, 99 n
Bernard of Clairvaux, St 105
Bernardus Silvestris 5
 De mundi universitate 6 n
Beulah 118
Bible 62, 129; Scripture 71
Binchois, G. 96, 97 and n
Bischof, A. 165 n
Blake, N.F. 39 n, 90 n
Blake, W. 132 n
 Descriptive Catalogue 115–28
 The Ghost of Abel 122 n
 The Marriage of Heaven and Hell 119 and n
Blanch, R.J. 81 n
Bloch, M. 165
Bloch, R.H. 6 n
Bloom, H. 78, 79, 81 n, 129, 132 n
Boccaccio, G. 2 n, 5, 19 and n, 20, 22, 25 n, 30, 31, 32, 33 and n, 34, 36 and n, 39, 129, 141, 142
 Decameron 18 and n, 21 and n, 23 n, 24 and n, 26 and n, 27 and n, 28 and n, 29, 31 n, 37
 Esposizioni sopra la Comedia 27 n
 Filostrato 67 n
 Teseida 51 n, 61 n
Bodel, J. 88 n
Boethius 4, 61, 72 n
 De consolatione Philosophiae 56, 58, 93
Boethius of Dacia 124
 De Summo Bono 127 and n
Boffey, J. 16 n, 57 n, 61 n, 89 n, 96 n, 97 n
Boitani, P. 18 n, 24 n, 43 n, 55 n, 139 n
Bokenham, O. *Legendys of Hooly Wummen* 63–79

Bolton Holloway, J. 4 n
Boni, M. 133 n, 134 n
Borges, J.L. 135
Bourbon 107, 110, 111
Bourchier, I. 65 n, 69, 70, 71
Bowden, B. 117 n, 120 n, 122 n
Bradwardine, T. 123
Branca, V. 20 n, 52 n
Brekenok, J. 94 n
Brereton, G.E. 22 n
Brewer, D.S. 12 n, 16 n, 139 n
Brie, J. de 88
Brink, J.R. 107 n
Britomart 108
Brown, M. 56 n, 57 n
Brown, M.P. 86 n
Brown, P.M. 31 n
Browning, R. 129–37
 'Childe Roland to the Dark Tower Came' 131–33
 Dramatic Lyrics 130
 Dramatic Romances and Lyrics 130
 Men and Women 130
 The Ring and the Book 135
 Sordello 129 and n, 130, 133 and n, 136
Brownlee, K. 9 n, 21 and n
Bruni, F. 24 n
Buchanan, R.W. 146
Buchthal, H. 52 n
Bühler, C.F. 87 n
Bunyan, J. *Pilgrim's Progress* 129, 132
Buren, A.H. van 98 n
Buridan 123 n
Burne-Jones, E. 151
Burrow, J.A. 45 n, 55 n
Byron, G.G. 129, 130, 133, 134 n, 135, 136 and n

Calin, W. 46 n
Calliope 73
Cameron, A. 77 n
Carnicelli, D.D. 54 n
Campbell, P.G.C. 95 n
Capgrave, J. 69 n
Caprasius 68
Carlyle, T. 129
Cary, H.F. 133, 134 n
Castel, J. de 95

Castle of Perseverance, The 105
Castorf, F. 167 and n, 168
Cavalcanti, G. 128, 130, 131 n
Caxton, W. 87 n, 90 and n, 140
Cecelia, St 65, 69
Cento Novelle Antiche 140
Cervantes, M. de *Don Quixote* 132
Champion, P. 43 n, 44 n, 49, 51, 61 n
Chance Nitzsche, J. 7 n, 9 n
Chandler, A. 129 n
Charlemagne 87
Charles I 113
Charles V of France 88
Charles VI of France 61, 87
Charles of Orleans (Charles d'Orléans) 43–62, 66, 73, 96 and n
Charlotte de Savoie 101 n
Chartier, A. *La Belle Dame sans mercy* 59, 62
Chase, R. 135 n
Chaucer, A. 60, 76, 81–101
Chaucer, G. 1–14, 43–62, 66, 81 n, 129, 130, 141
  Anelida and Arcite 15 n, 16, 73
  Book of the Duchess 46, 47, 48, 50, 53, 55 and n
  Canterbury Tales 15 and n, 16 n, 20 and n, 29 n, 37 n, 44, 58, 59, 60, 66, 115–28;
    General Prologue 65, 115–28;
    Knight's Tale 12 n, 15 n, 16 and n, 33, 51, 52; *Miller's Tale* 45, 65; *Man of Law's Tale* 15 n, 40; *Wife of Bath's Tale* 15 n, 34, 35 and n, 108; *Summoner's Prologue and Tale* 66; *Clerk's Prologue and Tale* 15–41; *Squire's Tale* 58; *Franklin's Tale* 15 n, 17; *Prioress's Tale* 15 n; *Monk's Tale* 58, 65; *Nun's Priest's Tale* 23; *Second Nun's Tale* 65; *Retractions* 78
  Complaint of Mars 51
  Complaint of Venus 51
  Fortune 50
  Gentilesse 33
  House of Fame 46, 50, 51 and n, 52, 55 and n, 56, 59, 73
  Lak of Stedfastnesse 38 n
  Legend of Good Women 46, 49, 55, 59, 64 and n, 65 and n, 66–79
  Parliament of Fowls 1 n, 3–14, 46, 48, 49, 51, 52 n, 53, 54, 55 and n, 57 n, 59, 65
  Romaunt of the Rose 34, 50 n
  Troilus and Criseyde 35 n, 44, 54, 59, 65, 73, 74, 75 and n
  Truth 15 n, 16 n
Chaucer, T. 76, 91
Chenu, M.-D. 5 n
Cherniss, M.D. 57 n
Chew, S. 105 and n, 112 n
Chiappelli, F. 130 n
Christ (Jesus) 21, 65, 68, 69, 70, 73, 105, 155, 158, 159
Christine, St 68
Christine de Pizan 60, 82, 100, 101 and n
  Dit de la Pastoure 88 and n, 89 and n
  Epistre au dieu d'amours 59, 62, 89
  Livre de la Cité des Dames 64, 81 and n, 86, 87, 89, 90 and n, 95 and n, 101 n
  Livre des Trois Vertus 101 n
Clanvowe, J. 59 and n
Clapton Denston, K. 65 n
Clark, A. 60 n
Clark, L. 91 n
Claudian 77 n
  De consulatu Stilichonis 6 n
Clémence of Barking 69 n
Cleopatra 68
Clio 72, 73
Clotho 73
Cobham, E. 96
Cobham, R. 96
Coleman, W.E. 61 n
Coleridge, S.T. 129
Collins, T.J. 130 n
Comberworth, T. 60
Combès, G. 124 n
Conlon, D.J. 89 n
Constable, A. 60
Constance 40
Constantia 68
Contini, G. 131 n
Cooper, H. 19 n, 88 n

Cornwall, J. 60
Court of Sapience 105
Courtenay, W. 124 n
Cowen, J. 57 n
Crawford, A. 86 n
Criseyde 49, 54, 65, 75
Cromek, R.H. 116
Crow, M.M. 58 n
Cumming, J. 17 n
Cunizza da Romano 133 and n, 134 and n, 135, 136, 137
Cupid 44, 46, 59 n, 65, 73, 111
Curnow, M.C. 90 n
Curteys, J. 99

Dagobert 155
Dahlberg, C. 9 n
Dante 25 n, 128, 130 and n
 Convivio 35 and n
 Divine Comedy 26 n, 134 n; *Inferno* 26, 27 n, 132 and n, 133 and n, 134 n; *Purgatorio* 133 and n, 134 and n; *Paradiso* 133 and n, 134 and n
 Vita nuova 130 and n, 131
Danz Stirnemann, P. 62 n
David 73
Davies, K. 1 n
Davis, N. 82 n
Davis, N.Z. 10 n
Day, M. 44 n, 46 n, 52 and n, 62 n, 96 n
De Angulo, L. 58 n
De Berry, Duc 106
De Bruyn, G. 164
Deguileville, G. 57 n, 91
 Pèlerinage de l'ame 60, 90
 Pèlerinage de la vie humaine 61, 87 and n, 90
Delany, S. 63 n, 81 n
De la Pole, J. 83 and n, 84 n, 86, 99, 100 n
De la Pole, W. Duke of Suffolk 51 n, 60, 76, 82, 83 and n, 84 n, 89 and n, 90, 91, 92 and n, 93 and n, 96, 97 and n, 99
Delisle, L. 61 n, 62 n
Dempster, G. 30 n
Deschamps, E. 50, 61, 66

Lai de franchise 67
Despenser, I. 100 and n
Desplanque, M.A. 97 n
Detje, R. 168 n
De Vane, W.C. 130 n
Dialogue of St Anselm 58
Dicts and Sayings of the Philosophers 87 and n, 90 and n
Dido 49, 68
Dinshaw, C. 34 and n
Diomede 54
Dioneo 24, 25, 26, 27 and n, 28, 29, 30, 34, 36
Dodd, J.A. 100 n
Donaldson, E.T. 131 n, 159
Donizetti, G. 110
Dorothy, St 63 n, 68
Dorst, T. *Die Schattenlinie* 168 and n, 169 n; *Merlin oder Das wüste Land* 154–69
Douglas, G. *Eneydos* 78
Doyle, A.I. 93 n
Dronke, P. 124 n
Dryden, J. *Fables Ancient and Modern* 117 and n
Duessa 107, 108, 109 n, 110, 111, 113
Dunseath, T.K. 108 n, 109 n, 110 n
Dupont-Ferrier, G. 58 n
Duxworth 58
Dyce, W. 151

Earle, J. 147 n
Ebert, G. 165 n
Echecs Amoureux 53 n
Eco, U. 153
Economou, G.D. 5 n, 6 n, 7 n, 8 n, 9 n
Edmunds, S. 98 n
Edward III 63, 64 n
Edward IV 43 n, 62, 83, 85 n, 90, 96, 99 n
Edwards, A.S.G. 57 n, 60 n, 93 n
Edwards, R. 46 n
Edwards, R.R. 22 n

Ehrhart, M.H. 52 n, 53 n
Elaine 141, 143, 148, 149, 150
Eliot, T.S. 43 n, 130 n
 Waste Land 154

Elizabeth I 104, 105 n, 107, 109 n, 110, 113
Ellis, H. 72 n
Ellis, S. 130 n, 134 n
Emden, A.B. 99 n
Emilia 25
Emily 33
Emmerich, W. 163 n
Emslie, M. 12 n
Engle, L. 32 n
Epicurus 126
Erdmann, A. 92 n
Erken, G. 155 n
Erler, M.C. 59 n
Esculapius 121
2 Esdras 105
Eto, J. 140 n, 147 and n, 150 and n
Euterpe 73
Evans, G.R. 2 n
Evans, R.D. 5 n
Eve 14, 113
Eye and the Heart, The 59 and n
Ezra 105
Ezzelino da Romano 133 and n, 134, 135

Faith, St 68
Farges, J. 124 n
Farrell, T.J. 30 n
Fastolf, J. 90, 95 and n
Fenn, J. 99 n
Fenster, T.S. 59 n
Ferrante, J.M. 7 n
Ferrier, J.M. 22 n
Ferster, J. 32 and n, 34, 35 n
Fetplace, J. 60
Fetyplace, W. 60
Fichte, J.O. 105 n
Finke, L.A. 81 n
Flegge, A. 65 n
Fletcher, A. 104 n
Fletcher, B.Y. 59 n
Fletcher, G. *Christ's Victory and Triumph* 105
Floure and the Leaf, The 50 n
Flügel, E. 77 n
Foot, M.M. 84 n
Ford, B. 85 n
Fortescue, J. 64

Fortune 9, 45, 46, 47, 54 and n, 56, 57, 73
Foulkes, A.P. 75 n
Four Sons of Aymon, The 89, 90, 94
Fourrier, A. 46 n
Fox, J. 43 n
Francesca 134, 135
Francesco da Fiano *Contra Oblocutores et Detractores Poetarum* 77
Franklin, C. 147 n
Fredeman, W.E. 139 n
Friedman, L.J. 8 n
Froissart, J. 67
   Le Dit royal 61
   Espinette amoureuse 53 n
   Meliador 61
   La Prison amoureuse 46 and n
Fühmann, F. 164
Fukuda, Y. 150 n
Furnivall, F.J. 87 n, 100 n

Gadamer, H.-G. 17 and n
Galahad 158, 159
Galloway, D. 97 n
Galopes, J. 90
Ganim, J.M. 31 n
Gautier *see under* Walter
Gawain 160, 162
Genius 3, 7 and n, 8, 9 and n, 75
Geoffrey of Vinsauf *Poetria Nova* 65 n
Gerson, J. 8 n
Geryoneo 108, 110
Giles of Rome *De erroribus philosophorum* 71 n
Gilson, E. 123 and n
Gilson, J. 43 n, 89 n, 94 n
Girouard, M. 129 n
Gloriana 106
God 1, 3, 4, 10, 14, 22, 23 n, 31, 32, 38, 74, 75, 103, 104 and n, 105, 106, 109 n, 111, 112, 114, 125, 157
Godiva 142
Goldberg, P.J.P. 83 n
Goldstein 162
Golenistcheff-Koutouzoff, E. 19 n, 21 n, 23 n
Göller, K.H. 57 n
Gourlay, A. 116 n

Gower, J. 7 n, 65, 66, 74, 123
  Confessio Amantis 56 and n, 75
  Vox Clamantis 72 and n
Grantorto 107, 111
Green, R.F. 87 n
Green, R.H. 6 n
Gregory of Rimini 72 n
Grey, A. Lord 112
Griffin, S. 1 n
Griffith, J.J. 15 n
Griffiths, J. 16 n, 64 n, 84 n, 85 n, 93 n, 95 n, 96 n, 99 n
Griffiths, R.A. 93 n
Grisdale, D.M. 73 n
Griselda 15–41, 142
  in Chaucer (as Griselde) 18 n, 29–41
Griselde *see under* Griselda
Grudin, M.P. 32 n
Gualtieri *see under* Walter
Gui de Mori 8 n
Guido delle Colonne 52 n
Guillaume de Conches 5, 124
Guillaume de Lorris 47 n, 124
Guinevere 135, 141, 143, 145, 146, 148, 149, 150, 151, 156, 157, 159, 160, 162, 163
Guinizelli, G. 35 n
Guy of Warwick 89 n
Guyle 108
Guyon 107

Habermas, J. 17 n
Haines, C. 26 n
Hamilton, A.C. 108
Hamlet 135
Hammer, K. 161 n, 165 n
Hammond, E.P. 15 n, 46 n, 48 and n, 59 n, 75 n
Hanawalt, B.A. 10 n
Hansen, E.T. 13 n
Harcourt, R. 82 and n
Hardy, E.L.C.P. 93 n
Hardy, W. 93 n
Hardyng, J. 72 and n
Häring, N.M. 5 n
Harling, A. 101
Harlow, E.M. 14 n
Harper-Bill, C. 71 n

Harris, K. 95 n
Harrison, A.H. 129 n, 130 n
Haug, W. 159 n
Hawkins, J. 117
Heffernan, C.F. 41 n
Heffernan, T.J. 16 n
Hein, C. *Die Ritter der Tafelrunde* 154–69; *Lasalle fragt Herrn Herbert nach Sonja* 165; *Schlötel oder Was Solls* 165
Helen 49
Hellinga, L. 90 n
Henry IV 95 n
Henry IV (of Navarre) 107, 110
Henry VI 89, 91, 93 and n, 96 n, 99 and n
Henry VII 43 n, 62
Henry, A. 90 n
Henryson, R. *Testament of Cresseid* 78
Hensing, D. 156 n
Herbert, J.A. 87 n
Hercules 73, 121
Herrtage, S.J.H. 86 n
Hieatt, C.B. 56 n
Higaya, M. 143 and n, 144, 145 and n
Hilton, W. *Of Angels' Song* 139 n
Hindman, S. 90 n
Hingham, T. 93 and n
Hissette, R. 123 n
Hoccleve, T. 17
  Letter of Cupid 59, 62
  Regement of Princes 88 n
Holcot, R. 124
Homer 113, 130
Honecker, E. 166
Honorius 77 n
Horstmann, C. 63 n
Howard, J. Duke of Norfolk 86 n
Howard, K. 65 n
Howell, M.C. 10 n
Hugh of St Victor 105
Humphrey, Duke of Gloucester 76, 96
Humphries, K.W. 98 n
Hunt, I. 65 n
Hunt, W.H. 147
Huot, S. 8 n, 9 n
Husk, T. 59
Hypermnestra 69
Hypsipyle 68

Index 177

Iden, P. 167 n
Innocenti, L. 132 n
Irena 104, 107 and n, 111, 112
Isabeau de Bavière 89
Isabel 64 n
Iser, W. 17 n
Iseult 49
Isidore of Seville *Etymologiae* 12 n
Ither 157

Jack, I. 129 n
Jacobus de Voragine *see Legenda Aurea*
Jacquetta of Luxembourg 89, 90 n, 101
James I of Scotland *Kingis Quair* 43 n, 56 and n, 57 and n
James VI 108
James, H. 137
  The American 135 n
James, M.R. 99 n
Janicula 35, 39, 40
Jankyn 9
Jansen, J.P.M. 51 n, 83 n, 84 n, 96 n, 97 n
Janssen-Zimmermann, A. 165 n
Jason 68
Jauss, H.R. 17 n
Jean d'Angoulême 36 n, 58 and n, 60 n, 62
Jean de Meun 1–14, 47 n, 124, 128
Jean de Waurin 93 and n
Jeanroy, A. 130 n
Jeschute 161, 162
Joan of Arc 93
Job 37
John de la Trémouille 93
John of Lancaster, Duke of Bedford 61 and n, 62 and n, 85 n, 89 and n, 90 and n, 97 and n
John the Baptist, St 100
John the Evangelist, St 105
Johnson, L.S. 32 n
Julian, St 126
Jünger, E. 167
Juno 52 n

Kane, G. 159
Kant, H. 164
Kaske, C. 111 and n

Katherine, St 69 and n
Keats, J. *Isabella* 129
Keep, A.E. 91 n
Keie 163, 164
Keller, E.F. 14 n
Kennedy, A.J. 89 n, 95 n
Ker, W.P. 142
Keynes, G. 115 n, 119 n
Kibler, W.W. 47 n, 48 n
King, Y. 14 n
Kingsford, C.L. 82 n, 84 n
Kiralis, K. 118 n
Kiriel, J. 60
Kirkham, V. 28 n
Kirkpatrick, R. 18 and n, 31
Klingsor 162
Klunker, H. 155 n
Knapp, G.P. 156 n, 159 n, 160 n
Knowles, J.T. 146, 147 n
Kochota, K. 165 n
Kren, T. 43 n
Kresnik, J. 167
Krohn, R. 154 n, 158 n
Krueger, R. 98 n
Krug, H. 160 n
Kühn, D. 153
Kunniware 162

Labalme, P.H. 7 n
Labroisse, G. 156 n, 160 n
Lachesis 73
Lacy, N.J. 141 n
Lady of Shalott 139 n, 143, 149
Laidlaw, J.C. 90 n, 95 n
Laing, D. 16 n
Lairesse, G. de 130
Lamer, J. 25 n
Lamorak 158
Lancelot 135, 139, 141, 143, 145, 146, 148, 149, 151, 157, 160, 162
Landor, W.S. 142
Landow, G.P. 139 n
Langbaum, R. 135 n
Langland, W. 66
  Piers Plowman 1, 105, 159
Latini, B. 5, 6, 9
  Il Tesoretto 3, 4 and n, 10 n, 62
Lavaine 148
Lawton, D. 16, 17 n

Lawton, L. 52 n
Lear 168
Lecoy, F. 8 n, 9 n, 47 n, 50 n
Lee, S. 92 n
Legenda Aurea 69 n
Leicester, Earl of 107
Leland, J. 84 n
Leonora 137
Lerer, S. 17 and n, 20 and n, 78 and n
Lewis, C.S. 103, 108, 131 n
Limentani, A. 52 n
Linneus, C. 116
Little, L.K. 5 n
Littlehales, H. 85 n
Litzinger, C.I. 25 n
Livre du Chevalier de la Tour Landry pour l'Enseignement de ses Filles, Le 21 n
Livre Griseldis, Le 22, 40 n
Locock, K.B. 87 n
Loest, E. 164
Löffler, S. 161 n, 166 and n
Los 122
Louis XI 101 n
Louis d'Orléans 61, 62
'Lover's Mass' ('Venus's Mass') 75 and n
Lowes, J.L. 67 n
Lucifer 158 and n
Lucina 72, 73
Lucrece 68
Lucy, St 65
Lydgate, J. 17, 48 and n, 49 n, 53 n, 57 n, 65, 66, 67 n, 73 and n, 76, 86, 91 and n, 98 and n, 100, 105
  Complaint of the Black Knight 48, 58, 73
  Exposition of the Pater Noster 73
  The Life of St Alban and the Life of St Amphibel 72 and n, 73
  Lives of St Edmund and St Fremund 88 n, 92 n
  Misericordias Domini 74
  On the Departing of Thomas Chaucer 73
  Pilgrimage of the Life of Man 87 and n, 90 and n
  Siege of Thebes 60, 92 and n
  Temple of Glas 15 and n, 56 and n, 58
  Troy Book 52 n, 73
  Virtues of the Mass 73, 92
Lynch, K.L. 35 n, 39

Macaulay, G.C. 56 n
MacCracken, H.N. 48 n, 67 n, 91 n, 92 n, 96 n, 98 n
Machaut, G. de 56, 57 n, 66, 67 and n
  Confort d'ami 53 n
  Dit de la fonteinne amoureuse 46 and n, 53 n
  Jugement dou roy de Behaigne 47 and n
  Rèmede de Fortune 47 and n, 48
Macrobius 5 n, 61, 124
Maddern, P. 83 n
Maddox, D. 61 n, 89 n
Maid of Ascolat 139 and n
Maid of Astolat (*see also* Maid of Ascolat) 148, 160
Malengin 108
Malfont 114
Malory, T. 132, 143, 145, 146, 147 and n, 149, 150
  Morte Darthur 139 and n, 140, 141 and n, 148, 151, 153, 159
Malthus 168, 169
Mancoff, D.N. 150, 151 n
Mankind 93
Manly, J.M. 16 n, 20, 30 n, 35, 36 and, 37, 40 n, 58 n, 60 n
Mann, J. 38 and n, 55 n, 122 n, 126 and n, 127 and n
Marchand, L.A. 134 n
Margaret, St 65, 67
Margaret of Anjou 89, 93, 94 and n, 95 and n, 96 and n
Marks, D.R. 56 n
Mars 73
Marshall, J. 81 n
Marsigli, L. 77

Marucci, F. 132 n
Mary (Virgin) 68, 86 n, 105, 158 n
Mary Magdalene, St 69, 70, 71, 75, 100

Mary Stuart 104, 107, 108, 109 and n, 110, 112, 113
Mary Tudor 105 n
Matsumura, M. 146 n
Maximus 65
Maynard, J. 130 n, 131 n
Mazzotta, G. 27 n, 28, 30
McCullough, H.C. 150 n
McGann, J. 136 n
McGerr, R.P. 60 n
McIntosh, A. 92 n
McKendrick, S. 98 n
McKitterick, R. 60 n
McLaughlin, M. 31 and n
McLeod, E. 43 n, 58 n
McWilliams, G.H. 24 n
Meale, C.M. 60 n, 61 n, 64 and n, 83 n, 95 n, 101 n
Medea 68
Mehr, M.T. 161
Melchiori, B. 132 and n
Melpomene 72
Menagier de Paris, Le 21, 22 n, 23
Mendelson, E. 14 n
Mephistopheles 156
Merchant, C. 1 n, 2 n
Mercilla 104, 107, 108, 109 and n, 110, 111, 112, 113, 114
Mercury 52 n
Merlin 148, 149, 154 n, 155 and n, 156, 157 and n, 158, 160
Mertes, K. 86 n
Metcalfe, C.A. 82 n, 93 n
Meyer, P. 89 n
Mézières, P. de 19 n, 23 and n
   Le Livre de la Vertu du Sacrement du Mariage 21 and n
Middleton, A. 19 n, 20 and n, 22
Millar, E.A. 31 n
Miller, R.M. 21 n
Milsand, J. 129 n
Milton, J. *Paradise Lost* 105, 112
Minerva (*see also* Athena *and* Pallas) 53 and n, 57, 71, 72
Minnis. A.J. 64 n
Mnemosyne 118
Montagu, J. Earl of Salisbury 95 and n
Montagu, T. Earl of Salisbury 87, 90, 91, 92, 95

Moody, E.A. 123 n
Morabito, R. 19 n
Mordred 143, 155, 156, 157, 158, 159, 160
   in C. Hein (as Mordret) 161, 162, 163, 164, 165, 166, 168
Mordret *see under* Mordred
More, T. *Utopia* 159
Morgause 158, 160
Morley, Lord
Morris, W. 129, 147, 151
Morse, C.C. 20 and n
Morse, R. 16 n
Mort Artu 139, 140, 141
Morte Arthur (stanzaic) 140
Müller, H. 164, 166
Muratori, L. 133
Muschg, A. *Der Rote Ritter* 153
Muses 118
Myers, A.R. 85 n

Napier, H.A. 83 n, 84 n, 93 n, 94 n, 96 n, 99 n
Nature 1–14, 45, 53, 128
Needham, P. 90 n
Neifile 25
Neutsch, E. 164
Neville, A. 101
Neville, C. 95 n, 101
Newell, R. 83
Newton, I. 116
Niccoli, N. 77
Nicholas of Autrecourt 123 and n
Niobe 73
Noakes, S. 24 n
Noll, D. 164
Norton-Smith, J. 48 n, 51 n, 56 n, 59 n, 75 n
Nümann, D. 167 n

Oberto 137
Ockham, W. 71 n, 123 and n, 124
O'Connell, M. 104 n, 109 n
O'Donoghue, B. 131 n
Oesterwik, C. 99
Oka, S. 147 n
Old Testament 105
Olson, G. 21 n
Omont, H. 94 n

Ooka, S. 150 n
Orgoglio 113
Orme, N. 98 n, 99 n
Orpheus 73
Othea 73
Ouy, G. 60 n
Ovid 2 n, 73
   Metamorphoses 71
Owen, A.E.B. 60 n
Owen, C.D. 16 n

Pace, C. 119 n
Pächt, O. 96 n
Pagnini, M. 132 n
Pallas (*see also* Athena *and* Minerva) 52 n
Palma 135
Pandarus 75
Panfilo 24, 25, 26, 27, 28, 29
Panofski, E. 123 and n
Paolo 134, 135
Paris 52 n, 53
Paris, G. 94 n
Parkes, M.B. 59 n
Parliament of Birds 59 and n
Parr, J. 92 n
Parzival 157, 161, 162
Paston, J. 96 n
Paston, M. 82 and n
Patterson, A. 109 n
Patterson, L. 12 n, 24 n
Paul, St Romans 72
Pearsall, D. 16 n, 36, 37 n, 49 n, 50 n, 52 n, 84 n, 85 n, 88 n, 91 n, 92 n, 95 n
Pepwell, H. 90
Persephone 68
Peters, E. 153
Petrarch, F. 18 and n, 21 and n, 22, 23 and n, 24, 27, 29, 30 and n, 31, 32, 33 and n, 34, 35, 36, 37, 38, 39, 40 and n, 131
   Epistolae Seniles 19 and n, 22
Petrina, A. 57 n
Pettigrew, J. 130 n
Phalaris 26
Philip the Good 93, 97 n
Philomela 69
Phoebus (*see also* Apollo) 70

Phyllis 64 n
Pietzsch, I. 166 n
Pikulik, L. 158 n
Piper, A.J. 93 n
Plant, J. 1 n
Plantaganet, E. 83 n
Plato 8 n, 72 and n
   Timaeus 71
Pliny 2 n
   Naturalis historia 12 n
Plowman's Tale 16 n
Plumwood, V. 1 n, 2, 3 and n, 13 n, 14 n
Poirion, D. 57 n
Polak, L. 8 n
Pollard, A.W. 141 n
Polyhymnia 73
Pugliatti, P. 132 n
Purcell, H. *Indian Queen* 160

Queste del Saint Graal 159
Quilligan, M. 6 n, 81 n

Radford Ruether, R. 1 n
Radigund 108
Raimondi, E. 134 n
Raleigh, W. 106
Rawcliffe, C. 91 n
Redcrosse 103, 111 n, 113
Renaud de Montaubon 87
René d'Anjou 95 n
Richard II 13 n, 38, 41
Richard III 99 n
Richard, Duke of York 63, 69, 70, 77
Richards, E.J. 81 n
Richards, I.A. 142
Richardson, O. 87 n
Richmond, C. 82 n, 83 n
Rickert, E. 16 n, 20, 30 n, 35, 36 and n, 37, 40 n, 58 n, 60 n
Rickert, M. 88 n
Riddy, F. 64 n, 83 n
Righetti, A. 132 n
Rinuccini, C. 78
Ripplinger, S. 167 n
Rizzardo di San Bonifacio 134 and n, 135, 137
Robbins, R.H. 16 n
Robert of Blois 98 n

Robertson, D.W. 79 and n
Robin Hood 153
Robinson, P. 59 n
Rogers, N.J. 83 n, 92 n
Rolandino da Padova 134 and n
Roman de la Rose 3–14, 47 and n, 48, 50, 61, 124
Roos, R. 59, 62 and n
Rose, D.M. 39 n
Rosenauer, A. 96 n
Roskell, J.S. 91 n
Rossetti, D.G. 129, 131 and n, 147, 151
Rossi, R. de' 77
Roth, F. 66 and n
Rougemont, D. de 131 n
Rowe, F.J. 141 n
Rowland, B. 16 n
Roy, M. 88 n
Rudel, J. 130 and n
Ruskin, J. 129
Rutherford, J. 148 n
Rutter, I.T. 27 n

Salinari, C. 24 n
Salinguerra, R. 137
Salinguerra, T. 135, 137
Salleh, A. 14 n
Salter, E. 88 n
Samient 108
Samuels, M.L. 92 n
Sandon, N. 85 n
Satan 109 n, 112
Saul, N. 98 n
Savelli, G. 36 and n
Scattergood, V.J. 59 n, 94 n, 97 n
Schichtman, M.B. 81 n
Schick, J. 15 n, 56 n
Schiller, F. 110
Schirmer, W.F. 73 n, 91 n, 92 n
Schmitt, O. 53 n
Schøyen, M. 93
Schreiber, E.G. 51 n
Science, M. 72 n
Scott, K.L. 92 n
Scott, W. 136
   The Betrothed 129
   Ivanhoe 129
   Quentin Durward 129

The Talisman 129
Scrope, S. 90
Seaton, E. 62 n
Secreta Secretorum 88 n
Seidensticker, E.G. 149 n
Seinte Katherine 69 n
Seneca 2 n
Serjeantson, M. 63 n, 65 n
Severs, J.B. 18 and n, 19 n, 20 n, 21 and n, 22, 32, 33 and n, 34, 35, 37, 40 n
Seymour, M.C. 88 n
Shailor, B.A. 86 n
Shakespeare, W. 78, 129
   Cymbeline 107
   King Lear 107
   Winter's Tale 19 n
Sharpe, W. 139 n
Sheingorn, P. 98 n
Shelley, P.B. 129, 130 and n, 135
Sherborne, J.W. 94 n, 97 n
Sheridan, J.J. 5 n, 47 n
Shikibu, M. 149 n
Shirley, J. 91
Shoaf, R.A. 75 n
Shoeck, R. 29 n
Sidney, P. 106, 107
Sieper, E. 53 n
Siger of Brabant 127
Silenus 121
Silvia, D.S. 16 n
Simone, F. 58 n
Singleton, C.S. 26 n
Sir Beauface 157
Sir Gawain and the Green Knight 132
Sir Orilus 157, 162, 163, 164
Sir Persant 157
Sismondi, S. 133
Skeat, W.W. 1 n, 59 n, 62 n
Sledd, J. 29 and n
Smalley, B. 72 and n, 74, 77
Smith, G. 94 n
Smith, L.T. 84 n
Soldan 108
Solera, T. 136, 137
Sordello 133 and n, 134 and n, 135, 136
Soseki, N. *Kairo-ko: A Dirge* 139–51
South English Legendary 93

Spearing, A.C. 57 n
Speght, T. 116 n
Spenser, E. 129
   Faerie Queene 6 n, 103–14, 149 and n
Spiazzi, R.M. 25 n, 26 and n
Spies, B. 164 n, 166 n
Spurgeon, C.F.E. 15 n, 16 n
Stahl, W.H. 5 n
Stearns, M.W. 50 n
Steele, R. 44 n, 46 n, 52 and n, 62 n, 96 n
Stevens, W. 132 n
Stewart, M. 153
Stothard, T. 116, 122
Stow, J. 84 n, 87 n
Stratford, J. 61 n, 62 n, 85 n, 89 n, 90 n, 97 n
Strelly, J. 89 and n
Strittmatter, E. 164
Strode, R. 123
Strohm, P. 17 and n, 58 n
Sturm-Maddox, S. 61 n, 89 n
Sullivan, R.E. 132 n, 133 n
Surrey, H.H. Earl of 46 n
Swinburne, A.C. 129 and n, 144, 151
   Laus Veneris 140, 141 n, 143 and n, 145
   Studies in Prose and Poetry 146 n
   Tristram of Lyones 147
   Under the Microscope 146 and n

Taillevent, M. 59
Takamiya, T. 15 n, 93, 139 n, 142 n
Talbot, J. Earl of Shrewsbury 89, 94
Tale of Genji 149 and n
Tale of the Heike 149 and n
Talus 108
Tanita, H. 147 n
Tannhauser 143
Tasso, T. 113
Tatlock, J.S.P. 35 n
Taylor, J. 5 n, 29 n
Tempier, E. 123, 127
Tennyson, A. 129, 142, 147 n, 148, 149, 150, 151
   Idylls of the King 146 and n, 151
   The Lady of Shalott 140, 141 and n, 147, 148, 149, 151

Lancelot and Elaine 139, 140, 141 and n, 148
Sir Galahad 151
Téravent, G. de 53 n
Theseus 69
Thisbe 68
Thomas, Lord Scales of Middleton 89
Thomas, W. 85 n
Thompson, J.J. 16 n
Thomson, J.A.F. 84 n
Thomson, J.A.K. 26 n
Thomson, W.G. 98 n
Thynne, W. 16 n, 62 and n
Tignonville, G. de 87, 90
Tiner, E.C. 97 n
Tirre (Torre) 148
Tirzah 122
Torti, A. 24 n, 55 n, 139 n
Trevrizent 157
Troilus 65
Trout, J.M. 5 n
Tuckerman, B. 147 n
Tuetey, M. 101 n
Tuve, R. 8 n, 103, 109 n, 110 n
Twain, M. 155
   A Connecticut Yankee in King's Arthur Court 157
Twycross, M. 51 and n, 52 n
Tyrrell, W. 116 n

Udall, N. *Respublica* 105 n
Una 113
Uriel 105
Ursula, St 68
Usher, J. 26 n, 28, 39 n
Usk, T. 66
   Testament of Love 73

Valterius *see under* Walter
Vasari, G. 130
Venus 15 n, 46, 51 and n, 52 and n, 53 and n, 54, 55, 56, 57, 73, 75, 143
Vérard, A. 88
Verci, G.B. 133
Verdi, G. 136 and n, 137
   Oberto, conte di San Bonifacio 136
Vere, E. 65 n
Vesce, T.E. 44 n
Vincent of Beauvais 98 and n, 99

De morali principis institutione 87
Speculum naturale 12 n
Virgil 26, 78, 113
   Aeneid 112 n
Visconti, V. 61 and n

Walker, K. 117 n
Wall, J.N.Jr. 106 and n
Wallace, D. 24 and n, 41 n
Walter 15–41
   in Boccaccio (as Gualtieri) 26–29, 31, 33, 37, 39 and n
   in de Mézières (as Gautier) 21
   in Petrarch (as Valterius) 19 and n, 20 n, 31–35, 37–40
Walton, J. 72 and n, 93
Wanley, N. 129
Wapnewski, P. 154 n
Ward, H.D.L. 87 n, 94 n
Ward, J.C. 13 n
Warner, G.F. 43 n, 89 n, 94 n
Warren, K.J. 1 n, 2, 3 and n
Wasserman, J.N. 81 n
Wasson, J. 97 n
Wathey, A. 85 n
Weber, G. 96 n
Weisheipl, J.A. O.P. 31 n
Westfall, S.R. 86 n
Wetherbee, W. 5 n, 6 n, 7 n, 8 n, 9 n
White, G.H. 92 n
White, T.H. 159
The Once and Future King 153
Wilkins, N. 97 n
Willard, C.C. 88 n, 95 n, 101 n
William of Moerbeke 25 n
William of Worcester 90
Williams, D. 43 n, 85 n, 92 n
Wimsatt, J.I. 46 n, 47 n, 48 n, 50 n, 67 n
Windeatt, B.A. 16 n, 46 n, 52 n
Wisdom 93
Wisniewski, R. 158 n
Wittkower, R. 53 n
Wogan-Brown, J. 64
Wolf, C. 163, 164
Wolfram von Eschenbach 158 n
   Parzival 153
Woodville, A. Earl Rivers 90
Woodville, E. 90, 94 n
Wordsworth, C. 85 n
Wordsworth, W. 115, 129 n
   Idiot Boy 132
Worsley, R. 97 and n
Wyclif, J. 66

Yamanouchi, H. 141 n, 142 n, 148 n
Yeager, R. 131 n
Young, A. 97 n

Zadek, P. 154
Zeeman, N. 88 n